Charles Rolls of Rolls-Royce

Writing a book is an adventure. To begin with it is a toy and an amusement. Then it becomes a mistress, then it becomes a master, then it becomes a tyrant. The last phase is that just as you are about to be reconciled to your servitude, you kill the monster, and fling him about to the public.

Winston Churchill 1949

Charles Rolls of Rolls-Royce

Bruce Lawson

YOUCAXTON PUBLICATIONS
OXFORD & SHREWSBURY

YouCaxton Publications
24 High Street, Bishop's Castle, Shropshire. SY3 8JX
www.youCaxton.co.uk

2nd Edition
Published in Great Britain by Bruce Lawson

www.charlesrollsofrollsroyce.com

Front cover : © Cover picture of C.S. Rolls by kind permission of
The Royal Aero Trust and the copyright holders.

ISBN 978-190964-472-4

Printed and bound in Great Britain.

Contents

Foreword

I am delighted that Bruce Lawson has written this new biography of Charles Rolls. Remarkably, it was as long ago as 1966 that I wrote my own volume on the subject. After a 47 year gap and with the recent centenary of Rolls' tragic death, it is perhaps timely that this most fascinating character should be re-examined for the benefit of the modern generation.

My father was good friends with Charles Rolls. Indeed they were both entrants in the Paris – Ostend race in 1899; the first Englishmen to enter a foreign motor race. Both won prizes in that event; Rolls came second in the touring class driving a Panhard et Levassor and my father finished third in his Daimler. Subsequently he had a close association with the Rolls-Royce Company, owning several of their cars from 1906 onwards and opening their new factory at Derby in 1908.

Charles Rolls was a man of many facets; pioneering motorist, racing driver, balloonist, business man and pioneer aviator. I'm sure that you will discover much of interest in this book. I wish Mr Lawson every success with this venture.

Montagu of Beaulieu

Lord Montagu of Beaulieu

Beaulieu
August 2013

From The Making of Modern Britain: Andrew Marr (MacMillan 2009)

Rolls and Royce found their common enthusiasm removed any social stiffness. Their lunch was a roaring success, as was the trip in the car that followed. From this meeting came, of course, one of the great British engineering success stories of modem times. Rolls-Royce would get it's first breakthrough in the frequent car races of the time, and it's second with the extraordinary Silver Ghost of 1906, which with 40 horsepower could do a top speed of 80mph, yet was remarkably quiet.

Though such cars became symbols of wealth and status, when they were first produced, it was their performance that flabbergasted even hardened automobilists. One wrote later 'There arrived at my house the most astonishing motor car I had yet seen. The length of it, the silence, the stately form of it were beyond anything the motoring world had yet known. It was, I was told, the work of a great engineer, one F.H.Royce. We glided through the traffic with an ecstasy of motion which left the passenger astounded. We floated up hills at top speed.'

A year after Rolls and Royce started working together, the plugged-in marketing aristocrat and the obsessed engineer, the number of cars on British roads had risen to 16,000… By the time the Great War began there were 132,000 registered vehicles… Royce was never much impressed by flying, but Charles Rolls was smitten. By June 1910 he was the best known aviator in the country, famous for his long distance flights.'

Marr wrote after Rolls's fatal crash:

'So a pioneer of British motoring died, a pioneer of flying, one of a small band whose efforts would produce the world's first air battles four years later.

… Rolls understood that breakthrough consumer products needed allure, a sprinkling of the magic dust of media attention. His circles and connections ensured that Rolls-Royce cars were winning prizes, were admired by the new mass media, and had a patriotic flavour… Had landed wealth and elan worked with northern engineering grit more frequently, the industrial history of modem Britain might have been more sparkling.'

Of the current book Andrew Marr writes:

'Charles Rolls was a great British hero, out of Central Casting and we've been missing probable good about him for far too long: this is a lavishly-illustrated and excellent read about one of the heroes of modem Britain' August 2014

Acknowledgements

Since reading Andrew Marr's portrait of Rolls in his book 'The Making of Modern Britain' I have had much help and guidance, which has assisted a first time writer through an experience, which at times seemed overwhelming. My heartfelt thanks and appreciation, in no particular order, to each of the following:

Philip Hall and Barbara Westlake at the Rolls-Royce Enthusiasts' Club – Hunt House
John Fasal – for photographs from his bookset The Edwardian Rolls-Royce (1994)
Tom Clarke – author
Mrs Elizabeth Bennett – author – *Thousand Mile Trial*
David Towers for his contribution on Sir Frederick Henry Royce
Roy Brooks
John Pulford at Brooklands and The Worshipful Company of Coachmakers and Coach Harness Makers for access to Rolls's Balloon Log Book.
Andrew Dawrant and the Royal Aero Trust, Hendon
Andrew Helme and the Monmouth Museum
Patrick Collins, Caroline Johnson and Jackie Bethel of the National Motor Museum
Bournemouth Library
Peter Bowen – bookseller
Hugh Meynell M.B.E. – great-nephew of Laurence Meynell
David Moore – Midland Automobile Club
Jim Coupe – Crosby Europe (UK) – concerning Harry Parsons
James Cowell – Royal Aeronautical Society
Paul Tritton – author, with particular thanks for allowing my use of his extract of the journey and meeting of Rolls and Edmunds with Royce in Manchester
Naomi Bishop of the BBC and the Heritage Motor Museum, Gaydon
Gwent Archives
The Hurlingham Club
Robin Wayne, Huw Lloyd and Kelvin Price of the Rolls-Royce Enthusiasts' Club – Welsh Section
Ian Campbell (for photographs)
Linda Kedward and Barbara Shelton of the Rolls of Monmouth Golf Club and Hendre
Brendan Lynch – author

My particular thanks to the Trustees of the Royal Aero Trust (the owner) and the copyright holders of the Rolls portrait by Cuthbert Orde that provides the cover for this book and also to Lord Montagu of Beaulieu for graciously agreeing to write the Foreword, a generous gesture indeed to a new author.

The book is self-published so my thanks to Bob Fowke who crucially edited my writing and also to his partner, Steve Edwards, of youcaxton.co.uk for hand holding during the production process.

My sincere thanks also to my very good friend, Roy Marthews, for sorting the photographs, many other kindnesses and coping with a computer illiterate – myself.

And finally to the ladies, my inestimable personal assistant, amazing Maggie Allen, for her enthusiasm during many hours of hard transcription, Jane Needham for genealogical efforts which bore great fruit and my oh so patient wife, Jo, for proof reading, final word processing and keeping us both sane, as we produced a book together, in an incredibly busy life. We hope you will enjoy the book in which I take sole responsibility for any errors, factual or otherwise.

Bruce Lawson – August 2013

Chapter One

Born with a Silver Spoon

Charles Stewart Rolls was born at 35 Hill Street, Berkeley Square, London on 27th August, 1877, in a house rented by his father for his mother's confinement. He was the youngest of four children. His elder brother, John Maclean, was born in 1870, his middle brother, Henry Alan, in 1871 and his sister, Eleanor Georgiana, in 1872.

They were a wealthy family, the wealth having been acquired a hundred years earlier when Charles's great-great-grandfather, John – occupation 'cowkeeper' – went from Monmouthshire and amassed a fortune buying and selling land in London, draining it where appropriate and building houses for London's burgeoning population. He was a cowkeeper with a farmer's shrewd eye to purchasing land. The houses built thereon eventually provided homes for around sixty thousand people. By marriage to Sarah Coysh, a doctor's daughter and heiress, in 1767, he acquired more land in the capital and in Monmouthshire, land sufficient for him to become High Sheriff. Now well-established financially, he started to build a London house of a size appropriate to his new wealth. Grange House, completed by his son, also called John, was a huge mansion on the site of the Old Kent Road, where the Prince Regent was once entertained.

Even the most thrusting of families have their ups and downs. John Rolls the younger, Charles's great-grandfather, was a gambler. One year he is reputed to have lost around £80,000 – over £10 million in today's money and, following this massive loss, he sold Grange House to pay his debts and lived more quietly. His son, Charles Rolls's grandfather, John Etherington Welch Rolls, then moved to Monmouthshire. Here John Allan Rolls, Charles's father, who later became the first Lord Llangattock, transformed Hendre from a farm and hunting lodge into an imposing family mansion where Charles was brought up.

John the gambler had lost some of the family money but not all of it by any means and Lord Llangattock was able to live in style. He was an avid breeder of shire horses, Hereford shorthorn cattle and Shropshire sheep and he was a Master of Foxhounds for seven years. Paradoxically, he was also a prominent member of the Anti-Vivisection Society and at one annual meeting of the Society he was attacked because of his hunting, shooting and fishing connections. The attack was unreasonable, there is of course a distinction between vivisection and blood sports – however bloody. His diary once recorded: 'the hounds killed at Whitehill', and on another occasion he and his guests shot one thousand six hundred and forty-eight pheasants, four hares and forty-three rabbits (with just six guns!). At another time, his guest, the Duke of York (later Edward VII), wore gloves because he had three loaders and the guns became so hot during the slaughter he would have otherwise have burned his hands.

At the time of Charles's birth, Lord Llangattock had a London rental income of around £30,000 p.a. (over £3 million today) and controlled 6,000 acres of Monmouthshire farmland. He also owned a substantial yacht, the *Santa Maria*, known in the family as *Saint*, which once travelled as far as St. Petersburg, but more usually made an annual pilgrimage to the Cowes Regatta. Shortly after Charles's birth, Lord Llangattock acquired South Lodge, Rutland Gate, Kensington as their London home, which the family kept for many years. The house was used by Lord Llangattock while attending Parliament, where he sat first in the House of Commons and later in the House of Lords. Meanwhile, Lady Georgiana Llangattock collected art and Nelson memorabilia. Her collection included works by Gainsborough, Hogarth, Holbein and Romney, a lock of Charles I's hair (cut off after his execution), and a death mask of Napoleon.

Such was the world into which Charles was born. Hendre, some four miles from Monmouth, was Monmouthshire's only full-scale Victorian country house, Monmouthshire being the least Welsh of Welsh counties (arguments have raged over its position as part of England and Wales until the Local Government Act of 1973 put it firmly into Wales) which is perhaps why Charles is not thought of as Welsh nor particularly recognised as a native in his home county. What a barn of a place he was brought up in! In the ownership of the Rolls family from 1767 until 1987, Hendre was built in the eighteenth century as a hunting lodge (or shooting box) but was vastly expanded throughout the nineteenth century. In 1872, shortly before Charles's birth, a coach house and loose boxes replaced the old stables and a billiard room, smoking room and dining room were added at the centre.

Entering the house through its massive front door[1], there remains today fine features throughout – marble fireplaces, stained glass windows, ornate ceilings, a magnificent library and a water organ on which Charles's musical brother, John Allan, played so expertly.

Outside, acres of magnificent parkland, with thousands of handsome trees, set off the huge house to perfection.

Having a much older eldest brother and another brother who was sickly, Charles passed a rather solitary childhood with much time to think and to invent. At the age of nine, he used an invalid chair as a soap-box Derby cart and would ride it on the long winding drive down to the big house, occasionally causing chaos and squashing the odd pheasant. Years later, in an interview for *Chums*, a scouting magazine, he remembered those early experiments:

'This bath chair, I remember, I rigged it up with a brake in the shape of a piece of wood, to be when required, jammed between the rim of the small front wheel and the fork'.

He was never shy of taking risks. Writing in May 1906, he described himself as the Benjamin of the family, saying: 'I was born in London in 1877 and set about trying to break my neck about as soon as I could walk. My ambition was to arrive at the Golden Gates on wheels. I was brought up… in Monmouthshire, and I think my first experience of self-propelled traffic was taking my governess for a sleigh ride, which intensely exhilarating while it lasted, ended in piercing screams in a half-frozen river' – not the only occasion on which his enquiring mind brought him family fury. On another occasion similar wrath descended on him for driving an Aveling steamroller, used for fixing estate roads, on a Sunday and ruining his best suit.

Many of these adventures took place during the summer holidays when home from boarding school. From the age of nine, Charles attended a small Berkshire prep school. One of his masters, writing to his future housemaster at Eton, the Reverend Daman, opined of thirteen-year-old Charles:

---

1 *The massive front door key has been missing since 27th August, 1977 – a surprising coincidence, since this was the hundredth anniversary of Rolls's birth. Does anyone know where it is?*

'Rolls, I regret to say, is still forgetful, irregular, sometimes even to the point of vanishing point, moreover his thoughts are far away in dreamland or vacancy instead of being on his work, but apart from this constitutional wandering, I am disposed to take a more cheerful view of his proceedings'.

Later, from Eton, Reverend Daman himself wrote to Lord Llangattock: 'I think he has considerable as well as inherent ability, as well as an interest in what I may now call his own line'.

Forgetful and irregular he may have been, but there was no avoiding his ability. Aged eleven he wrote home to his father urging him to install electricity at Hendre and Lord Llangattock did indeed install it – with the help of his son. It was the first house to be lit up by electricity in Monmouthshire, and no small house either. Legend has it that certain suspicious-looking devices such as dynamos were delivered and stored with instructions not to be touched until Master Charles came home for the holidays. Lord Llangattock was forward thinking, as evidenced by the early telephone installation at the Hendre. In this he was nagged by his impatient teenage son, who recognised the benefit of instant communication. His Lordship installed a telephone in his own room upstairs, which could be used without disturbing anyone and another just outside the pantry, under the stairs somewhere, which could be switched off if required.

John Allan Rolls, Lord Llangattock, Charles's father, was, at various times, a magistrate, a prominent Freemason, Mayor of Monmouth, High Sheriff of Monmouthshire and M.P. for Monmouthshire (under Gladstone) and was raised to the peerage in 1892. He had fought in the Crimean War and witnessed the battle of Alma and Inkerman.

His eldest son, John, being somewhat shy and the middle brother, Henry, being an invalid, their father, Lord Llangattock (family motto – 'Speed and Truth') began to realise that his energetic third son had more about him and may have come to regard young Charles as a bit of a favourite (which may help to explain his huge financial support later on).

Moving to Eton at thirteen, Charles was shy, gangling (he was eventually 6ft 5ins) and the descendant of a cowkeeper from the Old Kent Road, who liked playing with anything mechanical. One wonders what his contemporaries made of their country cousin. A tutor wrote: 'Charles does not run from the Army, but wishes to make electricity his career'. But his aptitude was noted by a private tutor, Mr. Herbert Pigg, engaged when Charles was seventeen before he went to university. Pigg wrote to Lord Llangattock: 'I am able to judge somewhat of your son Charlie's capabilities and to say that I have no doubt he will be able to matriculate at Trinity without difficulty, so as to begin residence in October next year (1895). He is working steadily and well. He seems to be much interested in mechanical engineering, and arrangements have been made for him to attend the workshop of the engineering professor'. That professor was Professor Downing of Cambridge University from whom Rolls was to learn a great deal.

And it was at Cambridge that Charles acquired that, oh-so-important, first car.

Chapter Two

Red Flags and Early Cars

In 1896 there were only ten cars in the entire United Kingdom. The French and Germans were a decade ahead. In the United Kingdom, the railways held sway – in years to follow, sporting balloonatics followed railway lines on early flights. Almost every town and village had a railway station and most parts of Britain had superb railway access. To complete the network, there were horse-drawn Hansom cabs in all towns to take passengers from stations to their local destination if they did not have their own transport. Trunk roads were almost unused, as we understand use today.

Trains were part of life for the wealthy, a few of whom, including royalty, had their own private carriages. Gentry had no need for cars, the journey was easy enough: back from London to the local station where an ostler and the carriage would be there to collect them, with family and luggage, to return home. Train coaches and private carriages were also discreet, no identification was needed. A rake's progress could be anonymous – and the breathalyser was irrelevant! Apart from trains, the horse reigned supreme, if odiferously so. It has been estimated that in the busier London streets, four tons of horse manure might be deposited on every mile of road in a twenty-four hour period.

The landed gentry in the shires, which included most magistrates, chief constables and other persons of substance and also the aristocracy, all relied on the horse. Furthermore, thousands of draught animals were used on the land. Horses gave livelihood and employment to tens of thousands and pleasure to others – classic horse racing had existed for over a hundred years – the St. Leger, having been contested at Doncaster since 1766.

Trains too had encountered opposition in their day. When the London and Manchester Railway Bill was debated in the Commons in 1846, one M.P., Sir Isaac Coffin, declaimed 'What will become of the coachmakers, horse breeders and horse dealers? Was the House aware of the smoke and noise, the hiss and whirr which locomotive engines, passing at the rate of 12mph, could occasion? Neither horses ploughing the fields nor sheep grazing the meadows could behold them without dismay. There will be the most complete disturbance of quiet and comfort in all parts of the Kingdom that the ingenuity of man could invent'.

Plus ça change..., fast forward to 1903 when Rolls and John Montagu, M.P. sought a new Motoring Bill. A dinosaur M.P. for the Orkney and Shetlands (surely hardly over-run with cars or likely to be) – Cathcart Watson – described motor cars as 'Those slaughtering, stinking engines of iniquity'. Neither this undoubtedly worthy gentleman nor Sir Isaac Coffin could have contemplated the M6 or the M25 today (especially on a Friday night!). Queen Victoria too was less than enthusiastic. She owned an electric car, which was acceptable, but with regard to the internal combustion engine, she commented to her Master of the Horse: 'I hope you will never allow any of these horrible machines to be used in my stable. I am told they smell exceedingly nasty and are very shaky and disagreeable conveyances altogether'.

Trains ruled but road steamers, the first cars, had been around for nearly forty years, subject to the Red Flag Act (correctly known as the 'Locomotives on Highways Act 1865'). This Act had effectively impeded their development. The key points of the Act were:-

i. *No motor car should be driven at any time at a speed exceeding 4mph.*

ii. *Three people at least should be employed in the driving of the motor car.*

iii. *While the motor car is in movement, one other person should precede the car by at least sixty yards carrying a red flag. He shall warn horsemen, drivers of carriages and shall assist them and shall give order to the mechanic to stop the motor car.*

iv. *For the driver shall not at such moment make use of the whistle or open up any taps in view of anyone passing on foot, on horse or in a carriage.*

v. *All motor cars shall immediately be stopped on the order of anyone passing on foot, on horse or in a carriage who indicates his desire by raising his hand.*

vi. *Every driver of a motor car shall cause to be placed two lights in front, one at each side of the machine, one hour before sunset until one hour after sunrise.*

The Act was poorly drafted and made no mention of rear lights or indeed the size of the flag to be used. Amendments made in 1878 allowed councils to decide whether the flag was needed, but the speed limits of 4mph, a brisk walking pace, in the country and 2mph, more of a saunter, in town were enforced everywhere. Motoring in Britain was at a standstill. The law made it almost impossible and only the most ingenious or persistent could hope to circumvent its requirements.

Henry Hewetson was a London motorist and coffee trader. His first car was a Benz, that cost him £80. In 1895 he drove from Charing Cross to Liverpool Street Station in the middle of the day and although not interfered with by the police, Scotland Yard took his name and address and told him not to do it again. He chose to drive with his son round London in quiet times with a youth preceding him on a bicycle. If a peeler was spotted, the youth would alert Hewetson, who would hand his son a pencil. On the end of the pencil was a small red flag – two inches square. A Penny Red stamp would have sufficed. The convoy of youth, son, pencil, stamp and driver with car would then proceed in a stately fashion past the constable, cocking a snook at the powers that be. On another occasion Hewetson lost a front wheel on Barnet Hill (where Rolls was later to have an accident). Being reduced effectively to a three-wheeler, Hewetson hired a large, fat navvy to sit on the car in the corner opposite the missing wheel. The car thus re-balanced, he drove home.

1896 was the year of the car, the year when nineteen year old Charlie Rolls found his destiny behind the wheel, the year the Red Flag Act was at last repealed – on 14th November – although even after its repeal it was an unwritten law that when a driver of a horse-drawn vehicle so indicated, a motorist should stop until horses were led past. Since some motorists behaved like Mr. Toad of Toad Hall[2], there was often ill-feeling between horsemen and motorists. Cars carried no identification and there was no known method to settle disputes later. It was not unknown for horsemen to set about a motorist with a whip, so please slow down for horses today – lest the spirit of yesteryear reasserts itself.

Rolls had become convinced of the massive future impact of motoring while on a visit to Paris and he already anticipated that the Red Flag Act would go. He wrote to his father: 'If you are willing to assist me in placing the order of the latest type, I propose running over to Paris for a few days after my exam in October (1896)'.

Once in Paris, he considered various cars and even sent Lord Llangattock a brochure, but new cars were fetching premiums. 'One firm', he wrote, 'has enough orders for two years… whenever one carriage arrives for sale, it is immediately pounced upon and fetches exorbitant prices'.

He settled for a used works-mileage car, a Peugeot, list price £270, for £225. He borrowed £140 from his father and paid the difference himself, the total being equivalent to £30,000 today. You could have bought two modest cottages in South Wales for £250. He wrote again: 'I stopped much longer than I had intended as I found the selection of an auto car no simple matter… there were a large number of cars for sale, which had to be hunted up in Paris, inspected or, if at all suitable, tested thoroughly… most second-hand cars are being sold for being out of date… when by lucky chance cropped up a magnificent Peugeot Phaeton of the latest type to date, new in September, with an extra-strong motor of three and three-quarter horse power… not a scratch on the paint, all as new'.

Bubbling over with enthusiasm, he explained that its first owner had died, the car had hardly been on the road and had a written guarantee. He had test-driven it and had it inspected by an unbiased English engineer. Fortunately he did not need a quote for insurance in those halcyon days. Aged just nineteen, it would have cost him a fortune today.

The car was shipped by boat train to Victoria Station and Rolls was almost immediately nabbed for 'no Red Flag'. The 'Emancipation Bill', as it became known, had been passed but a three month delay meant that it had not yet come into force.

---

2 *The Wind in the Willows – Kenneth Grahame, 1908.*

He wriggled free of the police's clutches with the help of parental influence on the Chief Constables of Hertfordshire and Cambridgeshire, and he proudly proceeded back to Cambridge at a stately 4mph, reaching the University in eleven hours. During this historic journey, Rolls is said to have given a beat policeman a lift. The latter sanctioned exceeding the speed limit: 'Just let 'er go as you please down this 'ere 'ill, for there ain't no one on the beat for another mile an' a 'alf'.

The Motor Car Club organised the Emancipation Run on 14th November, 1896 to celebrate the repeal of the Red Flag Act. The outlandishly ambitious Harry Lawson organised the event. Someone had to do it and it needed someone with his eye to a quick profit to take the initiative. The Daimler Company had been formed earlier that year with a capital of £100,000 and had bought premises in Coventry. Lawson's Great Horseless Carriage Company acquired working rights over Daimler and other patents. Lawson offered £250,000 for subscription as working capital, he and his fellow promoters grandiosely claiming that the company was formed to carry on and establish the great horseless carriage industry in this country. Extensive works with railway and canals adjoining had been secured in Coventry capable of an output of more than equal to the entire capital of the company in value every year. Investors should have run a mile, but they did not. It was the sort of company promotion that made Sir David Salomons shudder but that year over £2 million was raised to float motoring companies.

Various ideas were considered for the Emancipation Run. The organisers settled on a luncheon, followed by a drive to Brighton, followed by a celebratory banquet on arrival. *Autocar* (founded 1895) put out a crimson edition of its paper to celebrate the 'Liberty Day' of motoring.

The Motor Car Club issued instructions for 'The first meet of the Motor Car Club' and made sensible, general recommendations. 'Owners and drivers of motor vehicles taking part in the run should remember that Motor Cars were on trial in England and any rashness or carelessness might injure the industry:

(a) They should see that their motor cars appear in thoroughly good class order and are never left unattended on the route.

(b) *Should be fully provided with sufficient lubricating and motor oil.*

(c) *Should see that their passengers are provided with proper protection against bad weather such as macintoshes.*

(d) *Should use the greatest care as to speed and driving so as not to endanger ordinary traffic.*

(e) *Should treat the police and other authorities on the route with polite consideration.*

(f) *Uniform – Special Caps and armlets can be provided to members of the Club driving motor vehicles. Those who wish for them can apply to the Secretary.*

(g) *Pilot Car – Mr. Harry J. Lawson, the President of the Club, will drive the pilot car, from which directions will be given. Drivers are requested not to pass this car unless by necessity, so that directions may be communicated to those taking part in the run.'*

Harry Lawson's lead car was a Panhard et Levassor Daimler that had won the Paris/Bordeaux race in 1895. He exposed himself to a certain amount of friendly ridicule by wearing a special uniform, which he hoped would be adopted by members of the Motor Car Club. It consisted of a yachting cap, a double-breasted jacket and trousers to match – he was likened by one participant to a Hungarian bandleader or a steward on an excursion steamer. Meanwhile Charles Harrington-Moore, secretary of the Motor Car Club, had secured Herr Gottlieb Daimler as the star turn, to ride with Frederick Simms, who had formed the Daimler Motor Syndicate in 1893 to exploit Daimler patents in Britain. It was a colourful event: Hungarian uniforms aside, there were three Bollée motor tandem cycles, one steered by Leon Bollée, one by his brother and another by leading motoring writer, H. Duncan; a Daimler omnibus, an omnibus from

Harrods, two Duryea motor carriages, a Roger dog cart, a six seated car, a covered dog cart, an Arnold dog cart and a Pennington four seated tricycle. Sad to say all the cars were foreign. *Three Men in a Boat*, author, Jerome K. Jerome, was a participant.

Adversaries of motoring hooted at the Emancipation Run's slow progress. They pointed out that a coach pulled by four horses could do the Brighton run in just over three and a half hours, so what was the big deal about these new-fangled motor cars? They failed to add that the coach trip would require several changes of horses on each leg of the journey, and would be far more expensive. As today, enthusiasts and politicians can do anything with numbers. Despite the critics and the foul weather, huge crowds gathered along the route. Reigate put up a banner: 'Reigate Welcomes Progress' and the crowd in Croydon roared with laughter when two policemen on horseback gave chase (in vain) after a speed-limit-bursting car.

Two of the Bollées arrived in Brighton first after a run of just four hours – their nearest rivals took at least six hours. Of the fifty-eight original entries, thirty-three set out and twenty-two are assumed to have reached Brighton, although a lesser number were checked in at the finish and were in time for the celebratory dinner at the Metropole Hotel. This was hosted by the Mayor of Brighton and Lawson spoke of the demise of the horse and expanded on the future. Motors would not be tired nor all fall down nor bolt, he claimed. The Brighton coach needed five changes of horses to keep up with the cars, but was unable to do so. He said that trotters had passed him on the way down, but he had only motored at 12mph as the law allowed. He said it was the beginning of one of the greatest industries that the world had ever seen. Twenty years previously he had made the first safety bicycle in Britain and now cycle output was valued at £12 million (£1 billion today).

Lawson himself had only been delayed by a quarter of an hour on the Run, and he returned to London the following day in a very creditable four hours, honour satisfied. He did better than Rolls who did not take part. Rolls's car broke its back axle on its way to the start. Two of his passengers tumbled into the road but suffered only minor injuries.

The next day was a Sunday and some of the vehicles disported themselves in front of crowds along the front, but a planned parade was cancelled due to bad weather and because of the state of the vehicles. One vehicle, which had been intended to function as a parcels van and to carry spares in the event of breakdown, performed so inefficiently that it was deemed incapable of carrying anything heavier than an empty hat box. It had set out with the main flotilla at 9.30 a.m. and took eighteen hours to reach Brighton.

Thus ended the one really important event in the life of the Motor Car Club. The Emancipation Run put the public on notice that motoring was about to become a phenomenon. Unfortunately the motives of the Club and its founder held things back. Lawson's sense of his own importance invited criticism: his word 'was law', he intended to 'monopolise the motor car industry and all the relevant patents in the United Kingdom'. Those interested in the future of the motoring industry came to the conclusion that the Motor Car Club was Lawson's organisation and was purely for his own ends and the true dawn of motoring in Great Britain would have to await the Thousand Mile Trial three years later.

Rolls had failed to join the Run but he was jubilant about its impact. The 'car', as it became known, was here to stay, and Charlie Rolls was already one of its pioneer enthusiasts, notable for his aristocratic pedigree, youth and enthusiasm. He decided to drive home for Christmas – one hundred and forty miles in winter with no garages or satellite navigation available. In Rolls's own words: 'My next adventure was before Christmas 1896, a run… to my home town in Monmouthshire, which took me three days.'

At Cirencester they had to negotiate one of the steepest and most dangerous hills in England. Birdlip Hill[3] is still a severe challenge in the twenty-first century.

Rolls's own words tell the story: 'Had we known what we were in for, we would not have dreamed of taking on such a hill with the inferior brakes we had in those days. However, we started cautiously down the first and steepest part of the hill, which was almost like climbing down a precipice. The brakes

---

3 *Coincidentally, on Birdlip today, there is a well-known pub called the Air Balloon, and the author has always wondered why. From some time in 1784 onwards, balloon flights took place from this establishment, hence the name.*

had to be kept pretty hard on, and while we were still on the steepest part I felt my handbrake lever suddenly yield and go up against the top – a feather/key fractured and that was an end to the side brakes; it left a miserable foot brake, which pressed so hard that the lever bent and the pedal sat on the floor.

That settled it; away went the car down this awful hill, I did not know the road; I didn't know what curves there were and what might not be on the road. There was nothing to be done but to try and keep her on the road and trust to luck. The car kept on accelerating and swerved terribly from side to side, and we came to the first corner. She literally jumped around this corner, dashing across the road from one side to the other and then I hoped the hill was over. Not a bit. There was a long straight stretch ahead with a steady, down incline. To add to the difficulties we had a canopy, which made the car top heavy. We also had the front glass down, this coupled with the darkness that was just coming on, made it extremely difficult to drive and see which way the corners went.

While on we sped down this stretch wondering if we would get round the next corner, suddenly we caught sight of a light – right bang ahead of us. I said to myself... 'Now we're done for!'

We were swaying about the road so much that we could not possibly have got past a vehicle of any sort. We were gathering up speed, waiting for the crash, being by this time quite resigned to our fate, when I suddenly discerned another bend in the road and the light, happily for us, turned out to be a house on the side of the road. We dashed round this corner somehow and again came a gleam of hope that we might be saved; but still the road ran on downhill and downhill, until it really became a sort of a nightmare. Not until two more stretches were covered, two more bad corners negotiated did we find ourselves at last slowing up and then it seemed to us miles before the car actually stopped.

Such is the hopeless feeling of being in a car with absolutely no brakes of any kind – and when the car did actually come to a standstill we felt a relief which is now quite impossible to describe. It was the narrowest escape of our lives. I still do not know how we got round those corners. The hill turned out to be a mile and three-quarters in length and the car literally jumped from one side of the road to the other all the time. I think it was the fearful swaying of the car that checked its speed to a considerable extent and enabled the turns to be negotiated which otherwise could not possibly have been got round.

Walking up the hill with a lantern afterwards to look for a bag which had been dropped I noticed the very wide skidmarks which the car had made and sometimes went within a few inches of heaps of stones. There was a strong smell of burning when we stopped and all the brake leather was burnt so we adjusted them up as best we could and decided to put up in Gloucester for the night.'

But the 1896 Santa Run was far from over. Next morning, in the hotel yard, misfortune appeared yet again. In Rolls's own words:

'While the engine was running in the hotel yard, the clutch pedal stuck down and I stooped down in front of the car to release it. Stupidly I left the gear lever in the first speed, with the result that as soon as the pedal flew up, the car started ahead. Although I struggled to get out of the way, I had to lie down and get run over by my own car! I lay there for a moment looking a pitiable sight, wearing an old macintosh, the cape of which had been drawn over my head. I looked to all intent and purposes dead.

My friend was standing there and he told me afterwards of the thought that had flashed through his mind. He said: 'Here's a nice position for me to be in; there's a motor that has killed Rolls, it's running away, I don't know how to stop the thing, and there's Rolls like a sack of bones – dead as mutton – and I've got to tell his people that he's been run over by his own car; and I don't know them, and I don't even know where they live!'

All of a sudden, however, I jumped up and ran after the car just as it smashed into a dogcart. The whole situation was so comical that we spent the rest of the evening roaring with laughter in front of a fire, and so ended one of the most amusing and adventurous days of my life.

The following morning we spent repairing the dogcart and doing up our brakes; and after considerable difficulty in finding any benzolene in the town we at last got away. We made very slow progress that night, for we had trouble with the pump and got stuck on a long hill in a lonely part of Gloucestershire with the engine seized up. The worst of it was the lamps would not keep alight in the gale that was blowing and all our matches were soaked with rain, so we had to do all our work in pitch darkness. We spent all that night on the road and suffered extremes of discomfort – for the weather was bitterly cold and it was snowing and sleeting all the time. However, we finally got to Monmouth at 2.00 a.m. on Christmas morning where they had been waiting to see us pass through for two days and two nights! I have made many runs of a similar nature to this one; in fact in those days you never went out without knowing you were in for a lively time'.

Whether Rolls had the first motor vehicle to travel in Wales is unknown, but the Western Mail reported a Mr. Duncan driving a motor van on 4th January 1897, ten days after Rolls reached the Hendre for the first time.

Rolls repeated his Christmas journey from Cambridge University to the Hendre a year later, this time carrying three passengers and their baggage. A year's improvement in the performance and reliability of cars saw the trip made in half the time at an average speed of 11mph. But motoring remained an adventurous and uncertain activity. Rolls described a horrendously difficult journey in France, illustrating that a time should never be given to set out and a time of arrival to the exact day could not be guaranteed.

'The most eventful run I ever had in France was in the company of Colonel Mark Mayhew, Mr. Russell and Mr. Hutchinson. The car was an 8hp four-cylinder Panhard and we left Paris for Havre in the middle of winter with rather incomplete equipment of tools and spare parts; consequently all sorts of things happened of which I will only name a few. We took the best part of three days to get from Paris to Havre' (about a hundred and fifty miles).

On the first day we had an extraordinary number of water joints go from apparently no cause whatever and it being Sunday we could not get any assistance. We reached Rouen that night and on coming out to the car the next morning we found a huge rent in the outer cover, but after some delay with this and other things we got away on the road in a heavy snowstorm. Then we had more troubles and after darkness came on we lost our way. The reflection of the light from the lamps on the fine snow, which was continually flying off the front wheels, made it extremely dazzling to drive. Soon after we found our road a tyre went down and as we did not relish repairing it in the snow, we got into a place called Bolbec where we had tea and repaired the tyre.

It was now 8.30 p.m. and we were only forty kilometres from Havre, but we were destined to take all night getting there for now the fun began. Soon after leaving Bolbec, the car suddenly slowed up and gave a fearful skid. On stopping it we found that much cherished macintosh, belonging to one of the passengers, had caught in the chain and torn to shreds. The macintosh was destined to play an important part later on. The next thing was an ominous hiss from the engine; we thought an ignition tube had burst, we had no spare ones, but luckily it was only a nut loose.

Having put that right we started out again and then came the best part of the evening. The car suddenly slowed up and stopped and on opening the top of the bonnet we were horrified to spy the whole of the engine a glowing red. What had happened was this. Owing to faulty circulation and the extreme cold, the water had frozen up solid and the engine of course seized up. I tried the pump and found it jammed up with ice inside. Here was a pretty fix, right out in the country, ten o'clock at night, twenty degrees of frost and snowing hard'.

His friend, Hutchinson takes up the story: 'We wondered how far we would have to push the car. Before starting on mere brute force it seemed worthwhile to try a little experimenting. Petrol was cautiously poured on the pump and set alight. Petrol was also carefully dashed into the radiator and in great trepidation fire set to it.

Then we made torches of waste soaked in petrol, held on gas pliers and tried to heat up the pump and radiator. When the waste was exhausted we used Mayhew's macintosh. We soaked great wads of this in petrol and pushed them into the radiator and lighted them. All this was very anxious work as the flames were at times alarming. Presently the pump became moveable, very little water ran from the evacuating cap, and we knew the jackets were empty. A few minutes later a copious stream of water dashed out from the two places of the radiator showing it had burst. We at once started the engine and found that water was circulating, the engine was stopped and Rolls got on his back and with great difficulty made two very effectual joints with canvas and solution. During the first part of the job, water was trickling all over him and down his sleeves and freezing. When he crawled out from under the car his leather coat was stiff with ice.

While he was working one of us had been entreating him to come forth and leave the joint for a time so the engine could be started (he was lying just opposite the hole in the silencer) to keep the water from freezing again, and now when we again started the engine we found there was no circulation.

We had stopped two hours and used all the spare petrol and most of the macintosh. We decided to try and run the car on further with plenty of lubricating oil and with the bonnet open and stopping frequently. But – it may hardly be credited – no sooner did we start with this intention than an ignition tube blew a small hole and the next door lamp was extinguished. The tube was then after ten or twenty minutes more turned with the hole uppermost and we proceeded glad enough to sit down.

We presently came to a few houses on the main road. They were all of them in darkness with not a soul to be seen. It was agreed that Rolls and Russell should remain with the car and try, if they could, to obtain any water to put in the jackets. Mayhew and the writer turned at right angles down the road that seemed to lead to habitations. It was now about eleven. In a few minutes we suddenly came upon a silent, picturesque little town with crooked streets and irregular buildings and a market place, lighted with electric light. This latter fact gave us great joy, as there must be not far from us a man of probably similar tastes and with a fire and tools.

At last we found the electric light station. I knocked at the door twice and, hearing no response, opened it. The first thing I saw was an engine with a big flywheel, and then a man asleep in a chair, and an awful looking dog about the size of a piano lying by his side. It was asleep too. I softly closed the door.

On further knocking, the engineer opened to us. He proved to be an intelligent, pleasant young man. The car was brought up outside the engine house. Our friend brought us an abundance of boiling water, which we dashed over the radiator and pump. But this was to no avail. The radiator merely became covered with ice. We were told that there was no covered warm place available where the car could be thawed so we got the engineer to bring out shovelfuls of light coal, which he strewed with practised hands underneath the radiator and we fed the fire with oily waste and coil and the flames blazed under this costly car with its tank of petrol.

This treatment proved perfectly successful, the temporary joints held and we started up the engine and filled the jackets.

We now began to think of where we would spend the night. We left the motor running all night and went to have a look round the engine room. In about five minutes we heard a certain noise outside – a noise we had heard before during the last few hours. On going out we found the motor just stopping and one of the lamps out. The tube, which had burst before, had now burst in another place. Rolls set to work to try and remedy this and we again built a fire under the car as a preventative. Rolls took the tube off and went inside to tinker with it. Mayhew and Russell went back to examine the dynamo, etc. while the writer stayed outside to keep a watch over the fire. It was agreed that at one o'clock the engineer should go up to the inn for us and have some food put out, and as soon as the hour struck he stopped the engine and went off'.

The motor valve eventually ran alright. Hutchinson continued: 'We all drove up to the inn where the host had got some bread and cheese ready for us. He was a very good sort and would not hear of our apologies. The cold was awful and there were no fires alight. Russell, whose feet were very wet, took his boots off and endeavoured to warm his feet over a candle, causing intense amusement. Some of us were for going on and others, who by now had engendered in them a certain distrust, were for staying. However, we decided to make a start once more. We verified the circulation and having bidden au revoir at 2.30 a.m., once more started.

The car ran very well, but the cold seemed worse, it seemed to have come at us from everywhere. Before reaching Havre we actually had something else go wrong. Some oil got onto one of the brakes and we got down in the icy wind to try and wipe it, but we gave that up and descended slowly along the hill into Havre where we arrived soon after.

The only remark the hotel porter made when we arrived at that early hour was 'You Englishmen are very insanitary', meaning that he thought we were insane! We most certainly must have been'.

Rolls acquired his second car in 1897. It is unclear whether it was funded by his father or came from the proceeds of clandestine car dealing. He was bringing cars in from France and selling them at a premium of between thirty and one hundred per cent of their original cost. This second car was a 2.4-litre, four-cylinder Panhard which had won the Paris/Marseilles/Paris race in 1896.

He still had the original Peugeot which he used to convey guests to his sister, Georgiana's wedding to Sir John Shelley in 1898. He then road-tested a Duryea and a Bollée, and having discovered that the backfiring of the Bollée was almost lethal, he bought a third car, a new 6 hp Panhard – and, in addition, a De Dion tricycle, probably the quickest vehicle about. He had become a serious motorist. He attended the Paris/Dieppe race in France as a representative of the S.P.T.A. and was elected to membership of the *Automobile Club de France*, the most prestigious motor club in the world.

1900 presented Rolls with an unmissable chance to demonstrate motoring to Royalty. The Duke and Duchess of York, later King George V and Queen Mary, visited the Hendre that October for a five-day visit. The only cloud over this blessing on the Rolls family's status and local prestige and on Charles's opportunity to show off, was the death of a close relative, Prince Christian Victor of Schleswig-Holstein, great-nephew of Queen Victoria, which meant that plans for widespread celebrations had to be curtailed. Nevertheless, Monmouth and its citizens were not going to let a chance like this pass without *some* celebrations.

The weather, prior to the Royal visit, was indifferent and the local newspaper described how: 'All went to bed, though gloomy and despondent, and our slumbers were but fitful. We watched the dawn breaking and our hopes were raised as we saw the clouds being chased rapidly away by a strong wind. It must have been a Royal wind. Then the sun sent up its rays over the horizon and the eastern sky clearing prognosticated a fine day... The usual quiet streets of Monmouth became to look animated. The Mayor's request was ignored, and during the hours of Monday morning, private houses and residences blossomed out with flags and festoons and ingenious devices and mottos, bunting that made the main street the very picture of beauty. Monnow Bridge too looked pretty with its shields and festoons... and the old house of Geoffrey of Monmouth was bedecked with festoons and Chinese lanterns, the very pretty maypole, in charge of a group of very pretty children in holiday attire, stood in the square.

The welcoming party for the Royals consisted of Lord and Lady Llangattock, John Rolls as High Sheriff of the County, Lady Shelley-Rolls, and Charles Rolls himself.

The luggage of the Royal couple arrived at 3.29 p.m. and was taken straight to the Hendre. A regimental band played. The Royal couple arrived from Swindon by special train consisting of a saloon, an eight-wheeled coach and two brake vans. The Royal van came steaming into the Mayhill station at the minute. The Duchess was attired in a long travelling coat of black grey fur and high storm collar and black toque with white feather. The Duke was quietly dressed in morning coat and bowler hat… Their Royal Highnesses moved along the narrow, thickly peopled streets at a time when the sun shone out brilliantly, giving warmth and colour to the whole scene.

After welcoming speeches, the couple travelled by carriage to the Hendre'.

Charles Rolls took the Duchess on a motor tour of Chepstow and Tintern Abbey. At one point the Panhard encountered a small cart, but the two elderly occupants were more alarmed than the horse. *Autocar* reported that Her Royal Highness showed no sense of nervousness and seemed happiest when the speed was highest, and three months after their visit to Hendre the royal couple bought their first Daimler. In their thank you letter to Lord and Lady Llangattock when the visit was over, the royals made particular mention of young Charles, then aged twenty-two, and complimented him on his driving. But Charles was already more than merely a good driver. By 1900, he was already an expert mechanician, a designer, an adroit salesman and a leader in the new field of motoring. This was what set him apart from so many other aristocrats for whom motoring was just a jolly good sport.

Chapter Three

The Parliament of Motoring

The driving force behind the development of motoring in Britain was a members' club – the Royal Automobile Club, formerly the Automobile Club of Great Britain and Ireland – founded in 1897. Today, it has magnificent luxurious premises, providing accommodation, fine dining and a sumptuous swimming pool right in the centre of London. It has its own splendid, challenging golf courses at Woodcote Park, Surrey. Its facilities are enjoyed by seventeen thousand members – rather more than the hundred and sixty-three original founders, one of whom was Charles Rolls.

A few months before the Club was formed, the first motoring organisation in Britain, the Self-Propelled Traffic Association, had been founded by Sir David Salomons, one-time Mayor of Tunbridge Wells, High Sheriff of Kent and an accomplished engineer. Salomons had experimented with electric carriages and was a founder member of the French Automobile Club. The previous year he had organised the first ever motor show in Tunbridge Wells in Kent where just four vehicles took part. Rolls visited him a few months later, rode in Salomons's Peugeot car and wrote to Lord Llangattock that the experience: 'was delightful... I intend going in for one at some time, have been saving up...'

Harry Lawson's Motor Car Club (M.C.C. an unfortunate choice of initials), which organised the Emancipation Run, was founded shortly afterwards. Lawson successfully promoted a reception at the Imperial Institute, promoting the three month long 1896 Motor Exhibition, which was graced by the presence of the Prince of Wales, also known as the Duke of Cornwall, (later Edward VII). Meanwhile, one of the cars at the Tunbridge Exhibition, organised by Salomons, was owned by the Honourable Evelyn Ellis[4] whose brother was the Prince's equerry. Partly due to

---

4 *The Honourable Evelyn Ellis (1843-1913) is credited with driving the first car in England – a Panhard et Levassor – in 1895. It came into the country by boat and then by train to Micheldever in Hampshire. Ellis then drove it to Datchet, near Windsor, with Frederick Simms as a passenger – both being directors of the Daimler Motor Company in Coventry. They travelled fifty-six miles at an average speed of 10mph, well above the Red Flag limit.*

his influence, and to the Duchess's ride with Rolls in Monmouthshire, the Duke became enamoured of 'automobilism' and, after buying his first car in 1900, he announced: 'I shall make the motor car a necessity for every English gentleman'.

Lawson's Motor Exhibition certainly helped to headline the growing movement and that it ended in August 1896 when the Red Flag Act was repealed was more than coincidence, even if the Act did not become law until November. There were thus more than one contender for authority in the early world of motoring in Britain and this in part explains hostility to Lawson's venture in some quarters, the other part being Lawson's own inexplicable behaviour.

Rolls was fairly promiscuous in his loyalties. He wrote letters to the press as Charles Rolls, S.P.T.A. but his intention was also to ride in the Emancipation Run organised by Lawson's Motor Car Club.

After the Emancipation Run was over, Rolls bought Lawson's car, a Panhard, which had previously won the 1896 Paris/Marseilles race and in which Rolls led the parade along the Embankment in the very first Members' run of the newly-formed Automobile Club of Great Britain and Ireland (A.C.G.B.I.).

Lawson was riding high after the Emancipation Run. He was one of several sharp businessmen, who saw fortunes to be made and he attempted to monopolise motoring patents. Lawson considered that he held an exclusive right to import Peugeots and his British Motor Car Syndicate took out an injunction seeking to restrict Rolls from using his first Peugeot. They claimed breach of patent and threatened to confiscate or destroy Rolls's car. Rolls countered, saying that he had *tried* to buy a car from Lawson but Lawson had been unable to tell him either where he could buy it or when it could be delivered and that was the reason Rolls had imported one. Charles Rolls, with his youth, panache and monied background, was already well-known, and by taking him to court Lawson picked the wrong target. Lawson's stock fell sharply while that of the young aristocrat rose. The fledgling motoring press (*Autocar* and *Automotor Journal*) relished the dispute. Lawson won but it was a Pyrrhic victory. His syndicate received £15 damages – which Rolls described as his 'licence to use the Peugeot'. It was a public relations disaster for the M.C.C., and it certainly was not cricket. The Motor Car Club soon faded into obscurity, and people were not in the least surprised when Lawson was sentenced to one year's hard labour for fraud in connection with another matter in 1904.

Partly due to hostility to Lawson, Frederick Simms, who had founded the Daimler Motor Syndicate in 1893, and Charles Harrington-Moore, who had left Lawson's Motor Car Club, launched the Automobile Club of Great Britain and Ireland with a constitution copied from that of the French Automobile constitution. (It became the 'Royal Automobile Club' in 1907 after receiving royal patronage). Rolls joined the Committee in 1897 and remained a prominent member and committee member until shortly before his death in 1910.

Simms had been impressed by Johnson's flair at Lawson's M.C.C. Exhibition, and asked him to become the first secretary of the Automobile Club on a salary of £5 a week plus a commission of ten shillings for every new member recruited. The man, who was to become the 'Hyphen' in Rolls-Royce, was to stay Secretary for six years. Those six years saw an enormous expansion in motoring and saw A.C.G.B.I., despite being a members' club, established as the effective government of British motoring. It battled against prejudice within the establishment and among the landed gentry, many of whom were Members of Parliament and it soon became to motoring what the Jockey Club was to horse racing. It was once dubbed the 'Vatican of Motordom'. Through the Club, Rolls and Johnson became well-acquainted and since Johnson, universally known as CJ, met everybody who mattered in motoring, their contacts enabled Rolls's subsequent car sales business to prosper.

Claude Johnson's upbringing was very different to Rolls's. He came from a moderate background but his father's interest in art – he once arranged the Wallace Collection – rubbed off on his children. One became a composer, two became clergymen and, much later in life, perhaps less artistically, Claude's brother, Basil, became Managing Director of Rolls-Royce Ltd for a short time. Claude loved music and introduced musical events into the Club and, partly as a result of his imaginative endeavours, membership increased. The Club became the most exciting club in London. He seems to have thrown himself into his work to escape private regret. It was several years after his marriage and his wife had had several miscarriages before he finally became a parent, but meanwhile the marriage had deteriorated. The glamour and excitement of the Club contrasted with a less-than-happy home life.

Meanwhile the angels smiled on Charlie Rolls who lived in London at his parents' South Lodge home. Though not particularly sociable, his aristocratic background, his father's membership of the House of Lords and, more specifically, his extensive motoring knowledge, made him a very special member of the Club. He had a degree in engineering and all this meant that he could mingle, despite his youth, with the great and good of the day. His views on motoring and the motoring movement were widely sought after.

The objects of the Club – annual subscription was four guineas – harked back to a gentler time. It was to be a members club, independent of any personal, financial interest. Members could meet at its London premises where they could have access to all current motoring literature and information. The Club would organise lectures, races and competitions, with prizes where appropriate. The Club would observe, protect and encourage the new industry and liaise with other national motoring institutions.

The Club premises in Whitehall Court, which included a billiard room, residential accommodation and meeting rooms, were the hub of motor talk in London. Burrows, the butler/general factotum, became legendry in blue velvet tailcoat trimmed with gold lace, a striped waistcoat, crimson velvet breeches, silk stockings and patent-leather buckled shoes. He was ready to sort out any problem. 'Leave it to Burrows' became a Club slogan. The Club expanded rapidly and moved to 119 Piccadilly in 1902. £16,000 was subscribed in debentures to finance the move. It moved again to a spectacular new clubhouse on Pall Mall in 1911, which was built after Rolls's death and cost the equivalent of £30 million today[5].

Many founder members were professionals, lawyers, accountants, doctors, clergymen and London-area business motorists. Early members included: Henry Sturmey, *Autocar* editor, the first man to drive from John O'Groats to

---

5 *Two years after the Pall Mall Club opened, a country club was purchased at Woodcote Park, Surrey in 1913. A year later, with the outbreak of war, both clubhouses were put at the disposal of the armed services. During the hostilities, they provided bed, breakfast and baths for over two hundred thousand officers and served over two million meals. The Woodcote clubhouse was destroyed by fire in 1934, but rebuilt two years later.*

Lands End (in 1897); Harvey du Cros, who set up the first pneumatic tyre factory to exploit his acquisition of the patents of veterinary surgeon, John Dunlop; Paris Singer, playboy and sewing machine heir and one-time lover of American dancer, Isadora Duncan; Hiram Maxim, of machine gun fame, who later spent a fortune on unsuccessful aviation experiments; Custard King, Robert Bird; Mark Mayhew who founded the Motor Volunteers with Rolls; Rudyard Kipling who once described the car, as a 'Petrol Piddling Monster' and on another occasion described the horse as the 'Motorists' Hairy Enemy'; and there was Baron Henri de Rothschild, of the banking dynasty. Unsurprisingly, one journalist remarked: 'I doubt if there be collectively a wealthier club in the world'.

Not all of these illustrious members were technically capable, some were simply interested in the latest toy. Rolls's later ballooning partner, Frank Hedges Butler, was one of the least technically-minded and was wont to fortify himself, both in cars and balloons, with Bath Oliver biscuits and bottles of dry sherry. On one occasion when his car kept stopping and starting – because a wire was making only intermittent contact with the terminal, its securing screw having gone – the jovial vintner asked: 'Does that matter? That screw was always getting loose so I threw it away'. Rolls later declined the charms of Vera Hedges Butler. It is perhaps unfair to suggest that this was due to the mechanical illiteracy of her father.

Alfred Harmsworth (later to be enobled as Lord Northcliffe in 1905) was an early member and he and Claude Johnson became very good friends. Johnson enlisted and exploited Harmsworth's newspaper status for the benefit of the Club and motoring in general. Neither had been privately educated nor attended university and that was a common bond, given the Eton/Harrow/Oxbridge background of most Club members. The success in life of both of them was extraordinary. Both came from large families, although the bragging rights were with Northcliffe, one of fourteen children; Johnson was one of a mere seven. Johnson went to St. Paul's School in London and then art college and obtained his first job at the Imperial Institute at nineteen. Harmsworth was born in Dublin in 1865, son of a barrister, and only learned to read at the age of seven. He lived in Kent and wrote freelance articles for several London newspapers as a young man before joining the staff at the *Illustrated London News* thus beginning his long newspaper career. Like Charles Rolls, Harmsworth saw his first car in Paris and instantly realised the huge changes that cars would bring.

Motoring grew slowly. From perhaps a hundred cars at the end of 1896, half of which had taken part in the Emancipation Run, membership of the club spluttered up to two hundred and fifty by the end of 1897. Meanwhile, the Motor Union was set up to cater for motorists who were not interested in the London Club status of A.C.G.B.I. Rolls was on the executive of the Motor Union but was unenthusiastic because of its lack of direction. It was amalgamated with the Automobile Association in 1911.

Rolls, Johnson and Selwyn Edge, a racing rival of Rolls, later connected with the Napier car, served on the committee of the Motor Vehicle Users Defence Association, which aimed to help members accused of speeding and other misdemeanours. However, this did not suit Rolls because there was much talk and little action, and it soon became moribund. The original Self-Propelled Traffic Association was absorbed into A.C.G.B.I. when its founder, Sir David Salomons, accepted that there should be one combined voice for the motoring movement.

Back at the A.C.G.B.I., progress was slow and Johnson threatened resignation. Thereupon sixteen members paid a life membership fee of £25 and a Guarantee Fund was established. Contributors to this included Simms, the Honourable Evelyn Ellis, Salomons, balloonist Frank Hedges Butler, and the Australian Edge, and many others. Rolls, noticeably, did not contribute to the Guarantee Fund – which may have been an oversight but may also have been as a result of his notorious parsimony.

By the end of 1898 the Club had three hundred and eighty members, and in June 1899 there was a week long, three-part event at Richmond, including a hill climb and two runs, one for petrol and one for electric cars. A frivolous novelty was the Waistcoat Race, held over four laps. At the end of the first lap, the driver dismounted, took off his coat and put it on a numbered peg. At the end of the second lap, the driver removed his waistcoat and hung it on the same peg. Public modesty precluded further divestment so laps three and four reversed the process with waistcoat and coat being donned and fully buttoned. There was also a Ladies competition. Each vehicle had to carry one lady and, at a certain point, the carriage had to stop while the lady alighted to thread a needle before returning.

It was about this time that John Montagu, M.P.[6], later second Baron Montagu of Beaulieu, became a major motoring convert, as important a figurehead in the motoring movement as Rolls himself. Montagu was educated at Eton and Oxford, and in 1885 he became John Douglas-Scott-Montagu after Queen Victoria dubbed his father first Baron Montagu of Beaulieu. John became an M.P. in 1892 and was re-elected unopposed in 1895 and, along with Rolls, Royce, Johnson and Harmsworth, was one of the Famous Five of Edwardian motoring. Montagu bought his first car in 1898 and joined the Club immediately. He was originally refused entry to the Houses of Parliament yard in his car, but permission was soon given.

The Club, however, was in debt and it was Johnson and Harmsworth who had the idea of the Thousand Mile Trial, a three week rally around England and Scotland to promote the concept of the car. Johnson was fortunate in having in Harmsworth a wealthy man who was prepared to bail out the Club, underwrite the cost of the Trial and make prizes available to the winners and all those who completed it.

Harmsworth had prospered with several early newspaper ventures and bought the *Evening News* for a tenth of its development cost, but it was at the *Daily Mail* where he made his fortune. He bought up-to-date presses, and – after anticipating a first issue of a hundred thousand copies – had stunned the industry by selling over four hundred thousand on its first day in 1894. At a halfpenny a copy, the day's paper sales realised over £1,650, some £165,000 today, in addition to the advertising revenue.

Little did Rolls, Johnson, Montagu and Harmsworth anticipate the success of the Trial, which marked a turning point in the fortune of the Club and the development of British motoring.

---

6 *The existing Lord Montagu of the National Motor Museum is his son, having inherited the title eighty-four years ago in 1929.*

Chapter Four

The Thousand Mile Trial A Turning Point for British Motoring

In July 1899, Claude Johnson and Charles Rolls went to France. They watched a major cycle race[7] and they saw the Paris/St. Malo race, won by a Mors. Rolls was back in France shortly after with John Montagu, M.P. when they became the first Britons to race abroad, competing in the Paris/Ostend race of September 1899, a distance of two hundred and one miles.

Rolls's crew comprised Claude Johnson, barrister Staplee Firth and Robert Bird (of custard fame) in a Panhard. John Montagu drove his three-litre, Coventry-made Daimler, in which Montagu had initially been refused entry to the Houses of Parliament. One of the Montagu passengers was Julian Orde, who succeeded Johnson as A.C.G.B.I. Secretary and who persuaded the Isle of Man authorities to allow Tourist Trophy circuit racing there, in order to boost tourism.

Rolls led his class in the Paris/Ostend race until a tyre burst following a collision with a careless carter. His car finished second in their class. The 1899 Paris/Ostend race was the only major race ever to end in a dead heat – between the Frenchmen Girardot and Levegh.

Montagu was a busy M.P. and had to return home, but two weeks later Rolls was back. He competed in the Paris/Boulogne race for the experience. There was no separate touring class section so he had no chance of winning, but his last place result in the four hundred and forty-four mile event was disappointing. The race is notable because all motorcycle passengers had to weigh in at more than eight stone nine pounds. They were weighed on a 'franc in the slot machine' at St. Germain Railway Station, Paris.

---

7 *The major cycle race Rolls and Johnson saw was not the Tour de France, which started four years later in 1903. In those times there were fewer stages than today, but they were longer – up to two hundred and fifty miles. Cyclists had one to three days rest between each stage. They needed the rest. All the stages bar one started before dawn and the final stage started at 9.00 p.m. the previous night.*

Rolls was back again, in October 1899, for the one hundred and sixty-three mile Bordeaux/Biarritz event. Third time lucky. Despite pouring rain, Rolls was more steadfast and persistent than his rivals. *Motor Car Journal* reported: 'The engine suddenly turned stupid… Rolls was not the man to sit down and weep and promptly set out to remedy the defects… which ultimately ended in his disconnecting the governor spindle, and connecting the 'cut outs' with wire to be used when necessary, and although the misfortune was not temporarily adjusted until the night and early morning had been spent in unwearying toil, the reward was at hand and ended next day with victory for the car. There were a litany of incidents including two broken chains and trouble with livestock. The bag included five chickens, a goose, two dogs and a sucking pig'.

Rolls's activities were beginning to attract widespread newspaper coverage. Both the motoring journals and the wider press were alerted to the excitement of the new sport and Britain's finest exponent of it. Racers were news and tall aristocratic scorchers, like Rolls, major news.

Were there ever such things as time-traveller tickets I would certainly have bought one to be in Whitehall, London, in the early hours of St. George's Day, 23rd April, 1900. The weather was dull that morning but there was a chill of expectancy in the air. A phenomenon was about to erupt which would change all our lives, at first considerably for the better, but now, perhaps, for the worse.

The Thousand Mile Trial, arranged by the Automobile Club of Great Britain and Ireland, was about to start and nothing like it had ever been seen on the streets of London. An entrant described the scene:

'When we reached Grosvenor Place we found the entered and accompanying vehicles backed up against the kerbstone on the Park side of the road facing St. George's Hospital, giving the spot an open air market for autocars. It wanted five minutes to the appointed time when we arrived at the start and a slow prowl up and down the line revealed many personal friends, Club members and otherwise, to say nothing of new cars galore entered in the great round. A section led by A1, the privately owned vehicles and the quadricycles and several tricycles completed the line… but little time was available for greetings.

Before we had time to look round, Mr. J. Lyon Sampson[8], A.C.G.B.I. Committee man, had dropped the flag and the first great automobile tour ever made in England was underway'.

The number of vehicles assembled that April day was extraordinary. There were just eight hundred cars in the whole country at that time but sixty-one of them were entered for the Trial, that grey dawn. A revolutionary moment. In Britain, there had been no relaxation on limitations on car usage since the Emancipation Act of 1896, which raised the speed limit from a former snail-like 4mph to 10mph, and while inter-town races of hundreds of miles were being held on the Continent, in Britain the horse and the bicycle still held sway. The importance of the occasion was marked by the participants, who included most contemporary leading motoring figures. Together with their passengers, they numbered around two hundred. On that nondescript London morning, these strangely dressed figures made last minute adjustments to dress and vehicles, and down at Calcot Park, near Reading, the staff of Alfred Harmsworth, newspaper magnate, were setting tables for a sumptuous repast at the first stop on their journey.

Let us go back a few months. When the old century drew to a close, the A.C.G.B.I. was in trouble. It had lost some £1,500 (£150,000 today) on other activities and trials, and motoring in Britain had stalled. True, Charles Rolls and John Montagu had raced on the Continent, but in an age of few telephones and long before television, few people outside London had ever seen a car. Despite the work of pioneer engineers, particularly in London and Coventry where the infant industry was just learning to crawl and despite the efforts of other isolated mechanicians, Britain and the A.C.G.B.I. were in danger of falling behind their Continental rivals. Something had to be done.

The Thousand Mile Trial was the brainchild of A.C.G.B.I. Secretary, Claude Johnson. He developed the idea with Alfred Harmsworth, the newspaper tycoon, and John Montagu, the motoring M.P. Johnson felt that it was vital for the future of this new technology that the reliability of the car be accepted

---

8 *Mr. Sampson of A.C.G.B.I. was coincidentally to die in the same week as Charles Rolls as a result of an accident between a motor car and a traction engine.*

nationwide. Fortunately Alfred Harmsworth (later Lord Northcliffe) wanted to sell newspapers and could see the possibilities, so he agreed to finance the experiment. Harmsworth put up a number of prizes totalling £410 (£41,000 today), and these were announced at a dinner held to celebrate the anniversary of the Emancipation Run. Harmsworth only drove for one stage in the Trial due to work commitments[9].

The timing and route of the Trial were planned to show off the motor car as widely as possible:

23rd April, London to Bristol
25th April, Bristol to Birmingham
26th April, Birmingham to Manchester
30th April, Manchester to Kendal
1st May, Kendal to Carlisle
2nd May, Carlisle to Edinburgh
4th May, Edinburgh to Newcastle
7th May, Newcastle to Leeds
9th May, Leeds to Sheffield
11th May, Sheffield to Nottingham
19th May, Nottingham to London

Rolls recognised the importance of the Trial. He pointed out that few motorists had driven a hundred miles in a day, that proper stops should be made, so thousands could see the cars, that fuel should be on hand and had to be pre-arranged, for it would be hard to find for so many cars. Interviewed by *Motor Car Journal* he said:

'Racing made the industry in France, and one of the most hopeful signs of the present time is that English makers are turning their attention to the subject. The results should be seen in a higher class of car, for the maker, who could produce

9 *Harmsworth only drove for one stage in the Trial due to work commitments, although he entered two cars. He was reporting on the Boer War at the time, but his Irish friend and driver, Captain Hercules Langrishe, drove his car for the rest of the time.*

a vehicle to stand the strain of a great race, is best able to build one for ordinary touring or pleasure'.

Johnson was the prime organiser but Rolls, Montagu and Harmsworth were very involved and the quartet ensured that all was designed for maximum impact.

As they were all participants, they were not part of the impressive fifteen strong Judges panel for the event, which included W. Worby Beaumont (A.C.G.B.I. engineer) and Sir David Salomons.

The Committee of the Club was 'of the opinion that the Kingdom should not remain as it does at present in the rear of foreign countries as regards the new industry, and it is hoped that the passage of eighty (finally sixty-one) motor vehicles, over one thousand miles of the roads of Great Britain, and their exhibition at big centres of population, may have the effect of not only proving that the best of these vehicles are capable of covering long distances and mounting steep hills, but also demonstrating what are the respective capabilities of the various vehicles'.

There would be no Sunday driving and there would be rest days when, in some of the bigger cities, the cars could be displayed at pre-arranged exhibitions to best advantage. There would be three hill climb trials, at Taddington (near Buxton), on Shap near Kendal and on Dunmail Raise in the Lake District, and there would also be one speed trial, on the Duke of Portland's Welbeck Estate near Worksop in Nottinghamshire, which the Duke had kindly agreed to and which still stands, almost unchanged, today. On top of this, there would be many luncheon stops in the smaller cities where the cars would also be on display – the very first being the breakfast stop at Calcot Park.

Reconnaissance was carried out by Claude Johnson. He reconnoitred the route in December 1899 – hardly the best time of the year to travel a thousand miles throughout the highways of the kingdom, with roads in the state they were then.

Johnson was lent a car by Mr. Critchley of the Coventry Daimler company. His enthusiastic driver was a young adventurer called Montague Grahame-White, born in the same year as Charles Rolls. Grahame-White recalled: 'Mr. Critchley had received a request from Mr. Johnson who was responsible for the route to be traversed and to provide the Club with a car and a driver for this purpose. I was sent for by Mr. Critchley and he suggested that I should take the job. Needless to say I was flattered to be selected for this undertaking, although fully realising the probable difficulties to be faced under winter conditions in the North of England'. Little did he know.

Grahame-White's concerns were well-founded. The pair went up Shap on Christmas Eve 1899, a distance of ten miles, the road rising from 300ft. to 1,400ft, and they began the climb with three inches of snow already on the ground. 'Mr. Grahame-White, who had never seen the road before, drove me over it in the pitch black darkness of the night on Christmas Eve by the aid of two candles only' recalled Johnson.

Johnson was full of praise: 'On the summit, which was about 1400ft. above the sea, the County of Cumberland is entered and on descending a sharp turn is made to the left in order that the vehicle may pass over the Western Road constructed by the Manchester Corporation from which is obtained a view of Thirlmere. On the other side of the lake is Helvellyn, 3,118ft. This road… is beautifully engineered.'

They reached Keswick late on Christmas Eve and their enquiry at a local pub brought the landlady to an upstairs window.

'The George and Dragon has gone to bed' said the landlady when Johnson asked whether they could be put up for the night.

'I know that,' said Johnson, 'but get George to come down and let us in.'

George obliged and Christmas morning suddenly became brighter for Claude Johnson and young Master White.

It is a good story, but ten years later, through rose-tinted spectacles, Claude Johnson wrote a much kinder version about Mr. and Mrs. Scott, owners of the George Hotel. Taking up the story… 'We eventually made the steep descent into Keswick. We pictured to ourselves our arrival at the hotel at three o'clock Christmas morning. We blew our horn and timidly rang the bell. Suddenly a voice was thrown up and a cheery voice greeted us that the possessor would be down below in two shakes of a duck's tail and we would be welcome in his house.

We rubbed our frozen hands with delight, and in a miraculously short time the front door was thrown open and from it strode a great-coated form, bearing in one hand a candle and in the other a coach horn. 'And what are you lads doing here at this time of the morning? Bring your machine round to the yard and first to the right and a gate on the right'.

We arrived at the gate that was thrown open, a newspaper of the day was lighted in an exemplary bonfire to show us the path to the clubhouse. Bells were ringing inside the house. We were ushered into a splendid, old-fashioned flagged kitchen where the hostess was already engaged in re-lighting the fire, while her daughter was setting out huge joints of beef and ham, half a cheddar cheese and a cold plum pudding on the long kitchen table. Our host, on his bended knees, was unlacing our frozen boots, pulling off our socks and replacing them with his own homespun hose. Two huge beakers of hot toddy were poured down our throats, and within a quarter of an hour of our arrival, we were filling our stomachs, which had not known food for fifteen hours.

And that Christmas morning, the writer swore a solemn oath, which he has, of a certainty, most faithfully performed up to the present, and purposes equally faithfully to perform in the future as long as life remains in him, he will never pass the good town of Keswick without wringing, with gratitude, the hands of the hospitable Cumberland man, Mr. Scott, the owner of the George Hotel, and his good wife and charming daughter in remembrance of the surprising and much needed kindness on that ever memorable Christmas morning some ten years ago'.

Unfortunately, the landlord's daughter made the mistake of drying their boots overnight on the kitchen stove. Johnson's boots, 'thick soled, Scottish brogues', were shrivelled 'like Bombay ducks'... but owing to the courtly reception we had received, we said nothing and put on spare shoes... to go out and inspect the car after breakfast. The car too, was the worst for wear, due to the strain of crossing and re-crossing Shap'. They thought about asking the local blacksmith for assistance, but Johnson put the car on rail to Coventry and summoned a replacement Daimler instead.

Amazingly, given it was Christmas, on the 27th December, a 5.5hp Daimler was dispatched to Johnson and the tour continued to Newcastle with Mr. Ronald Outhwaite, its driver and a sportsman, driving.

Montague Grahame-White himself returned to Coventry by rail with the damaged car. By 30th December, another Daimler was substituted at Newcastle-upon-Tyne and Grahame-White returned to drive. They completed the tour back to London via Harrogate, Bradford, Wakefield and Sheffield, doing the last leg from Sheffield to London, a hundred and twenty-four miles in one day.

The following month, and before the Trial, after receiving the full report, the Prince of Wales ordered a 6hp Daimler for his own use – admittedly made in Coventry under a German licence, but a fillip to the fledgling motor industry nonetheless.

Following the reconnaissance and Johnson's report, the Trial was announced and entries invited. Interest increased rapidly as the start date approached and, gratifyingly for Rolls and the other organisers, entrants included many of the aforementioned leading motoring figures including the only lady driver, Mrs. Louise Bazalgette.

The entries were split into trade and private. Trade entries were numbered 1 onwards and private entries A1 onwards to differentiate their status.

Trade entries included Hewetson in a Benz (Number 1) and John W. Stocks, a renowned cyclist in an Aerial Quad. The Lanchester was driven by the company founder, George Lanchester (Number 21), J. S. Critchley and Montague Grahame-White, who reconnoitred with Johnson, both drove Daimlers. Herbert Austin, later Lord Austin, drove a Wolseley (Number 40), entered in the splendid name of the Wolseley Sheep Shearing Machine Company.

The thirty-three private entries were bold indeed. They represented the *Who's Who* of Victorian motoring. As individuals, they had little or no support although the likes of Hedges Butler (A2), Harmsworth (A7), Montagu (A11) and Rolls (A17) were all wealthy men.

Frank Hedges Butler, bon viveur, serial adventurer and wine merchant, accompanied his daughter, Vera, and both he and motoring M.P., J. S. Montagu, drove Daimlers, as did Siddeley, later of Hawker Siddeley; so did Claude Johnson, in his driving capacity of William Exe (an alias used for motoring).

Henry Edmunds participated in another Daimler (A12), which he called 'Rhoda', number plates being non-existent in 1900.

Mrs. Bazalgette herself drove a 3hp Benz Ideal (A25).

Charles Rolls, even at the age of twenty-two, saw it as his duty to take part regardless of expense. He had an engineering workshop at South Lodge and was not yet associated with the motor trade but he saw the Trial as a marvellous chance to review the best cars available, both at home and abroad, prior to a full-time foray into motor sales and service. He wrote to his father grumbling about the expense but noting that the motoring fraternity would expect him to take part. As an amateur car dealer, Rolls had made several trips to Paris in order to acquire cars for himself and for others. This included the car he was to drive in the Trial, which cost him £900 (some £90,000 today) and in addition he had to buy in spares and tyres for the trip. He reckoned that the tyres alone would cost £80 (£8,000 today). The 'Young Kaiser', as he was sometimes later known, was already watching the pennies, a trait for which he would become well-known.

Rolls was as keen as Johnson that the public be given the chance to examine the cars and hear from their drivers. In particular, his intention was that the Trial should test the machinery for reliability and safety more than the human endurance of the drivers. He wanted cars to become acceptable: 'People now take no notice whatever of a bicycle going along at 20mph; they've got used to it and it no longer shocks them, but when they see a heavy motor vehicle being driven by a man in a mask with a weird, shiny black jacket (bikers of 1900!), and an overall appearance of an armour plate travelling at 20mph, raising a cloud of dust and propelled by a force which they do not understand, and leaving behind a smell, which is sweeter than eau de cologne to the motorist, but to them abominable, they naturally say we are 'Madmen in motors, and that such practices must end in the deaths of thousands of people'.

Edge competed in a Napier for which firm he was General Manager and his mechanic was the fourteen-year-old school boy St. John Nixon[10].

St. John Nixon later became the youngest member of the Circle of Victorian Motorists. He had been brought up with racing in his blood – his tricyclist father held the John O'Groats to Lands End tricycle record for many years until 1923, and he must have been more than capable with motors to be asked to be mechanic to Edge at such a tender age and for such an occasion. Edge's decision

---

10 *The youngest passenger on the Trial, bar one – 'Bully', Edge's dog.*

to run a Napier, one of the first English cars, was a bold move. It was an unknown and untried car and this was the most severe trial ever conceived. His car was built from scratch in three months and it had already been sold to a Mr. and Mrs. Edward Kennard, he a hunting J.P. and she a Victorian novelist, who very sportingly agreed to lend it. Edge was, by this time, a renowned racing driver on a par with Rolls. The car was finished five days before the Trial.

Edge had originally entered the Trial as a trade entry, but his Napier was not completed in time.

Ironically, Rolls himself had counselled against 'scorching', given that there would be miles of empty roads and a sprint trial on the Duke of Portland's private estate at Welbeck, so off they went, for a three week trip, hugely ambitious for 1900. An acquaintance of the author, who ran in the re-enactment in 2000, said it was tough enough then, but a hundred years earlier it must have been gruelling.

Stories of the Trial are many. The first day's run to Bristol included a breakfast stop at Calcot Park. White waist-coated waiters served the motorists – dubbed the Motoring Missionaries by John Montagu – with salmon, quail, York ham and paté de fois gras, washed down with bounteous beakers of champagne. Just the thing for a day's motoring.

Harmsworth himself was furious when a photographer climbed up a ladder onto the roof of his stables to get an exclusive, unauthorised picture of the feast. When asked what he would have done, ever the newspaperman, the Press magnate replied: 'I should have dragged the ladder up after me'.

Rolls achieved nearly 38mph at Welbeck but nearly missed the start in London, repairs to his car being completed only half an hour before the start. Edge's car was bested by Rolls in the hill climbing trial at Taddington[11], near Buxton. Edge achieved 14mph, ahead of J. S. Montagu, but he was beaten by

11 *During the research for this book, the author found the Taddington course, which is on the current A6 between Buxton and Bakewell. The penny took some time to drop; there were not many cars on the A6 in 1900! The end of the run was at the Waterloo Inn, which still stands, as it did then. On my A6 visit I asked the present landlady if she knew anything about the Trial or the pub's significance in it. 'No' she replied, 'I've only been here six weeks'.*

Rolls's handsome 18mph, although Rolls himself came in second behind a power tricycle, powered by superman, A. J. Wilson.

Rolls won the Climb Trial at Dunmail Raise. At one point, Rolls lost Poole, his mechanic, when taking a corner too quickly on the Cat and Fiddle Pass. Poole fell out, as did some baggage, and Poole can hardly have been encouraged by Rolls's muttered curse, that if he fell out again he would not be retrieved.

Johnson arranged for a report to go back to London every day and Harmsworth's *Daily Mail* gave the Trial huge publicity, and so success was assured. The Press, however, as usual, looked for a fall guy. They called Rolls the 'Young Kaiser', somewhat unfairly, as he had six points on his licence or would have had if they existed at that time. He had collected three for failing to show a Red Flag in 1896 and another three for furious driving (30mph) in West Sussex some time later.

Meanwhile, crowds flocked to all the en route exhibitions including the Drill Hall in Bristol, Cheltenham Winter Gardens, Bingley Hall, Birmingham and Old Trafford Botanical Gardens in Manchester. Rolls, the expected and ultimate 'winner', recognised the chance to mix and promote his expertise and exuberance. He was just twenty-two and not a very sociable animal, drinking very modestly, but during the evening gatherings and the exhibitions, he must have found access to the *Who's Who* of the motoring world irresistible – providing his car was running well, which thanks to Poole and his own abilities, it was. He was able to promote his own interests as well as those of the motor car.

The entourage continued via Carlisle to Edinburgh, local newspapers reporting excitedly on progress and the public viewings of cars and personalities. Some employers allowed their men an hour off to see the cars go by. By now, the Trial had captured the nation's imagination. In Scotland the Lord Provost welcomed it in Edinburgh's Waverley Market – entrance money going to the Transvaal (Boer War) Fund and other charities.

The pace was telling but the remaining entrants were stalwart souls. One unkind soul described them thus: 'The motorist becomes a grimy one, in whose wrinkles the dust finds lodgings, and the general appearance is akin to that of an employee at the Corporation dust destroyer!' Flies, dust, no windscreens and untarred roads – stalwart souls indeed.

Turning south, the cars trundled one hundred and twenty-two miles to Newcastle via Musselburgh and Berwick on Tweed. On this stretch, Montague Grahame-White was unwise enough to let one of his passengers have a go at driving, and the novice promptly drove into a ditch and broke part of the steering gear. Standing on the off step with his left foot, Grahame-White kept his right foot on the hub of the off-front wheel end and, by pressure only, guided the car, over the fifty-two miles and for five hours to Newcastle. One newspaper commented: 'If this experiment in foot steering had gone astray, and a collision had occurred, when the car was running at third excessive speed (10mph), Mr. Grahame-White would not have received an unmixed tribute of admiration from a coroner's jury'.

The Trialists continued to Newcastle Drill Hall, the High Street packed and the Head Constable and his men keeping order where the crowd was thickest.

On the Newcastle to Leeds run, the *Yorkshire Post* reported: 'C. S. Rolls's progress from Darlington through Yorkshire on the southern leg was almost indecently rapid, and at Bradford, where children turned out to cheer the cars, any thought of a speed limit had manifestly been forgotten'. The vehicles paused at York for a brief exhibition, and the *Evening Press* solemnly reported a Mr. James Schumacher amongst the timekeepers – a hundred years on, one Michael Schumacher was undoubtedly a quicker champion.

Rolls continued to make the press, famously on the next run from Leeds to Sheffield, *Motor Car Journal* reporting: 'The Hon. C. S. Rolls has been going at high speed along the quiet country roads… between Otley and Guiseley his car had a neck and neck race with a North-East Express for three or four miles. The train made a detour through a tunnel, whereas the road was straight, and when the train came through, the car had forged ahead'.

And so to Sheffield and then on to Nottingham, the end in sight, but before that, the Welbeck Speed Trial on the Duke of Portland's estate although some entrants avoided it to ensure their completion of the journey. Works' entries had a point to prove on reliability however, so they were all keen to take part.

The Speed Trial took the form of a measured mile, with flying start – out and home – with an average then taken. The roads on the estate are good even today, and in 1900 they were as good as any in the kingdom. Rolls won the Speed Trial, averaging 38mph overall and 43mph top speed. Edge ran third in the Kennard's 8hp Napier. It must have been fun for the competing drivers, pedal to the metal after days of (ostensibly) adhering to 12mph (8mph in town) because the police (then as now) were inclined to pounce on 'scorchers'.

And so to London via Loughborough, Leicester and Northampton and with a final stop in St. Albans – and after a hiccup in Lincoln, sorted out by Claude Johnson, where a tollkeeper wanted four shillings per vehicle – Johnson cut a deal at one shilling and four pence a vehicle (four pence a wheel, excluding the steering wheel).

The cars arrived in London's Whitehall in the early evening of 12th May – there were forty-seven of them out of the sixty-one starters. Rolls was adjudged first with Edge in the Kennard's Napier just behind him. Rolls led the procession and, for once, his formal mask dropped and he is pictured with a beaming smile.

After Rolls and Edge, Farman's M.C.C. Triumph, the Ariel quadricycle of Stocks and Scott-Montagu were all in the leading dozen. Other well-known names to finish included Hedges Butler's Panhard, Johnson's Daimler, Mr. Hewetson's Ideal and the Benz of his friend, and only lady entrant, Mrs. Louise Bazalgette. Most of them were a little tired but triumphant at the end of their venture.

Mary Kennard, Victorian authoress and Napier-owner, waxed lyrical: 'The variety of motoring constitutes its principal charm. We were only small fry, shrouded in the generous dust of the flying Panhard (Rolls), swift Napier (Edge) and stately Daimler (Scott-Montagu)... they, we knew, looked down on us, we did not look down upon ourselves... we became a band of brothers, we of the De Dion Voiturettes, the Gladiator, the Wolseley, Triumph, etc.... we sympathised with each others misfortunes... we admired each other's feats of valour (*Motor Car Journal 19th May 1900*).

Mrs. Kennard had had an eventful time. S. F. Edge had borrowed the family Napier but she drove, not as an entrant, her own De Dion voiturette, following the Trial. She went up Shap Fell with J. W. Stocks, the famous cyclist, but came down in Mr. Holder's Daimler. Later in the Trial, her De Dion suffered a bad sideslip near Lincoln in which she was thrown from it. Shaken, but not badly hurt, she decided to retire from the 'race' as she lived close by in Market Harborough.

The Trial brought together key characters of the Rolls story. One such was Henry Edmunds, driving 'Rhoda'. He was a laggard by day, but at the exhibitions in the evenings he socialised with Rolls and the rest. So too did the adventurer, Frank Hedges Butler, and his nineteen year old daughter, Vera, whom Rolls entertained – the trio becoming ballooning partners a year later.

One sign of the success of the adventure manifested itself in changed signage of some Home Counties hotels, with repainted sign-boards offering 'Good accommodation for cycles – *and cars*'.

The event had been an unqualified success. One of the judges, Professor Boys, thought some three million people had seen the cars – one in twelve of the British population at the time. Selwyn Edge estimated that the engines of the cars had made six million revolutions in total and had proved the reliability of cars to potential purchasers.

Even today, if a car had covered a thousand miles in the previous three weeks it would be considered reliable for purchase; in 1900 such reliability was excellent publicity for the new manufacturers. Of the fifteen cars that dropped out, three-quarters were foreign made. Rolls's British mechanic, Poole, won the mechanic's prize (and many thought he should be sanctified for his forbearance in dealing with Rolls who was so very much a perfectionist).

Auto Car magazine summed up: 'Sixty thousand miles, twice round the world and no serious accidents even though almost all the drivers were on roads that they had never driven on before. Very few horses were frightened and most of them that were had been frightened by motorcycles. One man and a horse had been hurt and a motley mixed bag taken of seven or eight dogs, a cat, a hen, a little chicken and – a sparrow'.

A prize-giving gala dinner took place later at the Trocadero in London, presided over by Lord Kingsburgh, Chief Justice Clerk of Scotland, a participant. Lord Kingsburgh introduced Rolls, who among various anecdotes during his speech, described how he and his team had worked through the night for seven hours on the eve of the Trial to replace a four-speed-gear wheel, and he thanked Mr. T. P. Browne for the loan of Mr Browne's Panhard, which Poole and Rolls himself had stripped to extract the vital components. Interestingly, Rolls thought the most striking car was the Kennard Napier, driven by Edge, which had been assembled with incredible speed specifically for the Trial. Rolls wanted British cars to sell and mentioned £500 as a target purchase price for a new car.

The impact of the Trial was enormous, particularly on the horsey fraternity, and is encapsulated in an anecdote in *Auto Car* on 6th October, 1900: 'Lately I had a conversation with an old enemy of motors, bicycles and every kind of modern method of mechanical locomotion… imagine my amazement when I met him in Haldon driving an elegant little French motor. 'Oh yes' he said, I've come round. It was my infernal coachman who converted me. You know the kind of fellow I mean. He seemed to think that stables and horses are kept for him and not he for the horses… I sacked him at last and got another… sacked him too, sold the horses, carriages everything, bought four motors, and found myself master of my own property.

You can go anywhere and do anything at any hour… keep an engineer of course… even the butler and the boy can drive or lend a hand at a pinch.

I have been twenty-seven miles today, mostly uphill and have twelve to go. What price that in comparison with horses?

Take my advice – the advice of a man who started in active opposition – buy a motor and you will be glad of it'.

The 1900 Thousand Mile Trial had indeed achieved its objective and had largely established acceptance of the motor car throughout the United Kingdom.

However there were still more battles to be fought. The Club sought to counter proposals to further restrict automobile use. At Johnson's instigation, the Club decided to be proactive in the education of County Councils on the subject of motoring, which most Councillors knew little about. Deputations of County Councillors and Chief Constables were invited to the Club. Members drove them around and were under instructions to drive very slowly, and within the law, and only to speed up at the request of their passengers. A majority of local authorities were uneasy about car driving but this unease was caused by a minority – albeit a substantial minority – of selfish drivers.

The speed limit of 12mph-10mph in some places – was often flagrantly ignored, horses would rear and shy and be forced off the road. In a number of circulars, the Club told its members that they risked expulsion if they were found guilty of any such offence and these circulars were copied to the Chief Constables. The police were also asked for their opinion on registration plates or whether names on cars would continue to be effective. In 1901, registration numbers had still not been adopted, so names graced the cars. Rolls chose for his Panhard 'Petrolls' and Claude Johnson's car was called 'The Sluggard'.

The charm offensive continued. During 1901, a group, consisting initially of Rolls's friend, Mark Mayhew, and two others, began to transport Army officers. Although, in this instance, the charm backfired. Flak rose from the popular press. Why should Rolls, with his millionaire background, and other wealthy individuals receive thirty shillings a day (£150 today) and a petrol allowance?

The aptly named *The Critic* said it hoped Rolls, Mayhew and friends 'will invite me down to manoeuvres… at a pleasant resort within the reach of a town that might be agreed upon. In that case I promise them (the Army Reserve Volunteers) to give as warlike a display, with knife and fork, as the most valorous'. Journalists may like a free lunch – but expense accounts for aristocratic petrolheads were a fair target.

There were still plenty of critics. Augustine Birrell, K.C., a senior judge, wrote to John Montagu: 'Dear Scott-Montagu, I am sorry to be asked my opinions about automobilism, but I do not like withholding them from an old friend. As a 'bastard sport', which enables a great deal of idle folk to rush along public highways, at railway speed, to the annoyance, disgust and danger to the majority of ratepayers and their children, I regard automobilism with intense dislike and cannot honestly say that I hear of the frequent accidents that befall its devotees with any real regret'.

Rolls fought back, writing in the *Daily Mail* in 1901, 'It is pleasing to see the attitude you have taken up in the wholesale persecution of cyclists and motorists by certain small, narrow-minded bodies. At the early part of the last century serious endeavours were made to restrict the speed of railways to 8mph, and it's regrettable that there should still be a section of the community whose aims appear to be to hold back the country in the march of progress for the gratification of their own ignorance and prejudice'.

Meanwhile the Club went from strength to strength. By the end of 1901 it had a thousand members and Claude Johnson had pocketed over eight hundred ten-shilling notes. But Johnson was now in the firing line. He was fined for careless driving, (almost certainly only because of his profile in the Club). His predicament had been exacerbated by his London solicitor who advised him not to answer certain questions in Court. The offence and hearing were in Yorkshire where they claim to like plain speaking. Johnson was a careful driver and the consensus of motoring opinion nationwide was that he had been made a scapegoat. It was also noted that the Chairman of the Bench in Yorkshire might have been the brother-in-law of the Lord Mayor of Leeds, who had boycotted the Thousand Mile Trial earlier, one of the few local dignitaries to do so.

The courts were the battlefield where skirmishes over the future of motoring took place. Rolls had been involved in the setting up of the 'Motor Users Defence Association' (1900) to protect motorists from 'severe handling' in the Courts along with S. F. Edge, Claude Johnson and Charles Cordingley, the founder of the *Motor Car Journal*.

There was reason for concern. In an earlier case, a motorist had been prosecuted *after* having proved that he was not speeding in a particular county. The Bench, however, would have none of it, saying that he, therefore, must have been speeding somewhere else and fined him anyway. Scores of letters protesting against this decision were published in the press. Rolls wrote to Johnson asking that he enlist his friend, Harmsworth, to set out the current state of play and Johnson's letter to the *Daily Mail* describes in some detail how things stood in 1902:

'1. *Cars have come to stay.*
2. *They will shortly, to a large extent, replace the horse.*
3. *Our hereditary senses are shocked to see anything on the road faster than the horse… speed of itself is not dangerous, but the inability to stop is…*

It is, therefore, no good for people to get hysterical because cars are driven fast, as it is certain, up to a certain point, they will always be driven fast'.

Johnson suggested 'warning boards' on dangerous bends and zones and questioned the waste of police time in pursuing 'scorchers' who exceeded the speed limit of 12mph. He spoke of inexperienced drivers and of temporary (provisional) licences, as in France, of the numbering of cars, of the inevitable increase in traffic as cars became more popular, of an increase in average speeds from 10mph to 25mph. Manufacturers rather than 'turn out the fastest and most luxurious carriage, will have a far more simple problem to deal with, that of turning out at a most reasonable price, the most reliable and comfortable car, which will run on the flat at 30mph'.

The Automobile Association was founded in 1905. It was not a club but, to some extent, its activities complimented those of the Club. It was originally formed to help motorists avoid speed traps because there was a perception amongst its more militant members, including Mark Mayhew, Charles Jarrott and Selwyn Edge, that the Club was not doing enough in this area. At first, A.A. patrolmen on bicycles warned motorists of speed traps but this was outlawed following a 1910 Court case where it was ruled that such action constituted 'obstructing police officers in the course of their duties'. Thereafter, A.A. patrolmen would salute all passing cars that displayed an A.A. badge – if danger lurked, it being understood that an A.A. patrolman could not be prosecuted for failing to salute. The A.A. Handbook itself stated: 'It cannot be too strongly emphasised that when a patrol fails to salute, the member should stop and ask the reason why as it is certain that the patrolman had something of importance to communicate.' By 1939, a third of all motorists were members of the A.A. so presumably there was a lot of saluting[12]!

It was all rather typically British and confusing. When travelling with Rolls, a mystified Wilbur Wright observed that: 'we paid one lot of men to stop us from driving too fast, and paid another lot of men (the A.A. patrolmen) to warn us when we travel too fast, that there was a 'cop' around the next bend'.

---

12 *The Automobile Association was demutualised and sold to a commercial concern in 1999, ninety-four years after its formation, at almost the same time as the R.A.C. sold its motoring services arm (2000) and became a luxury, private members club again.*

The Association was more 'hands on' than the Club. By 1906, it had erected thousands of hazard signs, a vital contribution because local authorities did not take over road control until the mid-1930s at roughly the same time as driving tests were introduced. The comedian Rowan Atkinson, of McLaren GT41 fame, an ardent motorist and collector of cars, might be interested to discover, if he does not know already, that the first man to pass his driving test in the United Kingdom was one 'Mr. Beene'.

Meanwhile, back at the Club, Claude Johnson's departure to C. S. Rolls & Co. had left the Club with no one person at the helm, and disputes and misunderstandings became many. Johnson had had the foresight to realise that the Club had at least two factions as the car cult grew and the Club could no longer control them. Rolls was still on the Club Committee. Maybe this is why Johnson moved on, as well as to earn greater financial rewards. One faction thought the Club should defend the motorist at all costs against persecution at the hands of the magistrates, and that it was a jolly good members' club. The other faction thought about their wider, if duller, responsibility to the wider public and other road users, including pedestrians. How did you defend the indefensible? When one can do 60mph in a car, how does one avoid speeding, even under the new speed limit of 20mph, introduced in 1903?

That Australian bounder, Edge was particularly damning. He wrote in the Club Journal: 'We say we are the leading and controlling body in the automobile world, but to remain in that position it seems to me that it is absolutely necessary for us to have everyone in as members, who are willing to join, providing there is nothing to be said about their character, and their social position in life should have little or nothing to do with their joining'.

How could 'The Parliament of Motoring' justify itself before the real Houses of Parliament, when many of its members, who were also Members of Parliament, opposed number plates, which would enable 'scorchers' to be identified and dealt with? Magistrates were handing out fines for 'tearing madly about the country at breakneck speed'. M.Ps spoke of 'flying millionaires' while others said those who drove 'a ton of iron at excessive speed should be flogged'.

Even the clergy were seen as those whose word could not be trusted. The Bishop of Winchester was the first occupant of an Episcopal See to be involved in a motoring case. The story is a simple one. He was driving through Alton in Hampshire when a horse in an unattended brewer's van took fright and bolted. The police and other witnesses declared that the Bishop's car was being driven furiously and fast. Their testimony was accepted as against the evidence of the bishop, his chaplain and his motor man. If a Bishop's word, plus his chaplain, was to no avail, how could a common motorist expect to escape?

Nevertheless, Edwardian speed traps were fundraising as today, although not popular with the constabulary, who sought to meet their targets.

One constable related:

'I dropped in one evening to have a pipe with my friend, Constable Simmonds. He was sitting in his shirtsleeves by the fire, scraping great chunks of mud off his blue trousers with a big clasp knife. 'Dirty work sir, 'orrible dirty', he said, looking up as I entered. 'To think that a man of my age and respectability should spend his days hiding in a ditch like an 'unted rat.

Still, it's worth it, and it's only going to be for two days more… You may well ask sir. It's a little scheme of me own, about which I 'ave a right to be proud. Look at this map sir. Now here's a gentle slope and they come down that very slow, knowing 'ow it's a trap. Just at the bottom the road dips down very sudden for ten yards and then goes up again – kind of a switchback.

Well, sir, unless they take their brakes off for those ten yards, they can't get up the hopposite 'ill, and if they do take them off, they must do it in under a second. You could just work it out if you likes. Ten yards at one second is twenty and five-elevenths miles an hour unless I am much mistaken. They only want £500 for the rates now and a hundred motors pass through each day. The haverage fine is £3 each so there you are! Only two days more and the rates for this year will be paid and no more need to go ditch crawling'.

In 1903, the speed limit was increased to 20mph, in exchange for car identification, in part due to the heroic efforts of motoring M.P. and leading Club member, John Montagu, but it pleased very few. A members' club existed, the Automobile Club of Great Britain and Ireland, but not a club that could protect its members as most would have wished. The glory days of the Club, as arbiter, were over. It would still, in future, officiate in the Gordon Bennett and the subsequent races in Ireland. It would still inaugurate the Tourist Trophy races in the Isle of Man, to which we shall return shortly.

Its members might indulge their love of speed on the newly-built Brooklands track from 1907 onwards, but these commercial forces, including mass production of cars, were to bring the Club out of its own self-satisfied cocoon. It would cede some powers to other associations such as the Automobile Association, as motoring for the few, became motoring for all.

Grange House
Old Kent Rd area, London.

Lord & Lady Llangattock.

Rolls at eighteen – a keen cyclist.

The Hendre.

The Santa Maria.

Hon. Evelyn Ellis – the first car in England.

C.S. Rolls's first car – 3¾ hp Peugeot.

Before the red flag went.

The Tunbridge Wells exhibition.

Motor Car Tour to Brighton.

THE MOTOR CAR CLUB.

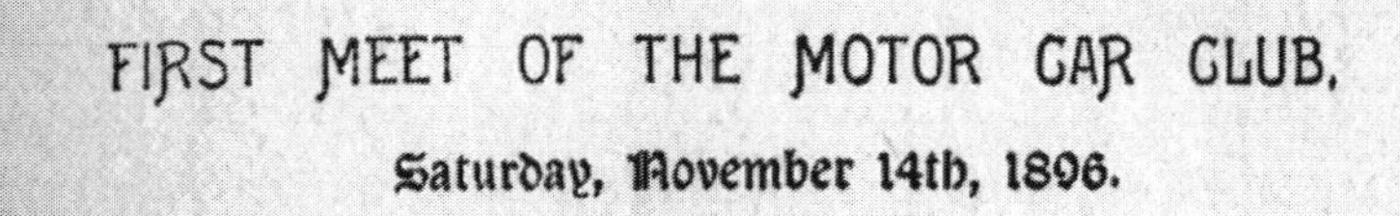

FIRST MEET OF THE MOTOR CAR CLUB,

Saturday, November 14th, 1896.

———:———

Instructions as to Route & Itinerary.

———:———

GENERAL RECOMMENDATIONS. Owners and drivers of Motor Vehicles taking part in the Tour

Should remember that Motor Cars are on their trial in England, and that any rashness or carelessness might injure the industry in this Country.

Should see that their Motor Cars appear in thoroughly good clean order, and are never left unattended on the route.

Should be fully provided with sufficient lubricating and motor oil.

Should see that passengers are provided with proper protection against bad weather, such as mackintoshes, etc., and with light provisions.

Should use the greatest care as to speed and driving, so as not to endanger ordinary traffic.

Should treat the Police and other Authorities on the route with polite consideration.

UNIFORM. Special Caps and Armlets can be provided to Members of the Club driving Motor Vehicles who wish for them on application to the Secretary.

PILOT CAR. Mr. Harry J. Lawson, the President of the Club, will drive the Pilot Car, from which directions will be given. Drivers are requested not to pass this Car unless by necessity, so that directions may be communicated to those taking part in the run.

OIL. A supply of motor oil (spec. 6·80) and also of lubricating oil will be found at the "White Hart Hotel," Reigate

WATER. Water can be obtained at the "Horse & Groom," Streatham, "Wheatsheaf," Thornton Heath, "Greyhound," Croydon, "Windsor Castle," Purley, "The Star," Horley, "White Hart," Reigate, "The George," Crawley, "Black Swan," Peas Pottage, "Red Lion," Hand Cross, "Queen's Head," Bolney, "King's Head," Albourne, "The Plough," Pyecombe, and the "Black Lion," Patcham.

MEET OF CARS. The Motor Cars should assemble in front of the Whitehall Entrance of the Metropole Hotel, not later than 9 a.m. Breakfast takes place at 9.30 sharp in the Whitehall Rooms of the Hotel Metropole. Tickets 10/- each, including Wine.

The Emancipation Run invitation.

En route to Brighton.

En route to Brighton.

Arrival at Brighton – Harry Lawson.

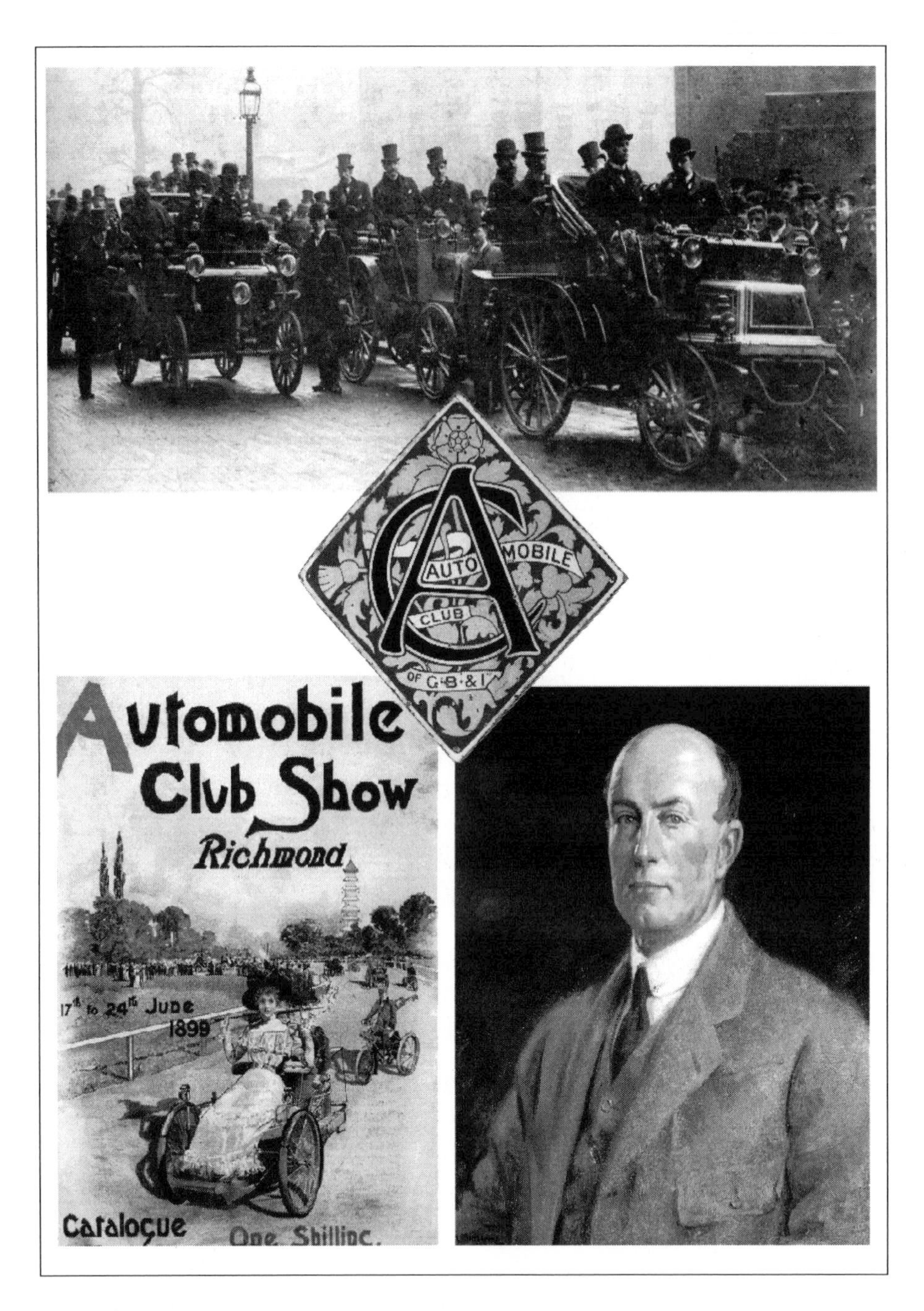

The first A.C.G.B.I. Club run-Rolls leading & the A.C.G.B.I Club badge.
The Richmond Show June 1899 & Frederick Simms – founder of the A.C.G.B.I.

The start of the Thousand Mile Trial.

Fuel for the journey – Pratts Motor Spirit.

N°.26 Friswell Ltd. – 8hp Peugeot.

Mrs Louise Bazalgette – 3hp Benz Ideal.

Frank Hedges Butler and daughter Vera.

Monday, April 23rd, 1900

LONDON TO BRISTOL

	Intermediate mileage	Cumulative mileage	Remarks
Hyde Park Corner . .			Start at 7 a.m.
Hammersmith . .	3½		
Brentford Town Hall .	3½	7	
Hounslow Trinity Church .	2¾	9¾	
Colnbrook, George Hotel .	7¼	17	
Slough, Crown Hotel .	3½	20½	
Maidenhead Town Hall .	5¾	26¼	
Twyford, King's Arms .	7¾	34	
Reading, St. Giles Church .	5	39	
Calcot Park, on right .	3¼	42¼	Breakfast
Theale	1¾	44	
Newbury . . .	12	56	
Hungerford . . .	8½	64½	
Marlborough Hill (summit)	8½	73	
Marlborough Town Hall .	1½	74½	Lunch
Beckhampton . .	6¾	81¼	
Calne (Market Place) .	6	87¼	
Chippenham (Market Place)	6	93¼	
Box	7	100¼	
Bath	5¾	106	Tea
Saltford (station) . .	4¾	110¾	
Keynsham . . .	2¾	113½	
Bristol	5	118½	End of first day's run.

Bristol, Tuesday, April 24th, 1900

One-day exhibition under the patronage of the Lord Mayor of Bristol, in the Drill Hall

The first day's route.

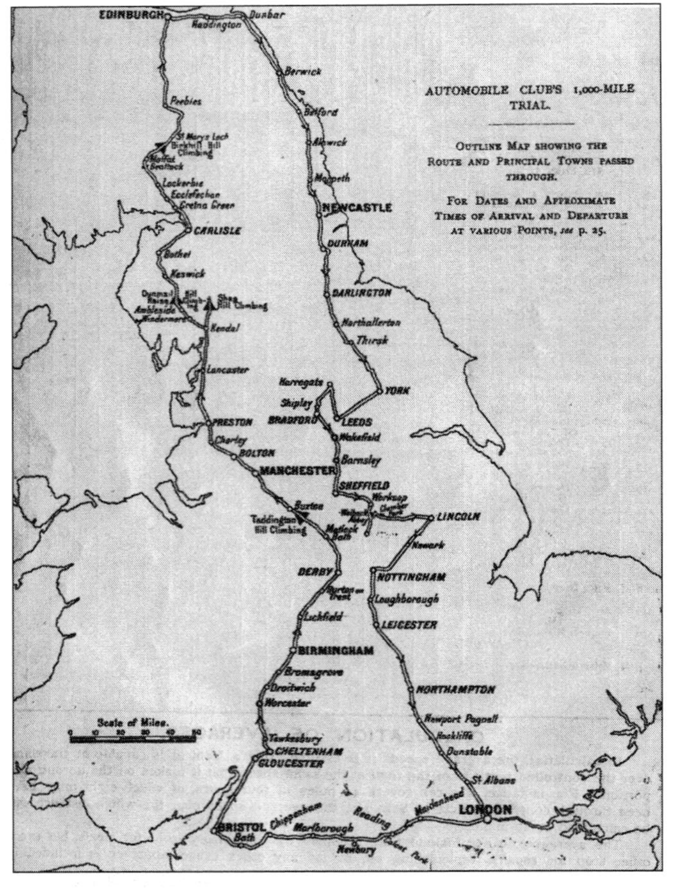

The whole Thousand Miles.

Calcot Park.

The Butlers and T.P. Browne's 6hp Panhard.

C.S. Rolls and his mechanic, Poole.

Ready to time trial at Welbeck.

A beaming C.S. Rolls – Gold Medal winner.

Driving the Duchess of York (later Queen Mary) October 1900.

Chapter Five

Rolls – The Racer

Charlie Rolls loved to race, to win fame, to test cars and to prove their reliability, he was a 'Man of Speed' as described by Laurence Meynell[13] in his book of the same name. He was not only Britain's first racing ace, but the first racing team's financier, manager and designer all rolled into one. Yet his racing career spanned just seven years, 1899-1906, and is largely forgotten when compared with his other achievements.

The Thousand Mile Trial had been a triumph, but 1900 continued to be memorable. Rolls competed in gymkhanas and domestic events and raced with S. F. Edge in a 16hp Napier in the Paris/Toulouse race that July. Edge had purchased the car, the first of its kind, for the Thousand Mile Trial, but it had not been completed in time. Since then he had undertaken to climb Porlock Hill in Devon, one of the steepest major hills in the country following a challenge from a member of the Stock Exchange, one Roger Fuller. Porlock Hill was half a mile with an average gradient of 1:6, but nearer to 1:4 around some of the corners. A large crowd of people collected. Edge described the event in his book 'Reminiscences'[14]. Edge: 'Before many yards had been covered we had left the horse and its owner, one Mr. Otter, in the rear and we never saw it again until we reached the top of the hill where we had to wait some time for its arrival'. This was the first time a motor car has been known to climb Porlock Hill and created a mild sensation.

Edge entered this Napier for the Paris/Toulouse race of July 1900. Rolls – not yet twenty-three – went as his mechanic, but only after Lady Llangattock had ridden in the car with Edge and entreated him 'not to bring his (Rolls) young life to an end'. Edge is somewhat coy about what happened in the race itself. It seems that he ran into Jenatzy's car and disabled it so that Jenatzy was unable to compete. Meanwhile he and Rolls were troubled by ignition problems. Edge had been experimenting with British-made coils because he was planning a bigger

---

13 *'Man of Speed' – Meynell (Published in 1953 by Bodley Head).*

14 *'My Motoring Reminiscences' by S. F. Edge (The Marshall Press).*

car to participate in the Gordon Bennett race of the following year, and the coil problem had to be overcome as all parts of Gordon Bennett cars had to be made in their country of entry. In fact, Edge, with Montagu Napier, was developing the first all-British racing car and he was effectively Napier's selling agent. The coil never worked properly, there was incessant misfiring, and it was almost impossible to make the car run on all four cylinders. Rolls and Edge abandoned the contest.

Rolls was far from being disenchanted with Napiers. He ordered a 50hp Napier racer because he too wanted a British car and the Napier was the only car capable of matching the French and German competition. However, delays in completing the car led him to cancel his order and he bought a Russian Blue 60bhp Mors instead and enlisted Claude Crompton for his drive in the 1901 Paris/Berlin race, an event that brought together Jarrott, Edge and Rolls, the three leading British drivers, for the first time as competitors. The *Tatler* described them: 'I think that Mr. Charles Jarrott comes nearest to my ideal driver. He's cool almost to imperturbability and yet he has all the dash, which carries a man successfully in a tight place. The skill and judgement are as perfect as may be and withal he is a most considerate driver. Selwyn Edge is another driver, who instils complete confidence in one. His grim determination gives the idea that he can carry through whatever he undertakes. In road knowledge he has no superior and his judgement is marvellous.

Charlie Rolls differs in many respects from both Jarrott and Edge. In the old days he was accused of recklessness by many critics, but here again sound judgement governed all his actions and he knew exactly how to deal with every difficulty which arose'.

The 1901 Paris/Berlin race assumed historic proportions. It was a gesture of reconciliation following the Franco-Prussian War thirty years earlier. The French racing authorities had been delighted that the German club accepted their suggestion that there be a seven hundred and forty-nine mile race from Paris to Berlin in June of that year. The race was to be held over three days, stages of two hundred and seventy-eight, two hundred and eighty-five and one hundred and eighty-six miles on consecutive days. The stages covered Paris to Aix-la-Chapelle, Aix to Hanover and Hanover to Berlin. Rolls paid his way as a private entrant.

Jarrott meanwhile had persuaded Harvey du Cros, who held the Panhard franchise for England, to secure one of the special racing cars that were being built for the event. Nobody else wanted it because it was numbered thirteen but Jarrott loved its racing green and waxed lyrical about the 'beautiful rich dark colour, which gave the car such a handsome appearance'. He wondered why no one else painted their cars green. British Racing Green was derived from this car and the subsequent Emerald-Isle Gordon Bennett team colours.

Charles Jarrott's book, *Ten Years of Motors and Motor Racing – 1896-1906*, describes the pre-race atmosphere on a Thursday night near Paris:

'I've never seen a more interesting and uncommon sight that met my eyes as in the darkness I made my way out to the start through the Bois de Vincennes at three o'clock on the morning of the race. Hundreds of cars and thousands of cyclists were rushing along in one continuous stream, miles in length, a great multi-coloured serpentine of light winding away through the trees. The cyclists were carrying paper lanterns of all shapes, colours and sizes. Fires were lit by the roadside and a scene of animation prevailed in the darkness, the like of which only those who have witnessed the start of a great continental road race can ever have seen. Many had camped out all night and were whiling away the time with song and music, and then as daylight gradually dawned, a vast concourse of people were assembled at the actual starting point. At four o'clock the first car was sent on its way, the rest following at two minute intervals'.

Jarrott and Edge met during the day. Jarrott was unfortunate enough to lose his mechanic, Smith, after about fifty miles; Smith was flung out of the car, narrowly missing a very solid stone wall. Jarrott collected him and the mechanic reminded him that there were seven hundred miles of fairly hairy driving to go and to be a little more circumspect.

C. S. Rolls also wrote about the event: 'My own experiences, however, were somewhat unhappy, chiefly due no doubt to my not having time to put my new Mors to proper test before the race. The vehicle was only properly finished at 11.00 p.m. the night before the start, which barely gave us time to get up to Champigny and find our places at the point of departure, owing to the enormous crowd of motor vehicles of every sort rushing along in one direction to take up their places on the road and watch the passing of the racers.

So continuous was the stream of motor traffic indeed that when we overshot our mark we were unable, for a considerable time, to turn round in the road until we got a number of men with lanterns to stand in the middle of the road and stop the run of the traffic for a moment.

No accidents, however, were reported at this juncture owing to the excellent police arrangements, although it was practically impossible for pedestrians to find an opportunity of crossing the road between the cars.

Fires were lit alongside the road and it was indeed a most wonderful and picturesque sight to watch the countless types of big cars, small cars, tricycles and bicycles, decorated with Japanese lanterns, speeding along through the night, many of them with their exhaust boxes detached… and we could scarcely tear ourselves away to get an hour's sleep in a hayloft, the sole occupant of which was a cat.

We were duly awakened at 3.15 a.m. and clambering down the ladder from the hayloft we mounted our car, moved into line and awaited the start. 'Quinze, dix, cinq, partez!' and we were off, speeding along the first stretch of bumpy road as fast as we could run without being jerked off our seats.

Soon after passing the first control, we came upon some ideal strips of road with a perfect surface and we passed some five or six cars in the first few miles. Before very long, however, we heard a cylinder missing, which produced the usual sinking feeling within one, so without stopping or slowing down, we next occupied ourselves in discovering which was the faulty cylinder. This done, we concluded the ignition was the trouble and my friend, Mr. Claude Crompton, who accompanied me as amateur mechanic, changed the coils to no effect. He then took out and replaced the 'inflammateur' on the cylinder, which was a difficult feat to do 'en pleine vitesse' (at full speed)… he had seven hundred shocks a minute to stimulate him.

Being unable to get the fourth cylinder to work, we decided to continue on three as far as the next control, where the Mors depot was situated with mechanics, petrol and spare parts awaiting us. We had lost a lot of ground through so running for some twenty or thirty miles, and two or three cars had re-passed us… When we got to Montmirail, another thirty-five minutes were lost in the control while the Mors men took out the induction valve, sparking maker, carburettor, etc., only to find at the end of it that an exhaust spring had jumped out. This was most annoying as it was one of the first things we looked for, but the hook of the spring had become displaced in such a manner that the latter appeared to be perfectly in its place, and the valve seemed to be working up and down alright.

This, of course, was rectified in one minute and we proceeded on our way.

At this time onwards, however, the car ran in a most wonderful manner and we caught up many others. We had no punctures that day, though we stopped a number of times to extract nails, which we felt in the tyres as we were moving along. The exhaust spring also jumped out again twice.

We arrived at Aix-la-Chapelle in excellent time and had done so well that it looked like us securing a good position in the race on the two succeeding days.

On the following day, however, exceeding ill-fortune awaited us. We started out at 5.00 a.m. in very curious weather, there being a thick mist in different parts of the road. This wetted one's coat and face with the result that when catching up with other cars, a thick layer of dust stuck to us all over. Driving under these circumstances was very difficult. One tried with the goggles on, one tried with the goggles off, and eventually found that one could see better without them as they became almost opaque in a mile or two.

During the second day of three we encountered many miles of atrocious pave, and over this, being accustomed to save our car, I went very slowly and allowed several other slower cars to pass us.

In spite of this precaution, however, a grave state of things was discovered on entering Cologne. One of the iron brackets supporting the water tank, having a flaw in the bolt, broke off and allowed the tank to drop onto the back axle, the action of which had battered a number of holes in the former and loosened the seams.

This was a heartbreaking situation as we had apparently got up to somewhere about seventh place according to classification. I felt like giving up the race, as the tank seemed irreparable, but Crompton, who takes after his father in knowing no difficulty, determined to make a shot at repairing.

First we took off the back off the car, opened up the manhole of the tank, and with great difficulty stopped up the holes with grease and canvas from the interior, by means of which we succeeded in getting the lower part of the tank to hold water, with only a slight leaking.

We then procured some strong, iron wire and bound the tank up to bits of wood projecting from the frame and attached, as best we could, and after this made up our minds to crawl into Dusseldorf, the next control where a Mors depot was established. I would here remark that the big makers in this, as in all important races, established depots at the outward control of most of the large towns en route, and the moment you arrive, one man hoses your tyres to cool them, another man fills your petrol tank, another the lubricators, etc. and any adjustments required are made in the most expeditious manner, during the one, two or three minutes that may remain before you are due to quit the outward control.

These men, however, practically refused to help us with the tank, saying it was impossible for us to proceed and recommending us to relinquish the race and wait for a new tank from Paris.

Rather than do this, however, we plugged steadily on, frequently repairing the interior of the tank and patching it up – an unpleasant job – for now and then it would suddenly commence to lose its water from the canvas and grease getting shifted inside, and Crompton nobly plunged his hand each time into the nearly boiling water to fill up the holes with more grease so as to save enough water in the bottom of the tank to run us to the next control.

When we had good surfaces we would go at full speed, but as practically the whole length of the route from here onwards comprised a villainous road… we did not dare go beyond the third speed throughout and generally were on the second.

We then had to content ourselves with seeing car after car and voiturettes pass us easily, having to curb the power of our big monster for fear of shredding our water tank altogether and thus losing any chance of reaching Berlin.

We got to Hanover of course very late and were much congratulated by our French friends, who had seen our apparently hopeless breakdown when they passed us at Cologne and were much surprised at our getting here.

Having only one and three-quarter hours allowed for Hanover, we could do nothing but remake the wire attachment of the tank, which had now broken a second bracket, leaving all the strain on the wire.

We took an extra hour out of our running time and made a better job of the attachment that we had on the previous day, although the Mors men again discouraged us from attempting to run to Berlin with a large water tank, which leaked everywhere and was only suspended by a few bits of wire attached to thin pieces of wood. On the final stage of the journey, besides starting very late, we had three punctures on the road (also one the day before but none on the first day), and what with the ceaseless trouble caused by the water tank and the dread of losing it over the rough surface, we were very grateful when Berlin was reached five hours after the first arrival.

So tired were we that during the three following days we fell asleep at all times during the day whether at meals, in a cab or at the opera, to say nothing about my talking in my sleep (about the car of course) in the night, a thing I have never been accused of before.

When the car was in the Exhibition, our repairs, the effectiveness of which I should say was due to the ingenuity of Mr. Crompton, were the cause of no little curiosity and the members of the Mors firm gave us their hearty thanks for the trouble we had taken on the road and our determination to get through somehow.

It is clear that a race of this sort is entirely a matter of luck, given equal cars – Fournier, both in the Paris to Bordeaux and the Paris to Berlin, having better luck than anyone else.

The Le Mans born driver had a great advantage moreover in being an early starter, as it is a matter of very great difficulty, and often impossibility, to overtake cars that are in front, owing to the dust which beats in your face like a blinding cloud of dense powder.

As we had got up from thirty-third to about seventh during the first half of the journey, we were told we must have been in the first three, if nothing had occurred to us, as two or three of those, who remained in front of us when an accident happened, never got through.

Having given up at Cologne the idea of being placed, having spent some four hours stationary on the road and having run miles from Cologne to Berlin at half speed, we were not a little surprised to learn that after all we were classed eighteenth out of a hundred and ten starters'.

Jarrott meanwhile, in one of his first major drives, finished a commendable tenth, and described the scenes at the finish: 'Huge laurel leaves were laid on the cars, tied with French and German colours. Altogether the scene, apart from being historic, was unique with regard to the enthusiasm displayed by everyone concerned.

... after a delay of three hours, the cars were lined up for a grand procession into Berlin itself... and the big Brandenburg gates, only opened up on great national occasions, were flung wide and the procession, led by the victorious Fournier, drove into the city'.

Rolls now owned at least three Mors racers. His Paris/Berlin car, that had cost him £1,200, he drove for his attempt on the kilometre record at Achères, near Paris, in April 1902, an attempt that was unsuccessful in 35.4 seconds (63mph), far slower than his Welbeck time.

His Mors for Paris/Vienna in 1902 cost him £2,000 and had coachwork similar to an upturned boat. He also drove it for a record attempt at Welbeck[15] and later during the Irish Fortnight of 1903, part of the Gordon Bennett celebrations of that year. It was later known to the staff of C. S. Rolls & Co. as the 'Easter Egg'.

Rolls's third Mors had an 11.6-litre, four-cylinder engine. In this car Rolls raced at the Southport Speed Trials.

At Bexhill he entered various cars, winning one head to head race against Edge but losing another to Jarrott. At the end of the summer, at the Welbeck Speed Trials, he won the day – but was then disqualified for having an inadequate complement of passengers.

---

15 *Welbeck, the home of the Duke and Duchess of Portland, was where the British cars would vie for the Flying Kilometre record, but the course was not flat and these world record times (at one time held by Rolls) were not recognised as the official world record, the adjudicators of which were the Automobile Club de France.*

The Paris/Vienna race was briefly threatened by the government of the Austrian Tyrol, which had forbidden cars to circulate on the mountain roads because they might frighten horses. The race was a monster – one thousand, one hundred and twenty kilometres (seven hundred miles). It contained within its serpentine length the entire Gordon Bennett race, which ended at Innsbruck. Jarrott, in a Panhard, had a rough trip and finished 'almost dead with fatigue'. One of his passengers, on reaching his rooms, 'flung himself on the floor and told his attendants to remove the remainder of his clothes… and take them away and never let him see them again'. And Rolls escaped serious injury when two tyres burst simultaneously. He told *Motor Illustrated*:

'Yes, I was unlucky, I usually am. It was the same in the Berlin race you remember when my petrol tank fell off and put me out of the race. I was very confident of success in the last contest, but after all its nine-tenths luck that gets a man through such an ordeal. My evil genius troubled me very early in the race. Firstly I had bother with the clutch, but that was not enough to seriously jeopardise my prospects of victory. I passed a nasty corner, where two cars had already come to grief, with ease, but directly afterwards my accident happened.

We were travelling well, probably at the rate of 60mph. Suddenly, as we were rounding a corner, both tyres on the left-hand side of the car collapsed. This was a most extraordinary misadventure, and I can only account for it by supposing that both tubes were punctured by the same horseshoe or jagged flint. There was no report and we drove on unheeding, but as the turning became more accentuated, the car refused to answer to the wheel, the deflated tyres caused it to run straight ahead, leaving the road, racing onto the grass, leaping two gullies into the field beyond. Then in a flash we were criss-crossing the road again and dead ahead of us was a stalwart tree, which we were approaching at the rate of an express train. We struck the tree with terrible force and in a second it was bent, cracked and broken down while the car had passed on, over it and beyond. Our speed saved us. It was the terrific impetus that destroyed the tree, so had we struck it at 40mph, we should probably have been killed. Directly afterwards the car buried itself in a soft bank and my mechanic and I alighted quite easily, comparatively unhurt. Curiously enough the seat, on which we had been sitting, was smashed to splinters, and pieces of it were actually sticking to the back wheel.

It was a miracle we were not fatally injured and it only goes to show how difficult it is to kill a human being. My sensation was not of fear, I only remember the great surprise I felt when the car stopped.

I broke a blood vessel in my wrist and, the skin not being broken, the hand swelled towards the size of my head. The crowd watching the race were more alarmed than I, they fully expected to see us killed. When we emerged from the ruins of the car with whole bodies, they fell upon us, wept and embraced us.

Nurses doctored my wound in a rough sort of way and, borrowing a bicycle, I rode into a town where I had it properly attended to. You can imagine how the other competitors stared when they saw me returned on two wheels rather than four. The tree I struck would be about nine inches in diameter. It collapsed just as though it were on a hinge. I feel no ill effect from the spill; I feel rather sore about my non-success in the race as my car was running so well at the time of the accident'.

England and France were the only two Gordon Bennett teams that took part, but the day belonged to Selwyn Edge, who, by sheer determination, took the 1902 Gordon Bennett trophy in a British car when all five others failed to finish. He alone reached Innsbruck. This gave the Napier marque the massive boost but created a problem with the A.C.G.B.I. because the rules meant that Britain would have to stage the 1903 race, and an even bigger problem for Charles Rolls. He wanted a British car to sell and Edge now had one – where would Rolls find a car to match the Napier?

Frenchmen, Charron and Girardot, both driving Panhards for France, had won the inaugural race in 1900 and the second race in 1901. The problem was that there was no racetrack in Britain and there was a 12mph speed limit. The head of the Racing Club of France, Count Zborowski and Claude Johnson, secretary of the Automobile Club, looked at a number of possible courses in Ireland. The Count was a racer himself, and had ordered one of the three originally conceived 50hp Napiers, one of which had been delivered to Edge, and the other being for Rolls although Edge's car was the only one delivered.

Zborowski and Johnson found out a course of three hundred and twenty-seven miles, centred on Athy, in the midlands of Ireland. It was made up of a figure of eight track, which was to be encircled three times, with an extra lap of the western loop to finish. The Irish tourism industry was thrilled at the prospect. Legislation was introduced in the British and Irish Parliament for a temporary repeal of the 14mph speed limit, which then existed in Ireland. The repeal would hold for the duration of the event.

Having lifted the Cup in 1902 the previous year, Edge was pre-selected as one of the three drivers for the 1903 race in Ireland. Jarrott was selected on the basis of his fine finish in the Paris/Berlin race and also his win in the Circuit des Ardennes in a Panhard. The A.C.G.B.I. was the only club to pick its team by way of a qualifying drive. Rolls, Mayhew and Stocks, all on Napiers, together with fourth driver, Lyall, on a Star were left to fight for the third place. Rolls's car did not come up to expectations. He had carburettor trouble. Stocks was chosen as the third driver to race for the Great Britain team in Ireland.

Nothing daunted, Rolls unsuccessfully tried to use his connections to obtain a drive for the German team. The national cars had to be composed of parts manufactured in that country but nothing in the rules said that foreign drivers could not drive for other countries.

Meanwhile, Rolls, together with Jarrott, took part in the most infamous race in history, the race that ended the great inter-town racing era. The Paris/Madrid race of 1903 became known as the Race to Death. It was a race in two parts: Paris to Bordeaux and then, the following day, Bordeaux to Madrid. The second stage to Madrid never started.

Early motoring is fortunate to have had Charles Jarrott as one of its afficionados. He was as good a writer as he was a driver and wrote a vivid description of the race. He started Number 1 in the Paris/Madrid race by dint of winning the Circuit des Ardennes shortly before. Louis Renault was Number 3, Lorraine Barrow Number 5, Philip Stead Number 18 and Madame Camille du Gast Number 29. Rolls was Number 59, and the winner of the first day's stage, Gabriel, was Number 168.

Jarrott started at the head of the race as part of a three-man all-English team consisting of himself, the Yorkshireman Philip Stead, and Lorraine Barrow, an Englishman and long-time resident in Biarritz. All three were driving French de Dietrich cars for which Jarrott's firm held an agency. Rolls was driving a Panhard.

After a prophetic last meal together, Stead, Jarrott and Barrow shook hands and left separately for the start. Barrow's jest was unfortunate: 'Let us eat, drink and be merry for tomorrow we die'. In less than twenty-four hours he lay dead in an indescribable tangle of metal, killed instantly. Stead too was gravely injured when he collided with another car, somersaulting into a ditch and becoming trapped under his car. He would have died but for the emergency first aid ministered to him by the legendary Madame Camille du Gast, who stopped to help him. Marcel Renault, one of the three founding brothers of Renault, was killed as were several others.

The series of disasters were largely due to undisciplined crowds and poor organisation. The cars were sent off at suicidal two minute intervals and were obliged to race through clouds of swirling dust set off by the cars in front and they were guided only by roadside trees and landmarks.

Barrow was travelling at 80mph when a dog strayed into the road. He jammed his steering gear and his mechanic was shot out of the car into a tree and was killed on the spot. Barrow was flung twenty yards and sustained fatal injuries. There were half a dozen other fatalities. In fact, there were so many other accidents that the French authorities stopped the race, ordering all the cars to be returned by cart or train to Paris.

Edge, in his Napier, had intended to follow Jarrott as a spectator and as a result was the only driver able to retrace his steps over the debris-strewn course because he was not a competitor. His description of Barrow's car is horrific: 'Barrow's car was about the worst. The remains of it lay there, smashed into fragments, the engine was not only torn out of the frame, but the cylinders were torn off the crankcase, leaving the pistons exposed to view. The terrific force of his crash into the tree can be gauged when I say that the front dumb iron was firmly embedded in the tree trunk up to the radiator… what had once been a racing car was in fragments, with hardly two parts remaining intact'.

Rolls, who drove an 80hp Panhard, got no further than Barbezieux, some three hundred and sixteen kilometres. He worked his way up to twelfth at one point, but engine trouble put him out. *The Daily Mail* reported that his engine parted from its frame and that Rolls and his mechanic, Crompton, managed to scrounge a lift on the step of another car to Bordeaux.

Jarrott, with his mechanic, Bianchi, escaped unscathed and drove unhindered to Bordeaux. Having started first, he had not been subject to the dust and had not seen the wreck-strewn road. Only two cars passed him and he wrote poetically about being the quarry of hundreds of cars in a chasing pack behind him. He was classified third and covered five hundred and fifty-five kilometres in just six hours. It was a creditable performance but was utterly surpassed by that of the winning driver. Frenchman, Gabriel, started in a hundred and sixty-eighth place and passed a hundred and sixty-two other competitors through blinding dust clouds, averaging 65mph over five hours fourteen minutes – and this in 1903.

Edge had concluded his description with what turned out to be the epitaph of the great inter-city races. Paris/Madrid was: 'a contest, which will go down in history as the blackest day in the annals of motor racing. In the minds of those who took an active part in it, it will ever remain a picture of death and destruction due entirely to bad, nay appalling, organisation on the part of the French authorities, who realised their mistake when it was too late and then proceeded to shut the stable door after the horse had escaped'.

Although he had failed to qualify as one of the three drivers for the British team for the Gordon Bennett, Rolls decided all the motoring action, for at least a few days, was going to be in Ireland. He travelled over to watch the main race on 2nd July, 1903, and to take part in supporting events arranged for the 'Irish Fortnight'. He took his Paris/Vienna Mors and was accompanied by J. T. C. Moore-Brabazon, who, given Rolls's notorious parsimony, had to pay all his own expenses.

Brabazon commented: 'When in Ireland, racing the Mors, we often slept under the car on the road, under the pretext that there was no accommodation. True, there was no first class, but certainly better than that. It was just an excuse to avoid a hotel bill. It didn't worry me, I could sleep then as now anywhere, but the droppings of oil and dirt from a racing car during the night do not improve one's early morning appearance'.

Rolls took part in speed trials in Phoenix Park, Dublin, where thousands came to watch the head to head racing. He was beaten by Hutton in a 60hp Mercedes. Later, at a hill climb at Castlewellan, County Down, he was runner up to another 60hp Mercedes driven by Campbell Muir. Muir's car had at one time been owned by Alfred Harmsworth and he had lent it to the German team following a fire in their factory early in June 1903.

During the Irish Gordon Bennett, Jarrott was in a major smash with his companion Bianchi, but finding a reserve of superhuman strength within himself he largely lifted the car off his trapped mechanic until nearby onlookers came to help. Jarrott collapsed and minutes later woke up under a white sheet where he had been laid out for dead. Thinking he had gone blind, he remembered where he was and then thought with horror that the sheet beside him concealed 'little Bianchi dead'. 'I called out to him', Jarrott writes, 'and to my relief he replied. I then asked him the somewhat superfluous question as to whether he was alive. He replied in a very faint voice that he thought he was alive, but he felt very bad'. They both subsequently survived.

The race was won by the 'Red Devil', Camille Jenatzy, the Stirling Moss of his day, in another 60hp Mercedes. For once, Jenatzy nursed his car a little and finished the three hundred and twenty-seven miles, averaging almost 50mph over rural Irish roads. This winning drive, his only major race win, took six hours and thirty-nine minutes, a mammoth feat of physical strength and mental concentration.

Once the big event was over, Rolls raced and lost a gentlemanly match in Cork against Montagu and then won the Cork Constitution Cup, gaining revenge against Hutton who had beaten him in Phoenix Park. Finally, towards the end of the Irish festivities, Rolls won the Kerry Sprint Cup in the far west, where one can imagine such racing caused a sensation.

Back in England, towards the end of the season the Mors achieved a very quick time at Welbeck of 84.6mph, faster than anything achieved in Ireland that year and only slightly slower than the official 'Flying Kilometre' record achieved by Duray on 5th November, 1903.

The Flying Kilometre attempts took place at Achères originally, on the south bank of the Seine. Average speeds rose rapidly from 39mph in 1898 to Jenatzy's 58 mph of April 1899. Until that time all the record holders had been electric cars although a Serpollet steam car briefly held the record at Nice. By the end of November 1902, the record was up to 77mph twenty-nine seconds in a petrol car – a 60hp Mors driven by Augieres.

Back in England, by March 1904 alcohol cars had pushed the record up still further to 95mph, and Rigolly, driving a Gobron Brillie, with a 100hp engine, broke the 100mph barrier in Ostend in July 1904, setting a record of 104mph, 21.4 seconds for the standing kilometre.

For the 1905 Gordon Bennett Race, Rolls was approached by Herbert Austin of Wolseley on the recommendation of Charles Jarrott. He agreed to drive a Wolseley in the Eliminating Trial which was held on the Isle of Man – giving Rolls very useful practice for the first TT race which was due to be held there the following September.

The Gordon Bennett race itself was to be held at Clermont-Ferrand following Frenchman's Théry's 1904 win in Germany. As ever, Rolls was very precise in practice and this was confirmed by the journalists, Swindley and Massac Buist. Buist wrote how: 'Many times we have stopped the car, shifted a broken branch of a tree and set it up as a point on a curving gradient, which was to be a sign to him on the day of the race precisely where he was to change into a certain gear, providing a peasant passing meantime had not thought the tree likely fuel for the winter'. Rolls had a near miss when a dog wandered onto the track. Rolls tried to avoid hitting it and nearly overturned. He was never a favourite to win but he mastered the two hundred or so major corners of the Isle of Man course, later the scene of his greatest triumph.

The British team that qualified at the Trial was made up of Clifford Earp on a 1904, 100hp Napier, Bianchi on a Wolseley and Rolls on another Wolseley. The race itself was held on the Circuit d'Auvergne. Rolls complained that he should have had more time to practise and that the team should have been selected earlier, but he praised the safety of the course, which was due in part to reaction to the Race to Death in 1903.

Rolls wanted more power than his Wolseley would give. He was hampered by too high pressure in the tyres and after a lap of dubious handling, he stopped to let some air out. Further, oil, due to be sent out from England, did not arrive in time and dirty French oil clogged the carburettors, then an offside rear tyre blew and Rolls limped in on the rim. If that was not sufficient by way of handicaps, the driver's seat broke up and the car finished with the driver supporting himself on the steering wheel and brake lever. Apart from that (!) the race went well and Rolls finished eighth out of a field of eighteen and went some way to justifying his mantra: 'To win you have to finish'. Théry (the 'Chronometer'), driving a Brasier, became the only man to win the Gordon Bennett race twice.

Rolls's racing career was giving him a great deal of information about many marques. It helped him prove their reliability, and furthermore helped him establish his London business as a major force, even at the age of twenty-eight.

Chapter Six

Two Smooth Operators

By the age of twenty-two, in 1899, Rolls already had an extensive workshop at South Lodge, Kensington with space to store several cars indoors[16]. Rolls was generous and let it be known that any members of the Automobile Club of Great Britain and Ireland (A.C.G.B.I.), breaking down near South Lodge, could count on help with repairs or a drop of petrol to see them home. A journalist who visited his workshop at the time described: 'a very business-like apartment, roomy and lofty and fitted with a variety of tools and appliances and a pit... while there is kept a duplication of motor car parts, which keep the owner free from some of the little worries associated with the pleasures of motor car possession. On the walls are arranged the numbers worn by Mr. Rolls in his various competitions'.

In January 1902, Rolls had begun to trade as C. S. Rolls and Co., Automobile Agents, from a former roller-skating rink at Lillie Hall, Fulham. He was just twenty-four, and the best-qualified man in England to sell cars.

So much has been written about Rolls's pioneer motoring, his racing, his meeting with Royce, his fascination with the Wright brothers, his double Channel crossing and his untimely death, that his business acumen is often overlooked. He was the best university-qualified and socially connected garage proprietor in Britain. He knew what the wealthy wanted, he had greasy fingers and could roll up his sleeves and do the work. He could sell with a driven charm and was able to drive a hard bargain. His London garage was also officially approved by the *Automobile Club de France* of which he had been a member since 1897.

He had youth, energy and friends in both Commons and Lords to call on which he did unashamedly. His central role at the A.C.G.B.I. was also helpful – and, miraculously, he had enough time to keep all the plates spinning. He even found time to write. He contributed to *Encyclopaedia Britannica* and, when Harmsworth decided to enhance his reputation as a leading motoring figure by publishing

---

16 *Garages barely existed and were originally called motor homes until the Hon. Evelyn Ellis coined the word 'garage' in 1899.*

the volume *Motors and Motor Driving* for the Badminton Library, Rolls was one of the specialist contributors.

He also wrote a small booklet *The Caprices of the Motor Car*, sub-title *Basic Tips On How To Fix Your Car At The Side Of The Road*, published 1902. It has a delightful simplicity. It was a guide to 'looking after a new car like a new horse' – that certain procedures and safeguards were important, but not every obscure disease must be anticipated. Writing about difficulties in starting, he broke problems down into basic causes: ignition, carburation, compression and moving parts. In the carburation section, he suggested that if petrol ran low, driving on to the opposite camber might help. He warned about stale petrol – shades of lawnmower frustration today. Water loss, he explained, was sometimes caused by our canine friends: 'The pump of a car has often been carried away by contact with a dog; in one case there was no trace of the pump or the dog, except a tooth, which the animal had left in the back tyre'.

Dogs aside, here was a logical, simple analysis path for the new motorist – and no one in Britain had more than five years experience anyway. Unusual noises were named and shamed – puffing, tapping, popping and bursting were all recalled and their cure analysed with aplomb. Always inclined to the whimsical, Rolls's 'Concluding Advice and Remarks' included nuggets of motorcraft:

'If your motor works well, leave it alone, although it may never seem to go fast enough. Many troubles arise from interference and undue curiosity.'

'Never pour petrol near a naked light; it is prudent to extinguish the burners when filling the tank of the car.'

'Do not spill petrol over your clothes and then strike a match to light your pipe.'

'Do not go out even for a short run without complete equipment of tools, spare parts, petrol and repair outfit or you may well be back late.'

'Do not pedal your tricycle (start it for half an hour before remembering your plug switch), unless your doctor recommends it.'

'Do not let the starting handle fly off and hit you on the chin.'

And finally, the author's favourite, even if unlikely today – 'Do not let a willing ostler fill up your petrol tank with water!'

Mechanics clamoured to join C. S. Rolls & Co. and learn the new skills. Rolls did not overpay them. Fellow graduates such as Moore-Brabazon worked and raced with him for nothing and paid their own way.

Rolls had the backing of his father, a very wealthy man, and had influence in the Army via the Motor Volunteer Reserve, and excellent contacts in the press through his frequent articles in motoring journals. His press contacts increased further when Johnson joined him. Further, he had his engineering degree and understood both engines and electronics and he had contacts at Cambridge, via Sir David Salomons. All this, and he was an entrepreneur who was prepared to take risks both on the road and in business. Until Johnson joined in October 1903, Rolls apparently managed his business, which employed some seventy people, single-handed.

At thirty thousand square feet, the Lillie Hall premises, acquired in 1902, was half the size of a football field. *Automotor Journal* inspected it in 1902 and confirmed that it could hold two hundred cars. Initially, Panhards were sold there – at premiums to their purchase price. Panhards were the mainstay of C. S. Rolls & Co.

Panhard was indeed the first big-car company in the world, employing six hundred and fifty people as early as 1897. In 1898 alone they built three hundred and thirty-six cars – while there were only twenty-five vehicles in all of Britain at the start of 1897.

Most motorists' homes did not have a garage, and it was a part of C. S. Rolls & Co.'s service that the cars they sold could be stored on the firm's premises. Indeed, in many cases it was essential. Cars had valuable lamps and other accoutrements and could be subject to vandalism. Cold starting was also a problem and most cars needed to be kept indoors and warm if they were to start at all.

By 1902 Rolls had owned makes such as Peugeot, Panhard, Mors and Locomobile and he had dabbled with Duryea. His enterprise supplied and repaired new and used cars and arranged for coachwork to be fitted to the bare chassis as the client required it. His repair shop carried out considerable insurance work. (Rolls became a business adviser to the General Accident Fire and

Life Assurance Company[17].) Cars were also part-exchanged and Rolls introduced hire purchase into the motor trade for the first time.

In addition, cars could be hired by the day, with or without chauffeurs – and sometimes they were lent informally which could and did cause trouble with subsequent purchasers. He sold fire extinguishers, sold and charged batteries, sold and repaired tyres and used the most up-to-date American machinery. He advised on the construction of garages – and he taught driving.

Lord Llangattock financed Rolls's foray into the motor trade. Papers at Monmouth revealed a £6,500 initial investment and then a further £11,000 when the showrooms were purchased. These sums were to be deducted from a legacy, which Charles would receive on his father's death. In addition, there was a £10,000 overdraft, guaranteed by Lord Llangattock. With considerable foresight, Lord Llangattock arranged that, should he himself die, the monies would not be repayable until Lady Llangattock died, and then monies owed would be deducted out of a second £50,000 legacy Charles was to receive at that time. The overall investment was equivalent to about £3 million today. This was a huge act of faith by the doughty Lord, and a tribute to the faith he had in his youngest son and the future of motoring. Rolls's business was further helped by his frugal lifestyle – outside of racing and ballooning. He lived close to his works and, with no family commitments, could work long hours.

There were setbacks of course. Not all customers were happy, although, Rolls being six foot and five inches tall in his socks, they were wise to be circumspect in their complaints. In one well-publicised dispute, Rolls sold an allegedly new, unused car to a Doctor Rutherford Harris[18], M.P. Previously, this car had been lent to Mark Mayhew to race at the Bexhill Speed Trials and had been used to

---

17 *General Accident Fire and Life Assurance Company (G.A.F.L.A.C.) was founded in 1861 after the Great Tooley Street fire in London. A great deal of dockland was destroyed and the company merged first with Commercial Union and then Norwich Union, ceasing to exist only in 2000.*

18 *Rutherford Harris, M.P. had been a colleague of Cecil Rhodes and involved in the Jameson Raid. He had also been an M.P. in South Africa before coming to Britain where he became M.P. for Dulwich. He was a tough customer and, therefore, a match for Rolls. Ironically, Harris eventually retired in 1906 and went to live in, of all places, Monmouthshire.*

drive aviator, Santos-Dumont, around London on a laudatory visit – and it had been hired out for a day's jolly to a member of the Rothschild family. Rolls alleged that the doctor had found unnecessary faults with the car and had changed specifications for work to be carried out and hinted that Harris was just plain awkward. The doctor dug his heels in, and the judge, possibly anti-motorist, thought the Young Kaiser had over-reached himself, and allowed Harris £900 off the deal, although both sides paid their own costs. Rolls was learning the hard way.

For three years the thrill of business absorbed him. Lord Montagu's biography[19] recalls: 'Rolls did all the demonstrating himself. His quickness of wit could match his skill behind the wheel on occasions. This stood him in good stead one day when showing off a Panhard to a lady customer.

Approaching St. Giles Circus from Tottenham Court Road Rolls had become aware that the policeman on point duty had suddenly shot up his hand. He jammed on the transmission brakes, whereupon the car turned right round. Rolls took the motor back smartly the way he had come. 'See' he remarked casually to his fair passenger, 'these cars are so handy, you can make them turn them on a sixpence'.

Little things mattered. Rolls once sent out for a seven shillings and sixpenny mirror to be used by his lady clients. Meanwhile, in the years 1902 and 1903, while he ran the business alone, Rolls raced fully, and was a captain in the Motor Volunteer Reserve. He was also on the A.C.G.B.I. sub-committee to the London Traffic Commission and joined the Motor Advisory Board, giving expert witness evidence on insurance matters.

His pace was unsustainable. Towards the end of 1903 he poached Claude Johnson from Paris Singer's City-and-Suburban brougham enterprise. At last he had an able colleague. Rolls's choice of Johnson as a senior manager was inspired. Rolls could sell and publicise, and Johnson was a brilliant organiser and a cultured man who excelled in public relations. Together, they would be a match for the all-conquering, British-made Daimler and for the ultimate driving machine of the day, the German Mercedes. Johnson had come a very long way since his appointment as secretary of the *Automobile Club*. Consternation

---

19 *Rolls of Rolls-Royce – The Right Hon. Lord Montagu of Beaulieu (Cassell 1966).*

reigned when he resigned, but presumably the Club Committee realised that they had stumbled on a very able man and had been lucky to retain him for so long.

Indeed, John Montagu, M.P., a friend of Johnson and also the owner and editor of *Car Illustrated* asked him his reasons for leaving his post as Automobile Club Secretary. Johnson simply replied that as a salaried employee of a club, he could never expect the rewards, which he felt he could earn in the burgeoning motor trade, and that it was time for him to move on.

Rolls needed all the help he could get. He had some seventy staff, a great set up and, through planning, parsimony and hard work had survived thus far. But what of the future? Panhards were becoming old hat. The very rich, such as Alfred Harmsworth, bought Mercedes from Germany or Daimlers (with the Royal Warrant) from Coventry. Napier was snapping at Rolls's heels with the first all-British car. C. S. Rolls & Co. were holding their own, but only just. Something else was needed. Rolls had created two more strands for sales; his ballooning activities, probably somewhat more than a weekend relaxation, and his activities within the Motor Volunteer Reserve, that had brought cars to the attention of high-ranking officers in the Army. Nevertheless Rolls recognised the opportunity that Johnson's appointment would bring. Johnson had access to the Harmsworth press, and though Harmsworth might campaign against the elitist motorist when it suited him (or his readers), he had championed the motor industry in general in 1900 and would again if the industry had a good British car to sell.

Little did Rolls realise that following his good fortune in recruiting Johnson, within months a second stroke of luck would follow, and he would discover an iconic, quality British car to sell, which could compete with any car in Britain, Europe or elsewhere.

C.S. Rolls's 80hp Mors.

C.S. Rolls's 110hp Mors which did 83mph.

C.S. Rolls's Paris-Berlin Mors.

C.S. Rolls's Paris-Madrid Panhard.

Camille du Gast's Paris-Madrid De Dietrich.

Lorraine Barrow's wrecked De Dietrich Paris-Madrid.

Charles Jarrott.

Gabriel's Mors – winner to Bordeaux, Paris-Madrid.

Rolls's Mors versus Hutton's Mercedes – Pheonix Park.

Stocks, Edge, Jarrott and others – Ireland 1903.

Earp, Rolls and Bianchi – Gorden Bennett team 1905.

Rolls in 1904 Wolseley – Gorden Bennett 1905.

C.S. Rolls & Co. exhibition stand – November 1906 Olympia.

C.S. Rolls & Co. exhibition stand – an earlier show.

C.S. Rolls mechanic at South Lodge 1900.

Claude Johnson joins C.S. Rolls & Co.

C.S. Rolls & Co. exhibition stand c.1903.

Lillie Hall – C.S. Rolls & Co.

Charles Rolls – the man in charge.

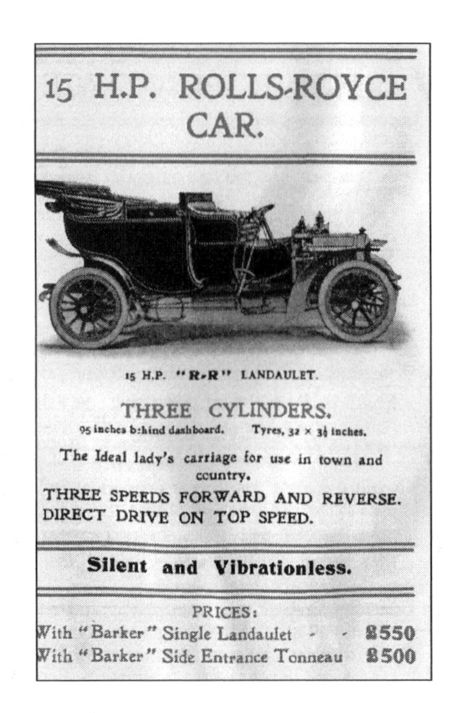

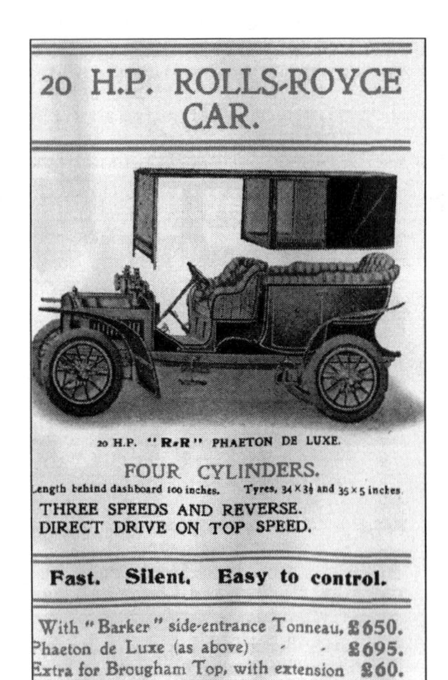

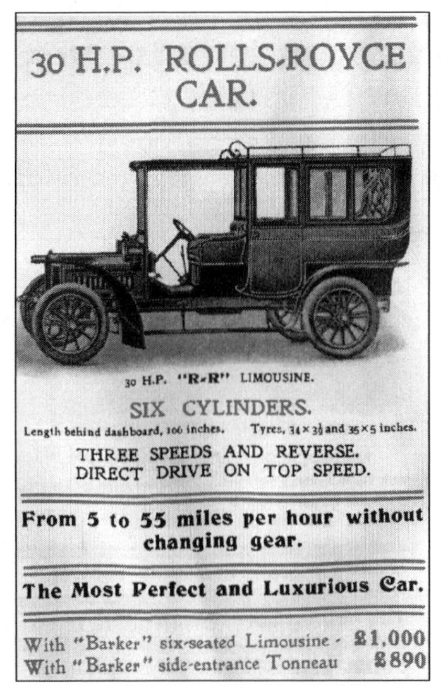

C.S. Rolls & Co. catalogue – 1905.

Chapter Seven

The Genius, Three Men and a Meeting

Frederick Henry Royce was born in 1863, fourteen years before Rolls. His early life was a struggle. Some of his relatives emigrated to Canada. His father, from a well-to-do milling family, introduced various innovations at the family flour mill prematurely and failed in business as pioneers often do. He did, however, fish young 'Fred', as Royce was known, out of the millrace in which he would otherwise have drowned at a very early age and is thus owed some thanks. As a consequence of the business failure, the family split. The mill at Alwalton, near Peterborough was demolished and Royce, the youngest of his siblings, was taken by his father to London at the age of nine while his mother and sister remained behind. His mother eventually went into service in London and Tunbridge Wells where Royce kept in touch with her, but saw little of her when a child, although later, when he prospered, he made a home for her where he lived in Knutsford.

It was a tough childhood compared to what it might have been if his father had been more successful. Between the ages of nine and fourteen Royce received just one year's schooling. To supplement his father's income, he sold newspapers for W. H. Smith on street corners and delivered telegrams. Eventually, an aunt came to the rescue and, for £20 per year, bought him an apprenticeship with the Great Northern Railway.

A Mr. Yarrow, in whose father's house Royce lived during his apprenticeship, described to Sir Max Pemberton, Royce's friend and first biographer[20], how 'Fred was a very quiet lad at that time and rarely went out at night. We couldn't keep him away from books. Although he had hardly any schooling he managed to teach himself a lot about electricity and algebra and something about foreign languages'.

In a workshop at the rear of the house, Mr. Yarrow taught Royce and his own son how to use a lathe and other basic engineering skills. Here Royce is said to have worked on his first vehicle – a modest wheelbarrow. But Royce's luck ran

---

20 *A Life of Sir Henry Royce – Sir Max Pemberton (Hutchinson)*

out and his apprenticeship ended when his aunt could no longer afford to pay for his indentures, and so the teenage Royce spent months traipsing the depressed North looking for work, despite excellent references. He finally secured a job in Leeds – fifty-four hours a week for a wage of eleven shillings, for a company that had an Italian armaments contract. At the same age young Rolls received an allowance of £500 per annum. Royce later always feared failure and financial hardship – and for good reason.

Back in London when a better job eventually arose, Royce attended evening classes in electrical engineering and it was here that he may have met Ernest Claremont, an equally qualified young engineer and future partner, in 1882 or 1883. Royce was by then twenty-one and Claremont a year younger.

About this time, Royce was lodging in the Old Kent Road, the source of the Rolls family's property fortune from one hundred years earlier.

Claremont and Royce became partners in 1884, setting up a factory at Cooke Street in Manchester with capital of £20 and £50 respectively. Royce had invented an electric bell, of which they sold hundreds. They were soon employing six female factory hands to assemble them. Following this success, they diversified and manufactured switchgear and electric motors, and then Royce invented a new dynamo that utilised a drum-wound armature and was virtually sparkless. The remarkable new gadget found a ready market in mining companies, mills, factories and ships – anywhere where sparks could cause fires. There was only one trouble with Royce's dynamo – it never seemed to wear out. The companies that bought it, loved it, but the firm that made it, could have done with repeat business orders, but there were very few.

Customers spread the word that Royce Ltd. built equipment to last. The firm developed electric cranes, both for export and for the domestic market and nine of which were used on the Manchester Ship Canal. By 1899, Royce Ltd. had orders on its books for £20,000 (around £2 million today).

Along the way, Royce and Claremont married two sisters, daughters of a London printer, who probably saw a chance to get them off his hands by a substantial investment in the capital-hungry business run by the two entrepreneurs.

Henry Royce, by now quite prosperous, built a home in Knutsford, which he modestly called 'Brae Cottage'. He worked all hours to the detriment of his health, pondered new designs – and tended his garden, by electric light if necessary, in the few hours remaining. Although prosperous, he was not a great businessman. Some of his designs were patented; some were not. Some were stolen by the Japanese; some were not. He became obsessive. Things that were not done precisely were intolerable to him. He scrapped imperfect work ruthlessly, and chastised his staff if they failed to live up to his standards.

Claremont was the son of a surgeon and privately educated. He understood the talent of the man with whom he was fortunate enough to be associated. Claremont, although equally qualified as an electrical engineer, sent out the bills, paid the wages, collected the money and let Royce give full vent to his genius, untroubled by such trivia. Claremont cut a gentle dash in Manchester society. He was a Lieutenant in the Fourth Volunteer Battalion of the Manchester Regiment, and having parted from his wife after just three years, was a ladies' man who prided himself on his appearance.

In 1899 he became a director of W. T. Glover, a Salford cable maker, whose products were used extensively by Royce Ltd., Glover's premises were adjacent to a second Royce factory situated at Trafford Park, Manchester, acquired because the firm had outgrown its Cooke Street premises, which it nevertheless retained.

In March 1903, Claremont succeeded Henry Edmunds (Edmunds was now fifty), as Managing Director of Glover's and Edmunds became company Chairman. Claremont arranged for Edmunds to exchange shares in Glover's for shares in Royce Ltd. Royce Ltd thus acquired Edmunds as another director and one with a wide range of contacts, which would shortly prove crucial to both Henry Royce and Charles Rolls.

Henry Edmunds was an innovator, an experienced dabbler, who should have become a very rich man but did not. He met Thomas Edison in America in 1877 and his biographer, Paul Tritton[21], recorded that Edmonds entertained passengers on the return crossing with stories of the first talking machine, and that he had with him two magnetic telephones, designed by Alexander Graham Bell. Edmunds and fellow passengers amused themselves by talking to one another from different parts of the ship along a cable three hundred feet long –

---

21 *The Life and Times of Henry Edmunds – Paul Tritton (Rolls-Royce Heritage Trust 2000).*

the first time the telephone had perhaps been used at sea. Edmunds had started a business in 1878, and by the new century had multiple interests, including the running of W. T. Glover, which had grown rapidly during the street-lighting boom as a supplier of cables. He had innumerable business contacts. Edmunds was involved in the explosion of Manchester business that followed the completion of the Manchester Ship Canal in 1889 when Royce Ltd. supplied significant lighting along the canal.

Edmunds was a very early motoring enthusiast and at the start of his association with Royce Ltd had had a long-time interest in motors. His first car was a De Dion motor tricycle and trailer, which he used to commute, driven by his gardener, now chauffeur, one Mr. Goody[22]. He bought his first car in France and sent Goody over there to learn how to drive. Once delivered, the car was a disaster and underwent months of repairs. Edmund dreamt of a reliable British car but none were available. He found the next best thing and bought a Coventry-built Daimler called 'Rhoda' – his mount in the Thousand Mile Trial.

Edmunds had been a member of the Automobile Club since 1900 and was right at the hub of motoring. In 1902 he donated the Club's first significant trophy for hill climbing, *The Automobile Club Hill Climbing Trophy*, also called the *Henry Edmunds Hill Climb Trophy*. It was a bronze statue of a motorist and his passenger, wearing goggles, caps and other motoring gear and was first competed for in Ireland, in 1903, as part of the Gordon Bennett celebrations.

Meanwhile, Henry Royce had bought a car, a De Dion quadricycle, one of three, which his doctor and Claremont had insisted upon, so that he would get out of the Royce Ltd. works for his health's sake. Royce went on a lengthy holiday and while away (in 1902) he studied a French treatise on motorcar construction. He bought a Decauville[23]. He took a tram to the station to collect his purchase but the car refused to start and he had it pushed back to Cooke Street by four strong men – whom Royce had to tip. The car was stored in a stable yard and fixed the next day.

---

22 *Henry Edmunds claimed Goody to be the first uniformed chauffeur.*

23 *It has emerged that he had an involvement in the design of an 'autocar motor'. This was in 1902 for a firm called Pritchett and Gold in London, and a drawing has been found in the Rolls-Royce archives to support this involvement.*

And to demonstrate that even a genius can sometimes err, Royce managed to run out of petrol the following Sunday, on a three mile drive from home.

Royce took the Decauville to bits with the help of two of his apprentices, Eric Platford and Tom Haldenby. A further apprentice was asked to make a drawing of each component while the car was dismantled. As each part of the Decauville was removed, the apprentice drew a picture from which Royce later reviewed its design and durability. Royce's little team worked incredibly long hours, starting at 6.30 a.m. each working day except Monday when they started at eight, and often worked late into the evening and on Saturday mornings.

The first engine was bench-tested in December 1903. By the Spring of 1904 the first car was ready and left the factory, having started without a hitch. The entire premises reverberated with a tuneless din of drumming with hammers, castings and anything that came to hand to celebrate. Royce drove and Platford and Haldenby followed dutifully behind in the Decauville, not that this was necessary because the very first Royce ran sweetly without mishap to Royce's Knutsford home.

Royce had obtained permission from his directors to make three prototypes. The ever cautious Claremont agreed, although he frequently cursed what he christened the 'two guinea an ounce job'. By February 1904, Royce Ltd. letterheads included Motor Manufacture as part of their activities.

Enthusiasts put up with hardship, to which Royce was no stranger. In his Decauville he drove fifteen miles to and from the factory and worked tirelessly. S. F. Edge had said of early cars in 1898: 'The public want a motor car, which they can, before going away in the morning, fill the necessary tanks with lubricating oil and petrol; and this engine will run throughout the day without any further attention... let us have a motor car which will go on day after day without stopping and will require a very small amount of mechanical skill to keep it in order'... and this from an ebullient Aussie in 1898. Too right mate!

Meanwhile Edmunds had become a Royce Ltd. shareholder, and in London, Rolls told him: 'I wish you would give me any information that you may get hold of relating to improvements in the building of motor cars. I have some ideas of my own, which I should like to follow up; and there may be opportunities of doing so'.

Edmunds was the ideal man for this sort of brokerage. He was not only a director of a very successful cable manufacturer, but he was a man who liked to deal in ideas. And events played into his hands. The Automobile Club had arranged a major trial for Potters Bar, North London, commencing on 18th April, 1904, just three weeks after the Royce launch. The purpose of the trial was to test devices designed to counteract sideslip, which was then a major problem. Tyres were nowhere as good as they are now and cobbled roads, greasy tram tracks and mud meant that cars would deviate far more than they do today. Paul Tritton's biography of Edmunds described how sideslip was: '… caused by failing to bite the road properly. The mud, when being in what is known as a greasy state, acting as a sort of lubricant, and presenting a film between the tyre and the road surface… so that the car has little lateral stability; and any deviation from the line of progress, whether caused by steering or the disturbing effect of brake application, results in a sideslip, more or less serious, according to the speed and general circumstances of the moment'.

A trial had already taken place a couple of months earlier in France, at Versailles, where a British invention 'The Parsons Non-Skidder' had not made a great impact. When the British trial, under the supervision of the Automobile Club, was first announced, Parsons were very keen to participate once again. The final section of the trial was arranged for a skidpan at the quaintly named Locomobile Garage Riding School. *Car Illustrated* reported a section of floor had been covered with mud and added gleefully 'the result was to form a surface that was villainous in its excess of sliminess and seldom was anything so vile to be encountered'…!' In March 1904, a board meeting of Parsons saw the resignation of one of its best-known shareholders, Paris Singer, and the acquisition of even more shares by Henry Edmunds, who was happily also a director of Parsons.

A full description of the non-skidder is inappropriate here, but the general idea was that the devices were interlaced with the tyres. Any loss of efficiency that followed was made up for by the improved additional grip of a skidder and a tyre to the road as one. It was for this reason that Parsons were looking into the lucrative market for non-skidders, the action of which was to cut through the grease and get a bite on the road with the tyre.

By 18th April. 1904, the event was imminent. It was to be more than just a Sideslip Trial, it was 'to be an endurance test over a thousand miles, each car having an official observer on board to see that no repairs are made' (*Automobile Club Journal*). 'Those devices that come through the trial would then be subjected to a sideslipping and brake test to prove their efficiency is not impaired by actual service. The sideslip test consists of a right-angle turn on a greasy wood surface followed by a zig-zag course, to be completed at a speed of 15-20mph'. *Autocar* commented that the combination of endurance test and sideslip would establish both effectiveness and durability of sideslip devices. A short-term answer was not enough.

The board of Parsons met in March and left the arrangements to Edmunds. He could supply one of his own cars or chance it with the new Royce, which had not yet run. Here was an opportunity to show off Royce's new car almost fresh from the drawing board and Edmunds took that chance. It would enable him to test the Royce's durability, subjecting it to an official trial immediately upon its birth. He outlined his plan in correspondence with Rolls whom he knew from the Automobile Club.

There were sixteen entries for the Sideslip Trials, but four withdrew leaving twelve participants. The Royce was taken to London, presumably by train or it may have been driven. Probably Edmunds, a capable driver, drove himself, accompanied by H. Massac Buist, a Cambridge University colleague of Rolls and by now a motoring journalist. The car ran under N-MR6, one of Royce's trade plates, car numbers having been introduced on the 1st January that year.

Buist also acted as the official Automobile Club observer when Edmunds drove in it from London to Margate and back around 18th April. There is an indistinct photo of the car in London. It can be identified as the first Royce by its number, N-MR6, the second and third prototypes being N-MR7 and N-MR8 respectively. The non-skidding devices are clearly visible, but not the driver.

The Morning Post was very complimentary: 'It's the first car to be built by the well-known Manchester firm of electrical engineers, and as it comes newly from their workshop, it is pleasant to be able to record its excellent running, whether on the level or negotiating long and steep hills, with four passengers on board, and the second and third gear speed. The engine is, at all times, very flexible, and it picks up splendidly after ascending trying gradients'.

The first Royce was now in London, ready to face the skidpan and the second Royce car – made available to Ernest Claremont as his own car, had just been completed in Manchester at the old Cooke Street works.

The Trials continued until 29th April. Perhaps because the car was referred to as a 'Parsons' on occasion, it was not singled out for particular attention, even though it was the only new make at the trial. Other makes included Panhards, Wolseleys and a Lanchester.

Before the Sideslip Trials, Henry Edmunds had been very keen to involve Rolls and had offered in his letter to come to London to see him, although Rolls had brushed him off: 'Very much occupied and, further, several other houses are in negotiation with him, wishing to do whole or part of the work. What he (Rolls) is looking for is a good, high quality car to replace the Panhard; preferably of three or four cylinders. He has some personal dislike of two-cylinder cars'.

A tired and irritable Mr. Royce might have told Mr. Rolls where to go at this point, but fortunately Royce left that side of things to Edmunds, both men recognising that they would not find a better sales agency in London than C. S. Rolls & Co., where, in addition to Rolls himself, Claude Johnson was now a senior manager.

Edmunds's letter to Rolls, enclosing photographs and a specification of the Royce, did the trick and Edmunds eulogised Royce saying: 'The point that impressed me most is this. The people (at Royce) have worked out their designs in their own office, and knowing, as I do, the skill of Mr. Royce as a practical mechanical engineer, I feel one is very safe in taking up any work his firm may produce'.

Rolls was astute enough to realise, that here was a complete British car, without any foreign components to complicate its patriotic British saleability. More importantly, the availability of spares and easy to access expertise in Manchester would be available to potential customers. He relented, and days later wrote: 'Dear Edmunds – can you come to Manchester any time next week?'

He and Edmunds travelled by train, probably on Wednesday 4th May, 1904, although the exact date is undocumented. On the train Rolls talked about his preference for selling British cars. He wanted the new marque to be as well-known as Chubb was to locks and safes and Broadwood to pianos. Paul Tritton's Prologue in Edmund's biography is very apt, and he has kindly given permission for its inclusion here.

A black locomotive, embellished with blue, white and vermillion stripes, a brass number plate and red buffer beams, steamed across the Stockport viaduct, high above the homes and factories of the busy cotton spinning town nestling in the steep valley of the River Mersey. It had been a long haul up from Crewe, but the remaining few miles were downhill nearly all the way. The train gathered speed, adding its own contribution of steam and smuts to the industrial haze, rising to meet the broken clouds drifting south-eastwards over the North of England's premier city.

An occasional shaft of spring sunlight brightened the scene, sparkling on the gold letters, L & NWR, on the sides of the carriages behind the locomotive. The train's travel-weary occupants stretched, yawned, folded their newspapers, gathered their bags and umbrellas and moved towards the doors. The serious business of the day would soon begin.

There was little to indicate that two of the men, who stepped onto the platform at Manchester's London Road Station a few minutes later, and jostled through the ticket barrier together, had much in common. The taller of the pair, clutching a forty-nine shilling first class return from London, was upright, alert and smartly attired in a dark suit. He had open youthful features of the kind that a dozen years later would gaze forth from black-framed portraits on the mantelpieces of countless families bereaved during the horrors of the Somme.

He was, as his bearing suggested, a young Army officer, a Captain in the Motor Volunteer Corps, but he was destined, not for battle, but for a sudden, early death on an aerodrome in peacetime.

The man at his side was a greying, less agile figure with a solemn, almost dour, expression.

A frequent visitor to Manchester, he strolled past the ticket inspector, proffering a trader's ticket, such as were issued to regular travellers, who ran businesses that provided the London and North-West Railway with valuable freight contracts. Although nearly twice the age of his companion, he would live to see the coming of age of the enterprise they were about to inaugurate. Today would see the successful culmination of his patient efforts to persuade the young man at his side to take a day trip to Manchester; it would also be an occasion that would change the course of motoring history.

As they stood on the forecourt and hailed a Hansom cab, the two men noticed that despite Manchester's reputation for perpetual drizzle, it was a pleasant day; calm, dry, with intermittent sunshine. It was also a little warmer than when they left London four hours earlier; the thermometer was now nudging 54° on the Fahrenheit scale. As always, the state of the weather was not far from the minds of those arriving in Manchester that day, but these two travellers had more important matters to think about.

Soon after leaving the station they arrived in the foyer of a nearby hotel to keep one of the most important appointments of their lives. Smiles of recognition passed between the older of the two men and the person with whom they were to have lunch.

'Mr. Royce" said Henry Edmunds, 'may I introduce you to Charles Rolls?'

Chapter Eight

The Legend Begins

Rolls and Royce had got on famously at their historic lunch in the Grill Room at the Midland Hotel, Manchester. Despite the difference in age and background, each recognised in the other their respective talents and that their engineering skills could be combined profitably. Rolls saw the car after lunch. Although he had misgivings about two-cylinder cars, these were soon dispelled and Rolls, apparently at Royce's insistence, drove it some way, murmuring his approval.

He is said to have noticed a car drawn up at the side of the road. The bonnet was open, a pair of legs protruded from underneath and various tools were scattered around the road, a common sight in those days. Rolls, obeying the unwritten law, pulled up and a head appeared. It was the local doctor who was on his way to see to a patient. His chauffeur had told him that the breakdown was serious and had walked on to the nearest village for help.

The car was a Mors, one of the principal makes sold by Rolls. The doctor informed him that he had bought it in London from people called Rolls and Company, whom he had been told were reasonably honest, if such a thing were possible in the motor trade! Royce, who had a great sense of humour, smiled broadly; Rolls, who had none, did not. The doctor wiped black grease from his hands and asked Royce if he knew anything about motor cars.

'Not as much as I ought to,' said Royce.

It took them less than a minute to find out that the car had run out of petrol and not much longer to empty the contents of a two-gallon tin into the tank. The doctor, who still had no idea who his benefactors were, thanked them profusely and the two 'mechanics' resumed their journey[24].

It took several months to finalise the deal. C. S. Rolls & Co. would take the entire output of Royce cars to be sold under the name of Rolls-Royce and Henry Edmunds would be 'umpire'. Royce Ltd. would produce the various chassis only

---

24 *From The Silver Lady – Neville Minchin, (Foulis), 1961.*

and C. S. Rolls & Co. would be responsible for the carriage work in which they had experience, having previously arranged this for their imported cars with the assistance of Barkers of Charing Cross, a firm with almost two hundred years pedigree. Johnson and Rolls were known to the firm's owner who was a member of the Automobile Club.

Royce would continue with his other business, Royce Ltd., and Claremont would continue to run Glovers but also be involved with Royce Ltd., and thus with the new car side. Claremont was perhaps looking to see how the arrangements would work out.

Rolls felt he could market the two-cylinder car more or less as it was, and was keen to sell some as soon as he could. It was agreed that nineteen would be supplied, but, in addition, there would be six three-cylinder cars, which Rolls preferred. There would be an interchangeability of parts because the same bore and stroke for each model would reduce costs. Rolls already believed that Royce was capable of producing a car superior to anything that he, Rolls, was currently selling.

The cars that graced the London Olympia Show were masterpieces of engineering but, in total, only three 10hp Royce cars were made. After that the engines were larger and they were called Rolls-Royce. Of the first three cars, numbers 15196, 15881, 15880 (the number of the last is not certain), sadly little remains except the engine of the second car, which Rolls probably saw during the first meeting in Manchester with Royce along with the third which was under construction in the factory that same day. The first car was in London for the Sideslip Trials with Henry Edmunds. Its bodywork had been made in Manchester, but it was scrapped, surprisingly early in its life, some of its parts being used in the second car.

It was this first car that was used by C. S. Rolls, accompanied by J. T. C. Moore-Brabazon to drive the Duke of Connaught, third son of Queen Victoria, along the South Coast on a tour of inspection in 1904, as part of Rolls's duties as a member of the Motor Volunteer Corps.

So sure was Rolls as to the reliability of the car, rather than driving from London down to Folkestone the previous day, he drove down on the morning of the tour, picked up the Duke, did the tour of inspection and returned to London on the same day, a distance of two hundred and twenty miles. The Duke and his staff were suitably impressed, as was T. E. Lawrence some time later[25].

The second car, 15881, seen and driven by Rolls after the Manchester meeting, nearly made it to posterity. It became Claremont's personal car and was never sold by C. S. Rolls & Co. – probably to placate Claremont about his doubts about the motor venture – 'the two guinea an ounce job', as he liked to call it. The car later passed to his estranged wife, Minnie, Royce's sister-in-law, and, later still, was used by Glovers' contract manager, a Mr. Anderson. Before his ownership, this was the car that was used for modifications when Claremont had it, and he had a metal plate made and fixed to the dashboard, bearing the legend 'If this car breaks down, do not ask a lot of silly questions'.

At the end of its useful life, Mr. Anderson, who by now owned the car, donated it to Manchester University which, in its infinite wisdom, decided to scrap it, keeping only the engine and gearbox – and this in 1921, by which time Rolls-Royce had achieved 'Best Car in the World' status. Would that someone like Roy Brooks of the Rolls-Royce Enthusiasts' Club, himself a motor-engineering lecturer, had been there to rescue the car for the enjoyment of future generations. For

---

25 *When the Great War broke out, Rolls-Royce became the most successful armoured car and was in continuous operational service, particularly in the desert.*

T. E. Lawrence (Lawrence of Arabia), wrote: 'A Rolls in the desert was above rubies; and though we had been driving in these cars for eighteen months, not upon the polished roads of their maker's intention, but across country of the vilest, at speed, day or night, carrying a ton of goods and four or five men up, yet this was our first structural accident in the team of nine. Great was Rolls, and great was Royce. They were worth hundreds of men to us in these deserts'.

The accident referred to was the fracturing of a rear spring shackle, to which a hasty but long-lasting repair was effected by Lawrence's driver, coincidentally, although no relative, one S. C. Rolls.

Whenever King George V or Queen Mary visited the Western Front, they travelled in Rolls-Royces, whose stamina enabled them to cope with terrible conditions.

After the Armistice, Lawrence was once asked if there was anything to be bought with money that he could not afford, what would he like? He replied immediately: 'I should like a Rolls-Royce car, with enough tyres and petrol to last me all my life'.

thirty years, the engine has been, and is still, on display in the Museum of Science and Industry in Manchester.

The third car was also scrapped, this time by Rolls-Royce themselves. It was sold to a customer, then re-purchased and used as a works hack until 1923. This failure to preserve two of the first three Royce cars may have led to a slight change of heart by 1923 when an Aberdeen owner, Doctor Gammell, returned a Twenty (chassis No. 20165) to the Derby works. He had bought the car in 1907 and by 1923 it had covered a hundred thousand hilly Scottish miles. With tears in his eyes, he explained that he had recently acquired a bigger car and had nowhere to keep his first Rolls-Royce. He had not the heart to sell it – and in any case the market price was negligible, a true Scot indeed. 'Would the firm', he asked, in a faltering voice, 'be so kind as to accept the car as a museum piece, a token of thanks for many years of faithful service?' Rolls-Royce Ltd. agreed although over the following years several other owners, with similar two-cylinder Rolls-Royces, came forward with the same offer, but the company was forced to turn them down. The doctor's car SU13 is still owned by Bentley.

Late in 1904, C. S. Rolls & Co. applied (in a ballot) for a space at the December 1904 Paris Salon, the premier motor show in the world at that time. Johnson and Rolls drove two of the small cars to Paris and took the engines for another two proposed models. In Paris, they ran a demonstration for the press and were awarded a special medal for elegance and comfort, an astonishing feat given that the car had been noisily rantanned out of the Cooke Street works only nine months earlier.

One press article described Rolls's influence in the new company:

'His long connection with the motor car industry and his intimate knowledge of all the best-known foreign and British automobiles, have no doubt proved invaluable to Mr. C. S. Rolls in perfecting the design and details of the new all-British car, which his firm, Messrs. C. S. Rolls & Co., has put on the market under the name of the 'Rolls-Royce car'. This vehicle, which occupies a prominent position in the Show, is being manufactured by Messrs. Royce Ltd. of Manchester, a firm of engineers, who have won a reputation for the high-class work they have carried out for the Admiralty.

The cars shown on the C. S. Rolls & Co. stand, included, amongst others, a 10hp vehicle exactly similar to one, which has already been driven for more than six thousand miles. There's also a six-cylinder motor and several examples are shown on the stand and the materials which are used in their construction.

The Rolls-Royce cars are capable of a very good turn of speed, but this consideration has not been allowed to influence the makers so much as the fact of simplicity, silence, ease of manipulation and comfort.

All these vehicles, whether of two, three, four or six cylinders, have the same sized cylinders, approximately four inch bore by five inch stroke; these are vertical and the engines are run at about a thousand revolutions per minute. Each cylinder has a separate casing, this giving room for additional crankshaft bearings. The carburettor is the automatic, self-regulating float feed type and the centrifugal governor acts upon the throttle valve. High tension' ignition is used, with commutator on the dashboard. The belt-driven lubricator is also fixed on the dashboard. The engine is excellently lubricated by oil rings as well as the 'splash' method.

The radiator is made of small brass tubes, passing through horizontal brass plates and is fan-assisted. Water circulation is effected by a rotary pump of the gear wheel type. An internal cone clutch transmits the power of the engine through universal joints to a three-speed gear of the sliding type, connected to a rear live axle. Special care has been taken to obtain the best design of driving axle, and it is noticeable that while in the 10hp and the 15hp car the wheels are keyed direct onto the tapered end of the steel-driving shaft, a different form of construction is used in the 20hp and 30hp types. In these, the steel tubes connecting the valves to the differential box prolongs and carry two hardened steel sleeves upon which the road wheels revolve; the driving shaft proper passes through the sleeve and has a dual clutch on the end of it, engaging with teeth formed on the outer end of the road wheel hubs. The differential gear is of the planetary type. Pressed steel frames are fitted to the larger and channelled steel to the smaller types. We were able to have a short practical demonstration on the 10hp RR car, and can speak in eulogistic terms of its flexibility, extraordinary quiet running and the unusual comfort of the body'.

Rolls and Royce complemented each other almost perfectly. Rolls recognised Royce's engineering genius and saw how Royce's persistence would improve the product; Royce recognised in Rolls the ability to understand what the market needed, how to sell cars and supervise their servicing. It has been suggested over the years that Royce had the brains, but Rolls had the money, and this is certainly a disservice to the young C. S. Rolls.

Sixteen two-cylinder Rolls-Royces were manufactured, all with the classic radiator shape, of which three survived. They were followed by six three-cylinder cars, of which one survived and then by about forty 20hp cars, the Light and the Heavy. And finally, in this early multiple-model period, another forty or fifty Short and Long cars were manufactured.

Autocar said in December 1904: 'We are interested to hear that the new British car made its first bow to the world in the Paris Motor Show and has not been shown there in vain. Up until Tuesday (mid-December 1904), twenty-seven cars were positively ordered and deposits paid'.

So, at last, C. S. Rolls & Co., as a firm, had the prospect of a great British car to sell. Rolls pushed on with his ballooning and the contacts it brought. The firm adopted agencies for Minerva and Orleans to bridge the widening gap in its range. They built on the success of the Paris show, and then another huge opportunity, a plum, fell into their lap. Although it involved racing, it is described here, being a significant event as the Rolls-Royce success story evolved.

As background... The Gordon Bennett Race in Ireland had generated a huge response and the public wanted more. The A.C.G.B.I. at one time considered Lincolnshire but Claude Johnson's successor as Secretary, Julian Orde, travelled to the Isle of Man on a mission to convince the authorities there that a race would generate huge interest in the Island and help tourist revenue. The Tynwald parliament had it's own law making powers. Orde had an invaluable ally on the Island, the Governor, Lord Raglan, himself a keen motorist.

Nevertheless, landing on a foggy day in February 1904, Orde may have felt nervous about the prospects. The Island, just thirty miles deep and twelve miles wide slumbered in the last days of winter – a haven of tranquillity, it's peace not yet shattered by the noise of racing engines.

As the Industrial Revolution had gathered momentum, annual mass vacations, sometimes known as wake weeks, sprang up and whole towns took time off for fresh air and fun. Some adventurous souls ventured beyond Blackpool or Llandudno to the Isle of Man tempted by ferry fares as low as sixpence. Lower taxes meant the Island could offer cheap meals and accommodation, and also, as a Victorian guide book chortled, 'spirit at a penny a dram'.

Theatres in Douglas featured stars of the day such as Irish tenor, John McCormack, and music hall favourite and male impersonator, Vesta Tilley. There was a pier, San Francisco-style trams and a mountain railway to Snaefell – the highest point on the island.

However… seasonal success depended on the weather… so how to start the season earlier – and if possible extend it. Lord Raglan had a plan, and seized his opportunity.

Julian Orde was driven round the island in Raglan's Daimler. Over the next few years he recalled he did sixty-nine circuits but came up with the first proposal, a course of fifty miles that took in Ramsay in the north, Castletown in the south and the formidable heights of Snaefell.

A public meeting was quickly held, after which a deputation successfully sought Lord Raglan's blessing. A special session of the Tynwald, doubtless with a few hotelier members within it, approved the first race to be held. By 23rd March, Julian Orde and members of the A.C.G.B.I. Racing Committee motored round the circuit and within a month 'had gone across' back to it's London headquarters, and were discussing the rules for the first race.

One can scarcely imagine the excitement on the Island in the second week of May as the racing cars arrived. There were five Napiers, three Wolseleys (in early British Racing Green) and three Darracqs from Scotland. Three scheduled Huttons failed to show. This caused a somewhat caustic Charlie Rolls in London to mock Hutton, whose current argument was that more cylinders meant more trouble, for his inablility to produce a car for the Eliminating Trials.

Any overweight car had to be slimmed down to the 1000 kilogram weight limit. This amputational surgery was strangely known as 'adding lightness'. Five hundred temporary Special constables, mostly farmers, were sworn in and temporary grandstands sprang up around the circuit.

The track itself was in turn very muddy, full of potholes and oh, so dusty when dry. Ten cars started that memorable day, Tuesday 10th May. The drivers included Rolls's motor volunteer colleague, Mark Mayhew, and the Gordon Bennett heroes of 1903 and the leading drivers of the time, Selwyn Edge, Charles Jarrott and Jack Stocks.

All drove for more than seven hours to complete five circuits of the fifty-mile course with Clifford Earp emerging as the fastest. However other factors were considered and Edge, Jarrott and Sidney Girling were selected as the Gordon Bennett team. The Island would no longer slumber undisturbed.

Meanwhile in England, working with his new collaborator, Henry Royce, Rolls must have watched the Trials with a pang of envy for his not being there. However, there would always be next year.

So it proved. Charlie Rolls had raced little, since the 'Race to Death' in 1903. His dream of a world beating British car was emerging with Royce making stunning progress in design and development. Claude Johnson could 'mind the shop' at Lillie Hall – so 'why not?'

One of the early Rolls-Royce cars was the Heavy Twenty, later to be known as the Twenty Long. Wealthy Bradford customer, Arthur Harry Briggs, bought one. He was so pleased with it that he suggested it would be suitable for the new Tourist Trophy race scheduled for September. Why didn't C.S.Rolls and Co. enter a car? They did better than that, they entered two – and were the first entrants.

Charlie Rolls had in fact been to the Island, at the request of Herbert Austin (later Lord Austin), to take part in the 1905 Elimination Trials in a Wolseley. With an eye to the Tourist Trophy event later he readily agreed and joined four Napiers, another Wolseley, two Stars from Wolverhampton, a Siddeley and a Darracq.

Anyone this year, 1905, allowing a horse, cow, sheep or dog onto the roadway faced a £20 fine (£2000 today). Ridge-Whitworth wire-spoked wheels made their first appearance and cars were weighed in on the public weighbridge (not in the coal yard as previously). 'Adding lightness' to overweight cars was a feature yet again.

Rolls duly qualified for the team in the Wolseley, together with Clifford Earp in another and Cecil Bianchi in a Napier. Just as important, with masses of notes on the circuits' twists and turns, he had done his homework for September.

Race week arrived, and the first Tourist Trophy to be held over four laps of some fifty miles each. Petrol was limited to eight and a half gallons per car for the precise 208 miles distance.

The chassis weight was to be 1300 pounds minimum and 1600 pounds maximum. The load on the chassis itself was to be no more than 950 pounds including driver, mechanic and extraordinarily, 600 pounds of loose sand as ballast in the two unoccupied rear seats, on top of which were placed coats and refreshments.

The rules also stated the price at which the car would be sold to the public – a motoring selling plate, in racing terms. Despite the strict conditions fifty-eight cars entered, a public relations opportunity for the manufacturers. This was what what Briggs had spotted and which Rolls, Royce and Johnson were keen to exploit.

There was to be no overtaking in the villages. Quaintly, all cars were provided with the times that various trains would cross the open level crossings en-route – marshalled conscientiously by you have guessed it – men with red flags.

There was a starting paddock and the cars were rolled down Alexander Drive to join the main course before Quarter Bridge; this with a cold engine until momentum was sufficient to let each driver 'bump start' his car.

Bad weather conditions resulted in the organisers increasing the fuel allowance to nine and a half gallons.

Rolls's debut – he was first away – was less than propitious. The Twenty 'failed to proceed', the odds-on favourite falling at the first. St.John C.Nixon, of the Circle of Victorian Motorists and a protegy of Selwyn Edge described the debacle. 'He (Rolls) tried to get his car into his third gear but could not do so; then he tried his top with the same result, so he came back and tried third again: there was a crash in the gearbox and he was out of the race'.

Wisely, under the circumstances, C.S.Rolls & Co. and Rolls-Royce Ltd concentrated their marketing on their second car driven by Percy Northey. This was indeed a triumph, finishing second, without stopping, over the two hundred and eight miles averaging 34mph at 25 miles per gallon. In doing so the Rolls-Royce Light Twenty beat other more established makes of car including Cadillac, Darracq, Napier, Peugeot and Wolseley.

The race was won by an Arrol-Johnston driven by it's designer John Napier. Another entrant J.C.Dennis (later to design and build fire engines) finished gallantly after eight and a half hours with his plucky wife beside him as passenger

And Rolls? Mr. Grumpy on this occasion did not endear himself to the world's press after the race. He initially alleged that his car had been sabotaged: 'I found a certain number of broken, loose nuts at the bottom of the gearbox which, as far as I can see, must have been put through a hole at the top. This is the sort of thing that happens frequently in France, but I hardly thought it possible in this country. The effect was that as soon as I started running by the gravity of the car downhill, using no power, the pieces caught in the gearing and broke the gearwheels'.

There had been sabotage in continental events, but the press did not like that sort of complaint. *Car Illustrated*, owned and edited by John Montagu, cried very sour grapes indeed! Rolls was lampooned by a wickedly ironic tail (!), told in the paddock, 'concerning a certain Manx cat, which committed suicide by jumping into the gearbox'. Not all comment was hostile, however. He found support from the young St. John Nixon, who, in his book *'Romance amongst Cars'* (R.A.C.)[26]: 'There was a strong suspicion that there had been a certain amount of tampering with some of the cars, as Arnott on an Orleans car – also entered by C. S. Rolls & Co. – had found his carburettor needle bent and both porcelains in his plugs cracked'.

A few days later, Rolls had calmed down enough to write a personal letter to his father's secretary: 'But the gear was broken up at the start owing, I think, by some loose pieces having got into the gearbox somehow'. A cloud of mystery hangs over the whole business. Surely Royce would have had something to say or perhaps, for once, silence was golden – 'least said, soonest mended' for the marque, but Rolls compounded his error by protesting that the winning Arrol-Johnston had had a dangling silencer, which came adrift in mid-race, giving the winner extra horsepower and breaching A.C.G.B.I. rules about silencers. A rather feeble complaint. This petulant effort was rebuffed by Napier, who explained that the loss of his exhaust reduced horsepower, and that anyway Rolls

---

26 *'Romance amongst Cars' by St. John C. Nixon (G. T. Foulis 1937).*

was bluffing about silencer rules because there were none. Napier 1, Rolls 0. Rolls took a step back using the charm he could turn on when he had to. He congratulated Percy Northey on his second place out of forty-five cars and his new associate, Henry Royce, on his brilliance in designing such a reliable car. Rolls gave each of Northey and Royce a cigar box as a momento (his speech at the Trocadero in London to celebrate the 1905 success is quoted in full at Appendix 1).

Rolls had strong views about where matters stood between racing cars and cars for the motorist: 'Racing pure and simple has proved its purpose, and the construction of special racing machines, which are of no use to the ordinary motorist... It involves enormous expense... but the object of the Tourist Trophy was the improvement of motor cars... which is useful to the ordinary purchaser'.

C. S. Rolls & Co. now really had something to crow about and Johnson's gift for public relations went into overdrive. True, in December, 1904, only the original cars were complete, but the Tourist Trophy success proclaimed the progress made in such a short time.

The firm had held on to the Minerva as a mid-range Belgian car, for which they had the agency and which sold for around £300. Johnson captured the Orleans car agency and those cars cost around £600, so by the end of 1905 you could spend £300, £600 or £900 in buying a new car at Conduit Street, on hire purchase if necessary.

Johnson then produced a twenty page, pocket-sized brochure in early 1905, masterful for its time. Some pages are reproduced here, but at that early time, before the switch to a one large car policy, the brochure referred only to two, three, four and six cylinder cars of 10hp, 15hp, 20hp and 30hp. The least expensive car, with a Barker tonneau body, was £395. The most expensive, a six-seater Barker limousine, described as 'the most perfect and luxurious car', was a 30hp, six-cylinder model, with three speeds and a reverse and a direct drive on top speed at a price of £1,000. The brochure claimed the car could do 5mph to 55mph without changing gear.

The brochure described the Works: 'The car is manufactured exclusively for C. S. Rolls & Co. by Messrs. Royce Ltd. of Hulme, Manchester, established in the year 1884, a firm of the highest standing in the engineering world'.

For telegrams, Conduit Street was 'Rolhead', and for Brook Street, later closed on the grounds of cost, a more jaunty 'Rollicking' was preferred. Repairs were still done at Lillie Hall on all makes of cars, although the firm announced in November 1905 that they would only supply, as new, the Rolls-Royce range.

Pictures of the various of tonneau, landaulette, phaeton and limousine style were shown, with detailed price lists. The brochure repeated they still repaired all makes of vehicles and that they were repairers to the War Office and the A.C.G.B.I.

Finally, the interchangeability of parts was stressed. The cylinder dimensions were the same for two, three, four and six-cylinder cars, so valves, pistons, connecting rods, etc. were the same on all types and were thus interchangeable. Spares could be dispatched immediately. And finally, the 'RR' became the company logo, and the fact the cars were 'ALL-BRITISH' was emblazoned on the front and back cover of the brochure.

A list of C. S. Rolls & Co's customers were included deliberately, giving the impression they might have ordered a Rolls-Royce, but it was, in fact, a list of C. S. Rolls & Co's customers back to the inception of the firm. Patrons included the Crown Prince of Romania, the Duke of Sutherland (President of the A.C.G.B.I.), the Duke of Manchester, Lord Raglan (Governor of the Isle of Man), Sir David Salomons and several other notables. Moore-Brabazon, a long-time friend of Rolls, pulled no punches when he described Rolls: 'A snob too. The way he used his super-powers of salesmanship to float early Rolls-Royce cars to the aristocracy of England, left every other firm an also ran'.

However, that did not prevent the King, Edward VII, taking delivery of a 20hp Daimler, bodywork by Hooper & Co., to the dismay of Claude Johnson, who called the Daimler 'The Unmentionable Car'.

In the publicity, Johnson was given equal billing to Rolls, and their separate achievements eulogised in the brochures. As to the cars, simplicity, engine, ignition, cooling, power, brakes, carburettor, weight, economy and tyres were all described. The car was easy to drive and look after, so that it was 'not necessary to employ a skilled and expensive chauffeur'. Both Rolls and Johnson were experienced and seasoned drivers and could and did teach novices to drive – there was no specific driving test until the 1930s. Here, however, Johnson and Rolls differed in one respect – Rolls thought ladies should and could drive, whereas Johnson felt they should stay at home and leave driving to the men. The silence of the Rolls-Royce car was stressed, and the fact that 'the car is sent out with a full kit of tools, two magnificent brass headlights, with double lenses and regulation tail lamp (without extra charge)' was trumpeted.

Customers were required to pay one-third of the purchase price upfront and a three month guarantee was given to replace and repair any original Rolls-Royce part. Barker bodies were recommended and fitted to customer specification and, with a slick reference to that, the brochure confirmed that Barkers were coachmakers to the King (albeit on the chassis of another well-known make of car).

Trading Standards might have nit-picked today, but hey ho, it was 1905 and Rolls and Johnson were indeed two smooth operators.

There were still hurdles to overcome. Rolls trialled unsuccessfully with the Dufaux at the Brighton Speed Trials, but this potential addition to his stable became a very unfunny joke. The beast was 150hp but achieved just 49mph – about half the speed of Earp's winning Napier, which ran at 91mph. Its pathetic performance was lampooned in the press. *The Globe* reported: 'Mr. Rolls's 150hp Dufaux proved to be an unpleasant monster to meet at close quarters, vomiting both flame and clouds of smoke on the few occasions when one or two of its four cylinders consented to fire for a few seconds. The motor, probably the largest ever fitted to a car, certainly looked as if a good-sized boy could easily find room within its huge cylinders'.

The Morning Leader also weighed in: 'Mr. Dufaux had a cold or indigestion or something mortally wrong inside. He came up the course, making more noise than an infuriated snark. He was firing like a Maxim gun, roaring like a bull and covering himself and his driver (Rolls) with clouds of black smoke'.

Unsurprisingly, C. S. Rolls & Co. abandoned any idea of selling the Dufaux.

At the 1905 Olympia Motor Show in February, C. S. Rolls, on Stand 65, presented for the first time the new all-British Rolls-Royce motor cars alongside the Belgian Minerva and the new Orleans. They were sole concessionaires for the Minerva and sole London agents for the Orleans. On the stand was a 30hp seven-seater Pullman, previously described in the brochure at £1,000, and a 15hp, three-cylinder 'Silent Landaulette', priced at £550, both with Barker coachwork.

Johnson's marketing strategy was to make the car as glamorous as possible, a fashionable toy for both *arriviste* and established. He actively encouraged pieces such as appeared in the *Evening Standard*, 5th June 1905:

' Midnight Motor Meet – Theatrical parties novel run after the curtain fell:

An altogether fairy-like adventure was the Midnight Motor Meet of London actors and actresses and their friends, who gathered at Oddeninos in Regent Street directly the plays were over on Saturday night, and they rode through the first dawn of June to the Riviera Hotel at Maidenhead. It had been announced that a start was to be made outside the New Walsingham Club in Coventry Street on the stroke of twelve. As a matter of fact, supper pardonably intervened and it was not until one o'clock that eight spic and span cars and a bright little party of some thirty or forty brave and fair emerged into Piccadilly Circus, empty now and silent save for the convocation of tired policemen, who looked quite dazzled as the cars came gleaming and 'toot-tooting' round the Gilbert Fountain.

Gay as each car was, with pretty frocks, the little procession proved indeed a sight at that witching time of night to make the solitary fireman rub his eyes in wonder. Several of the cars were piloted by quite distinguished amateur motorists. At the helm of the Rolls-Royce car that led the way was the Hon. C. S. Rolls himself, fresh from his triumphs in the Gordon Bennett trials…

Amongst the actresses, who had joined courageously in the midnight run were several well-known stage favourites…

The weather proved perfect, nothing could have been more wholly delightful after a stuffy evening in the West End than a little spin along dim roads between dreaming fields in the cool, fresh air of the early morning.

As the cars reached Maidenhead between two and three, when twilight had almost merged into the day, the little crowd of Maidenhead people on the bridge, who had apparently stayed up all night to greet the motors with a cheer, seemed to belong to some of the mysterious world. Anyhow they mistook Mr. Rolls for Sir Henry Irving (hardly likely as Irving was then in his late sixties!). It may be added that the whole party spent the most enjoyable weekend at the Riviera Hotel with its beautiful garden and its lawns.

Sloping down to the river where an alfresco concert was held. They were, too, as was promised, photographed in the cars. The photographs will duly appear in tonight's biograph at the Alhambra'.

Before their second attempt to win the T.T. Race in 1906, ever the publicist, Claude Johnson had taken on board the impact of Charles Jarrott's Monte Carlo run. Jarrott had run a 40hp Hodgkiss from Monte Carlo to London in thirty-seven and a half hours and asserted that his time would never be beaten. Rolls and Claude Johnson were confident that Rolls's new 1906 Light Twenty could do just that.

Rolls's passengers were an old Varsity chum and journalist, Massac Buist, Eric Platford from the Royce works and a tyre man from Dunlops. The team had a good trip over and, on the way down, arranged with railway-crossing keepers to open key gates as they returned. That May, Monte Carlo was awash with British socialites who gave Rolls a warm send-off at noon. Progress was rapid for the six hours. Rolls then woke his mechanic team to check the car and change tyres and had a glass of bubbly, before heading off to change.

All seemed to be going swimmingly. However, the night drive became a nightmare. Pouring rain reduced the maps to pulp, one French crossing-keeper thought even the English would not be mad enough to drive in such conditions and had to be dragged *'Mon Dieu'* from his bed to open a crossing; Rolls took a wrong turn and added scores of miles to the seven hundred and seventy-one mile route. He drove to Dijon, changed again and by 4.00 p.m., twenty-eight hours into the journey, finally reached the ferry. He had gained three hours on Jarrott, but he still missed the ferry, and whereas Jarrott had had one waiting, Rolls and his team had to wait three hours. They eventually crossed 'Le Manche', and hammered on to London in darkness, guided by no more than instinct and the Pole Star.

A pre-arranged pilot car met them in London, but that too went awry when its driver got lost in London's back streets. The Rolls-Royce crossed Blackfriars Bridge just ten minutes inside Jarrott's time, reaching Big Ben just before 1.30 a.m. and beating Jarrott by one and a half minutes but this after a three hour wait at Boulogne. It was a new record and was seen as a triumph, providing publicity and kudos for the new marque.

Rolls was coming to the end of his racing career. His swan song in Britain came the following summer at the 1906 T.T. Race. He was fortunate that, after his effort with Wolseley in the 1905 Gordon Bennett trial, he knew the island circuit well. The 1906 course was one hundred and sixty-one miles, four laps of forty miles via Douglas, Peel, Ramsay, Quarterbridge and Snaefell and then back to Douglas. Fuel was again rationed, one gallon for twenty-two and a half miles, and each car carried nine hundred and fifty pounds. There was a test to start and stop on a gradient of one in six, and competitors also had to be able to cover a measured half mile in top gear at 12mph. Rolls wanted wire wheels rather than wooden ones. Royce was reluctant because of cost. He had been poor once and dreaded being poor ever again, but Johnson said it was vital. It was agreed that the still independent C. S. Rolls & Co. would foot the bill at an equivalent cost today of £4,000.

The race was already a major tourist attraction and there was huge interest across the United Kingdom. The papers sent special correspondents. Harmsworth (now Lord Northcliffe) of the *Daily Mail* had recruited the crime writer, Edgar Wallace[27], following Wallace's return from South Africa to escape his creditors. Claude Johnson put two Rolls-Royce cars at the disposal of journalists to ferry them from London to Liverpool. Some reporters had commissioned an aerial platform beneath a balloon.

The island was agog. Thirty-one cars were to race, including the 1905 winning Arrol-Johnston, which was favourite alongside the two Rolls-Royce entries. Rolls was fourth away, Northey fifth, but this time it was the latter's turn for failure. 'Spring broken, heartbroken' read the cryptic telegram back to England. Meanwhile, Rolls averaged just under 40 mph on the first lap and overtook the Arrol-Johnston on lap two, which he completed in sixty-one minutes. On lap three his goggles were smashed but he took those of Platford, his mechanic,

27 *Harmsworth was later to bitterly regret his involvement with Edgar Wallace, which cost him £60,000 in the first decade of the new century, as Wallace was hopeless with money. During that time Wallace developed the well-known crime series featuring the Four Just Men, and later wrote 'Sanders of the River', which became an iconic film. His best-known work of all was his co-authorship of the story and screenplay for the early film, 'King Kong'.*

and roared on. Four hours and ten minutes from the start Rolls and Platford, averaging 39mph, took the race by twenty-seven minutes, the Arrol-Johnston having suffered puncture trouble. With only one pint of petrol left, the Rolls team had judged the race and fuel consumption to perfection. Their time was 6mph faster than the previous year's winner, a tribute to the continued design improvements of Royce.

Rolls's triumph gave a huge boost to the morale of the new company. The lads in the Manchester works received telegrams on progress from De Looze, the company accountant, and down in London, Johnson placed a large blackboard in the showroom on which the lap-by-lap positions of Rolls and Northey were displayed. After the race was over, three hundred Manchester employees hammered on benches and anvils and one man produced a cornet and played a celebratory tune. An embarrassed Royce was carried shoulder high through the works. He then gave the entire workforce the rest of the day off – for the very first time ever.

Rolls was presented with the Automobile Club Tourist Trophy – a silver casket, supporting a golden figure of Hèrmes – by the Lord Lieutenant Governor of the Isle of Man, Lord Raglan. It was quite a party that night. Rolls and Platford drove the winning car into the ballroom of the Mona Palace, the largest hotel on the island, which was crammed with almost five thousand guests.

From late 1905, Rolls-Royce embarked on a project to develop an eight cylinder V8 car at the behest of Lord Northcliffe – formerly Alfred Harmsworth – who had been enobled during the year. There appeared to be a market for a car that would keep its owner away from the possibility of speeding and exceeding the 20mph limit. Lord Northcliffe was very keen on this, and Royce felt he could design such a car. Its speed would not exceed, either on the level, uphill or downhill, the legal limit.

It was this car that was introduced to the public in a splendidly comprehensive and well-produced catalogue, issued in 1906. Another aim of the new technology was to produce a vehicle to succeed the electric brougham, which would be noiseless, shockless and odourless.

At the London Olympia Show in 1906, Rolls's winning car occupied pride of place, and a further brochure was launched, capitalising on the company's development and the year's Isle of Man triumph. The brochure featured only Rolls-Royce cars, and this has since become a collectors item. It contains testimonials from patrons such as the Duke of Argyll and A.C.G.B.I. consulting engineer, Mr. Worby Beaumont, and others. There were testimonials too from newspapers, which stressed fuel economy, 25mpg on Northey's run in the 1905 Tourist Trophy for example.

The brochure contained anecdotes and well-presented details such as a topographical map of the Isle of Man Tourist Trophy course, with lengthy extracts from the motoring press. There were glamorous pictures, including no less than nine Rolls-Royces at the Duke of Westminster's Eaton Hall home in Cheshire. The catalogue listed seven available models, 10hp and 15hp, Twenties, Long and Light, six-cylinder Thirties, Short and Long, and the ill-fated Legal Limit, inspired by Alfred Harmsworth, which, not surprisingly, never caught on.

You could have a limousine, landau, a Double Victoria or a shooting brake version. There were about twenty types of cars depicted from the simple 10hp at £395 to the Tatton Bower, the writer's personal favourite, a snip at £1,140, about £100,000 today, a gorgeous looking conveyance.

1906 was the year in which the efforts of Manchester and London were combined in the financial sense. With the steady hand of Claremont and the backing of Glovers to help, the financial transformation proceeded quite smoothly, but for one short period of concern, as we shall see.

March 1906 saw the incorporation of Rolls-Royce Ltd.

Royce Ltd. itself continued to trade until the Thirties, with Royce remaining a director. This hiving off must have reassured Claremont, who was very dubious at the outset about the car venture.

He was also heavily involved in Glovers, a much larger company, making cables. Undoubtedly their reputation added kudos and support to the infant Rolls-Royce company. C. S. Rolls himself subscribed £10,000 of the £60,000 capital of the March 1906 issue.

It was by this time that Royce and Johnson had realised the need for a new factory. Leicester and Derby were short-listed. Derby Corporation promised a long-term contract for reasonably priced electricity, and this proved a deciding factor. Other advantages were that the Derby site was new and away from others, so the chance of workers moving and then defecting elsewhere was much lessened. In addition, Leicester was also short-sighted enough to indicate to Rolls-Royce that they thought such an enterprise would introduce severe local competition for skilled labour.

Henry Royce proved not only his planning foresight in designing a purpose-built works, but also in shrewd land buying. The company bought and obtained options on some eleven acres of land, almost a million square feet, and even by 1914, although they occupied five times as much as the area when they moved in, they had used up only half the site.

The second phase of the company's development was the absorption of C. S. Rolls & Co. in late 1906, which was agreed on Rolls's behalf by his father, Lord Llangattock while Rolls himself was away in America.

Rolls received some 12,000 ordinary and 14,000 preferred shares in exchange for C. S. Rolls & Co. and its associated interests. Rolls liked the idea of the merger even if it meant later that he was not to have his own way, for the first time ever, over the issue of aero engine development.

Having left his father to do the deal, he wrote on shipboard to New York in October 1906: 'It's principally a matter of bargaining for the best price for the business and goodwill. There's probably no doubt that the manufacturing end would, in any case, enlarge if they make two hundred and sixty cars annually (the proposed target). We, CSR & Co. – if we had remained separate – would have to have more capital to sell that number.

So on the whole, the amalgamation is good as it does not involve having to find any capital at my end... and I shall have a good shareholding in the company, with a certain salary plus commission on profit, and be released of a great deal of responsibility'.

At the same time, it was agreed to raise £100,000 of outside capital for the proposed new factory. The minimum subscription was to be £50,000, but because of a number of motor company flotations, and a certain lack of information published, at one stage only £40,000 had been raised. Failure to achieve the minimum subscription would have been calamitous for the infant company, had it not been overcome.

The financial press commented that: 'An estimate of future profits is about as tangible as the Aurora Borealis'. This was barely inspiring as was the further comment that: 'An appeal so bereft of any formal inducement, outside of personal confidence and the personalities, that appear on the directorate, should be made at an appropriate season'.

Another paper, *The Financial Review*, made an even gloomier comment, describing the prospectus as: 'A vague proposition, which does not lend itself to comparison with any existing concern'.

It must be remembered that one is looking back on the Rolls-Royce success with the benefit of a hundred years of hindsight. There were dozens of small United Kingdom car manufacturers. While Rolls-Royce was and is excellent, there existed older, established names like Napier, Daimler and others, which had a longer pedigree. Extravagant claims might be made in a prospectus, but would firms be there in five years or ten years to support their manufactured wares with back-up and replacement parts?

Coventry and London were the centres for car manufacture. Royce Ltd of Manchester made excellent cranes did they not and did not everything about their manufacturing development depend on one man – would their car operation survive, many had not.

Claremont must have been very concerned and self-justified about the lack of enthusiasm, but fortunately the accountant to the firm, John De Looze, remembered the wealthy Arthur Briggs, who had purchased the first Twenty from the firm, and who had suggested the Tourist Trophy entry. A dash to Yorkshire by De Looze secured a cheque for £10,000 without demur, and the subscription was saved. Mr. Briggs got what turned out to be a spectacularly successful investment and was asked to become a director of the firm. Such was his faith in the firm that when he died in 1919, the annual report of the company appeared with a black border as a mark of respect.

At the other end of the scale, Eric Platford, an apprentice, famously subscribed ten sovereigns, and other workers in the firm backed the issue, thus showing their faith in the future of their company and the motor industry.

Royce was to become Managing Director and Claremont, after a slight delay, became part-time Chairman. He still had major responsibilities at Glovers.

Rolls and Johnson became Technical Managing Director and Commercial Managing Director respectively on a salary of £750 each plus 4% of the profits. Royce was to receive £1,250 per annum plus 4% of the profits.

Profits rose steadily from £5,390 in 1907 to £37,761 in 1913, a remarkable feat since the period included the acquisition and move to the Derby site and the development of all the cars.

The Board was further strengthened by the recruitment of Lord Herbert Scott, D.S.O. He was the son of the sixth Duke of Buccleugh and a cousin of Lord Montagu. He resigned his commission in the Army to join the Board in January 1907, and later, in 1936, became Chairman of Rolls-Royce until his death in 1944.

The company felt confident enough by the end of 1906 that Rolls-Royce could sell every car it could manufacture, and decided to explore the American market.

If Charles Rolls instigated this initiative, it may well have been partly due to his fast-growing interest in aviation. For several years he had followed the developments towards powered flight and, in particular, had kept in touch with American developments concerning two cycle shop owners, Orville and Wilbur Wright. He wanted to meet them and a sales trip to America seemed the ideal opportunity.

In October 1906 he set off to the States with two Light Twenties and a Thirty. After a satisfactory crossing, he exhibited a car at the New York Motor Show at Madison Square Garden. He then entered the Light Twenty, which Northey[28] had driven in 1906 for a five mile race at the Empire City Track. He told motoring journalists that his race strategy was to risk everything on the first ten corners and put the wind up all and sundry, who were minded to put it up on him.

Rolls won the race in New York by superb handling on the corners. His powerful American rivals had been eager to upset the 'Limey Lord' but had failed.

On the commercial front he received orders for three 30hp, six-cylinder Rolls-Royce models, appointed a Canadian agent and sold Northey's 1906 T.T. car to a Texan, one Captain Hutton and loaned Roy Macready to help Hutton race at Ormond Beach in Florida. There the car established a new world record (for a car

28 *Rolls's own winning Tourist Trophy car was occupying pride of place back in London at the Olympia Show, and he had taken Northey's car to America.*

of less than 60hp) over five miles and won a trophy for Britain described as the 'Bronze Statue' at the World's International Touring Car Championship. Meanwhile, Rolls mixed with American aristocracy. He demonstrated cars to the Vanderbilts and to the Astors and Mrs John Jacob Astor IV[29] purchased a Rolls-Royce.

Rolls was not to be aware of it then, but he had raced for the last time. Developments in Rolls-Royce technology were to mean that there would not be a suitable car to race on the Isle of Man in the Tourist Trophy in 1907, and the New Year saw the withdrawal of Rolls-Royce Ltd's entry for the contest.

By the time Rolls returned from America, Rolls-Royce Ltd. had become a substantial integrated business. Johnson and Claremont had decided in which way they were going to take the business and how they were going to protect the company's principal asset – the genius of Henry Royce – and although Charles Rolls's technical input was valued, other members of Royce's design team had matured, and Rolls's diminishing influence in the affairs of the company can be traced back to this time.

---

29 *Her husband, John Jacob Astor IV, reputed at the time to be the richest man in the world, was to perish on the Titanic in 1912.*

Chapter Nine

Best Car in the World

Rolls-Royce's reputation was, before Charles Rolls's death, largely built on the development of its six-cylinder car known as the 40hp/50hp.

From 1902 onwards, and particularly from 1903, Selwyn Edge and the Napier Motor Company began to promote the idea of a six-cylinder car. This was before Rolls and Royce joined forces. A six-cylinder (four stroke engine) has the smallest practical number of cylinders to give up an overlap of power impulses and a smooth flow of power[30].

Although Rolls-Royce initially lagged behind Napier in the development of six-cylinder engine technology, they realised its importance and a long conflict within the British motor industry took place between Rolls-Royce and Napier. Napier had developed a six-cylinder engine, and supplied customers as early as 1904, and Rolls-Royce would surely follow.

Acres of newsprint were expended in correspondence back and forth between car manufacturers such as Hutton, Edge (of Napier) and Claude Johnson. Rolls had been critical of other manufacturers such as Hutton, who contended that more cylinders meant more trouble. Replying to a press jibe from Hutton during the so-called 'Battle of the Cylinders', Rolls wrote: 'Sir, Mr. Hutton is so pleased with his little joke about the twenty-ninth valve that he has sent it to every motoring journal… When one calls to mind the unfortunate attempt Mr. Hutton had, at one time made, to build his own car for the Gordon Bennett Trials, one is surprised that he should talk of complications when criticising the products of a successful manufacturing firm'.

Development on a 30hp, six-cylinder Rolls-Royce commenced in late 1904, and a part-finished engine was exhibited at the Paris Salon in December 1904. The first public showing of a 30hp, six-cylinder Rolls-Royce was at the Olympia Show in February 1905. This was a seven-seater Pullman limousine, and by the 23rd May, 1905, the first production chassis left Manchester and was sold to a Mr.

---

30 *C. W. Morton, 'The History of Rolls-Royce Motor Cars, Volume I, 1903-1907'.*

Cliff of Leeds. After the February show, the *Automotive Journal* said: 'All the cars are fitted with three speeds and reverse, with direct drive on top speed'. Later *Autocar* commented on the car: 'All ordinary hills are mounted with ease on the top speed with direct drive'.

The 30hp, six-cylinder, was intended to be the top of the range, but was less accomplished than the smaller models. It was not big enough to be really luxurious in order to compete with cars like the Napier and it also had some technical short-comings. The wheel-base was too short and the big six-litre engine had to be mounted well-forward. This put a lot of weight on the front axle, and, with the type of worm and nut steering then used, this made the car heavy and awkward to drive. Royce also used the 20hp gearbox, and, unless handled with skill, it could not cope with the extra power and was prone to failure.

Nevertheless, it was given official blessing, effectively, by W. Worby Beaumont, then consulting engineer to the A.C.G.B.I., who gave the 30hp car his very solid seal of approval. Napier countered by driving one of its six-cylinder cars four hundred and forty-six miles from London to Edinburgh on direct drive, and hit back with its own publicity. However, *Autocar* commented in November 1905: 'If you saw a six-cylinder car, but could not hear its engine, it must be a Rolls-Royce'. The advert also used the phrase 'The Best Car in the World', to the chagrin of the Napier management and Selwyn Edge.

However, the major weakness of the Rolls still lay in the engine. It lacked stiffness, and the slender crankshaft, based upon the basic dimensions of the smaller cranks, could not cope with the torsionals of a six. Crank failures occurred. This was not helped by mounting the main bearings in the lower half and having three pairs of cylinders. The ignition system was exposed to the elements and in wet weather missing fire was commonplace.

The 30hp had to be replaced quickly, and it does not take a very educated guess to believe that Rolls, with his blend of society connections, technical ability and racing experience, was able to indicate to Royce the type of motor car that should be produced.

Meanwhile, the Battle of the Cylinders still raged on, and eventually both a 30hp Rolls, driven by Johnson, and Captain Deasey's four-cylinder Martini car took part in the June 1906 Scottish Reliability Trials, which covered over six hundred miles of gruelling motoring in the Scottish Highlands, with severe hill climbs and loose mountain roads. The route to and from Scotland was also made under the Automobile Club's observation. Points were awarded for speed, hill climbing, gear changing, fuel consumption and reliability, judged by A.C.G.B.I., and four stockbrokers judged the cars for silence and absence of shock and vibration. Following the Trial, Claude Johnson's 30hp six-cylinder Rolls-Royce was the only six-cylinder car to lose no marks, and won the Battle of the Cylinders against Captain Deasey's car by a huge margin.

Claude Johnson also drove the 30hp car, accepting a challenge concerning the turning capabilities of six-cylinder cars in narrow streets. In April 1906, The *Autocar* reported: 'Johnson got the Rolls-Royce car to turn round (without reversing) and had eight foot to spare on a road forty feet wide'.

The new 48hp, seven litre car (which later became known as the Silver Ghost series) was unveiled at the November 1906 Motor Show. Even by that time their progress had been judged unstoppable. The *Autocar* said: 'I take it almost every visitor came to the Show fully intending to visit the Rolls-Royce exhibit... their meteoric rise to the position of one of the first three firms in England is proof of it', the other firms presumably being Napier and Daimler.

The bigger car had a seven litre, six-cylinder engine, at 4.5 inch bore and stroke. The robust seven bearing crankshaft, much stiffer in torsion – crankshafts had been the previous problem – was located in a new rigid, aluminium crankcase, providing massive front, centre and rear main bearings.

The unique feature of the car was a pressure lubrication system, probably the first on a production car. For the quietness of operation, Royce chose a side-valve layout, with cast-iron, integral blocks and heads in two groups of three. Dual ignition was fitted with plugs in the valve caps. Care had been taken to keep the electrics dry and not subject to the weather. A further feature was ease of maintenance and the ability to change the valves quickly. The valve system had two expansion chambers close to the exhaust ports, with two downpipes feeding a common tailpipe.

The engine was mounted in the chassis with two feet at the rear and a front location to isolate it from frame deflections. There was also a new gearbox of larger dimensions, having a direct third and a geared-up fourth speed. With normal final drive ratios, these gears gave thirty-eight miles and forty-eight miles per hour per thousand rpm. There was a new steering, with worm and nut operation, with oil lubrication in the sealed steering box. As with the engine, ease of chassis maintenance had been carefully considered.

Time had not permitted a radical re-think of the suspension, and Royce recognised that more needed to be done on this later.

The plaudits began immediately. One paper, describing the Rolls-Royce stand at Olympia, said: 'If a visitor wanted to see a car into which the designer had really put brains, let him closely examine the exhibits on the Rolls-Royce stand. He will not only find features and novelty too numerous for us to mention here, but he would be thoroughly educated as to the reason which led the makers to adopt certain practices, for on no other stand has so much care and thought been expended in order to provide intelligent information for all who seek it.

Naturally the actual 20hp Rolls-Royce car on the stand, the car that won the 1906 Tourist Trophy race, was regarded with interest, as was also the very ornate Pullman, with its daring colour scheme, clerestory roof, and oval-shaped windows in bevelled edge glass, but the most interesting exhibit is undoubtedly the latest six-cylinder, 40hp/50hp chassis, the chief points, of which attention should be directed, are as follows:-

The method of casting the cylinders so that the water jackets completely encircle each one; the number of bearings, providing for the crankshaft and the manner in which they are kept lubricated; the new commutator, which is of ingenious make and break type instead of the wipe system as before; the efficient, but very simple, carburettor, which affects such a saving in petrol; the method of attaching the front end of the engine to the frame so that the slight twisting of the latter, when running over rough roads, cannot place undue strain on the base chamber. These, and many other features, will commend themselves, even as much to the novice as they do to the expert motorist'.

Autocar started its review: 'No other manufacturer in the world could produce such a car within three years of producing his first one'. They were wrong; it had taken just two years and eight months since March 1904.

One of Rolls's disappointments at about this time was the withdrawal of Rolls-Royce from competition. No car was being made in 1907 that could race in the

Tourist Trophy, so the Rolls entry was withdrawn and Rolls never had a chance to repeat his 1906 triumph[31].

However, the directors, at the end of 1906, could reflect that the businesses had now been combined financially. The existing cars were selling well in America on the back of the Tourist Trophy victory, and orders for the new 40hp/50hp car were such that it was fortunate the decision had already been made to construct a purpose-built factory somewhere in Britain to meet the unprecedented demand for the cars.

After Christmas, Claude Johnson thought that massive publicity could be obtained by competing in the 1907 Scottish Trial, and entered car chassis no. 60551 in the Trial. It was the thirteenth 40hp/50hp to be made, and Johnson arranged for Barkers to build a four-seater, open touring body, finished in aluminium paint. All the exterior and interior fittings such as head lamps, windscreen, grease cups, wheel hubs, door handles, etc. were silver-plated, and Johnson had a silver plaque made, which was fitted on a scuffle, bearing the words 'Silver Ghost'.

Following a successful trial, in which the Ghost covered two thousand miles, Johnson arranged for the car to undergo further trials under observation by the R.A.C. The plan was to drive the car fifteen thousand miles continuously backwards and forwards between London and Glasgow. He drove the first four thousand miles, and then the car was driven in turn by C. S. Rolls, Macready and Platford. It had one momentary stop, with six hundred and sixty-nine miles covered, when a jolt turned off a petrol tap… the delay was thirty seconds… the car then ran continuously for fourteen thousand three hundred and thirty-one miles, breaking the existing record, held by a Siddeley car.

An official RAC report stated: 'A standard 40hp/50hp six-cylinder Rolls-Royce was in 1907 submitted to a Royal Automobile Club road test of fifteen thousand miles, for reliability, durability and the cost of upkeep. It was also decided to

---

31 *Probably the next race that Rolls-Royce would compete in would be the 1913 Spanish Grand Prix – a hundred and ninety mile race won by the then Spanish Rolls-Royce agent, Señor Salamanca, in a Silver Ghost. Eric Platford finished third driving another Ghost, with orders to ensure victory for a Spanish driver on home soil.*

ascertain the cost of putting the chassis into a condition as new, by replacing all parts, which showed any sign of wear measurable by micrometer. Briefly, the results of the trial were as follows:-

Reliability: The distance of fifteen thousand miles was covered with only one stop for a short duration to turn on the petrol tap. Fourteen thousand three hundred and thirty-one miles were covered without any involuntary stop, the longest official run without any voluntary stop ever accomplished.

Durability: So excellent was the chassis at the conclusion of the trial that the total cost of the new parts to replace all the parts showing any sign of wear was £2 2s 7d.

The total cost of running the car, including petrol, oil and tyres and repairs sufficient to make the car equal to new was four pence halfpenny a mile. Of this, tyres amounted to three pence a mile and petrol, oil and all repairs one and a half pence. The petrol consumption… averaged 15.7mpg.'

Other leading motor journals were also fulsome in their praise: 'One of the most conclusive trials of downright merit in touring car construction the world has ever seen' – *The Automotor.*

'A triumph in engineering construction' – *The Autocar.*

'The best object lesson on the durability of the modern motor car that could possibly be given' – *The Motor.*

Claude Johnson, ever the publicist, wrote to *The Car* magazine, concerning an experiment carried out in the presence of Lord Herbert Scott of the Irish Guards. He stressed the absence of vibration in the new car: 'One side of the bonnet of the 40hp/50hp six-cylinder Rolls was raised so as to make a level table, the other side was raised so as to form a suitable background for a photograph. On the horizontal place of the bonnet, a plank was laid and on the plank were three tumblers, filled to the utmost with water coloured with red ink, green ink and black ink respectively. The starting handle was removed and a revolution counter was put on the front end of the crankshaft.

The car stood in a badly-lit portion of the Conduit Street garage, and when the engine had been started, the photograph was taken, an exposure of exactly four minutes being given during which the engine revolved four thousand six hundred times at the rate of eleven hundred and fifty revolutions per minute.

The photograph showed, by the absence of the outline of the tumblers, that the vibration was practically absent. Furthermore, it shows that although the tumblers were filled with liquid to the utmost, not a drop was spilled'. Johnson then went on to say 'that the experiment would be repeated today for the benefit of the press'.

The Silver Ghost itself, registration number AX201 (chassis number 60551), which participated in the Scottish Trial of 1907 and the Fifteen Thousand Mile Run, was first tested in April 1907. It was finished in silver and was described as a Windham detachable side entrance tonneau with Barker coachwork. It was Claude Johnson's trials car, originally painted green and later painted in silver, with silver fittings. After a supremely successful 1907, the car was exhibited at the Olympia Motor Show. It was sold in 1908 to a Mr. Hanbury of Eaton Square, London. Rolls-Royce re-purchased it in 1948 and it was lovingly restored. It has been used as a publicity car, and travelled all over the world – as recently as 2005. Its insured value was then reported to be $35 million (*Motor Trend* magazine) but it is literally priceless.

Rolls sold cars steadily and Royce finished his home at Quarndon near the new Derby factory site, and kept an eye on the factory contractors, Handysides, while continuing to refine the 40hp/50hp Rolls-Royce car. (Rolls himself had a 70hp model, one of the few that were made.)

Meanwhile, Johnson organised a competition for 'best chauffeur', and began to institute a programme of free inspections to owners and continued to fret as to how to overtake Daimlers – the choice of English royalty as a supreme marque.

On 13th March, 1908, with the development of the factory almost complete (it was due to open in three or four months), Johnson put forward a startling proposal to his fellow Board members. He suggested that the firm concentrate on one model. He was persuasive. Claremont sensed that this policy would give Royce some respite from his excessive labours. Royce himself was somewhat neutral about the proposal and did not understand why it was necessary to abandon things just like that. Rolls himself felt that the 20hp and 30hp were popular so why stop selling them, but put up little fight on the issue. The one car policy was approved.

On 9th July, 1908, fifteen months after starting, the Derby factory was ready, and John Montagu, now Lord Montagu, was invited to open it.

The Opening Day programme records that Derby was chosen on account of its central position and being close to the various sources of materials such as Sheffield and Birmingham... and because the Midland Railway provided an excellent service between London and Derby.

The factory was split into two sides, with the Safe Side, on one side of the roadway, consisting of the main shop and comprising raw materials stores, machine shop stores and finished parts, fitting bays and a large erecting bay. On the other side of the roadway was the Dangerous Side, including the smiths shop, the case-hardening shop, the sheet metal works, the pattern shop and the store, boiler house and chassis running/testing shop. The idea was that if there was a fire on the Dangerous Side, it would leave the Safe Side unscathed.

The programme spoke about 'horses drawing massive blocks of steel, the heavy rods and metal bars into the factory' and yet also spoke of new automatic machine tools, which could 'spit out finished parts with marvellous rapidity and accuracy'. It continued about the individual bays having their own single phase current, a far cry from the time when Royce used a 40hp/50hp engine power unit to power the works for a month in Manchester, night and day, when a power unit itself broke down. The programme then continued about metallurgy and a hill climb test facility within the factory compound that could test cars on an incline of up to 1:4.

At the opening ceremony, Royce, the quiet genius, kept in the background. Rolls opened the formal proceedings. He told the assembled guests that Rolls-Royce Ltd. was going to turn out a comparatively small number of cars by the very best and most careful methods of manufacture.

Continuing this theme, he said: 'In the first place the class of man, who would be quite acceptable in ordinary engineering works, would be unsuitable for us and for our standard of work. To produce the most perfect cars, you must have the most perfect workmen, and having got these workmen, it is then our aim to educate them up so that each man in these works can do his particular work better than anyone else in the world.

We have always believed that the construction of a motor car, which while possessing every degree of necessary rigidity and strength, was of less weight than other similar cars, is largely a metal question. We consider the success of the Rolls-Royce and its extraordinary durability and low cost of upkeep, as exemplified in the Fifteen Thousand Mile Trial of last year, is entirely due to the scientific design to the original research work and a close study of metals, which has been made by Mr. Royce, and his assistants in the physical laboratory of this company'.

Rolls went on to say that the company regarded this as the most important department in the works, but he could not show it to the visitors in view of the confidential development that was going on within it. The truth was somewhat different because that was where all the rubbish and scrap had been hidden out of sight of the assembled guests for the day!

Rolls then introduced John Montagu, who made fulsome praise of Messrs. Rolls, Royce and Johnson, describing Rolls as the most skilled driver, Royce as the mechanical genius and Johnson 'the man of business'. Montagu concluded: 'There is one reason why I think Rolls-Royce is the best car in the world and that is because I have just ordered one myself'.

A politician's opportunism? Montagu was now a peer and had known and liked Rolls for years and he respected Royce. In addition, he had had a Rolls Twenty since April 1906. With that, he threw a switch, the factory came to life and they went off, after a brief tour of inspection, for tea or something stronger. After the break, the Mayor of Derby had his five minutes of fame, and then Henry Royce presented Eric Platford with a momento to celebrate his Scottish Reliability Trial success.

A few weeks after the Derby factory opened, Johnson was planning again. He wanted Royce away from the works. Royce could inspire loyalty, but his man-management was more than erratic – Royce was wont to sack anybody whose work was not perfect. Johnson wrote to Claremont from Conduit Street: 'This brings me to the point that one cannot help wishing that a portion of Mr. Royce's time', as Johnson still referred to the maestro, 'should be spent right away from the works so that his brain might have the chance of producing Rolls-Royce something better... He insists on being worried with all the small, pettifogging details, which must surround him as long as he superintends the works'. Johnson felt that if Royce could be kept away, it would be a much better use of his (Royce's) time for the benefit of the shareholders.

The one-car policy meant that Royce could pursue perfection across a reduced sphere, and within a short while would refine the 40hp/50hp car to become the 'Best Car in the World'. It was just a case of sell, sell, sell. By 1909 Johnson was able to report that Rolls-Royce had sold every car it could make in that year and this before the end of September. The proposal was thus accepted, and the one car policy was indeed now fact.

By 1910 Royce's health had benefited, and his move, deliberately engineered by Johnson, meant that labour relations could improve in the factory while Royce could still monitor quality of design, but from a distance, and thus maintain his ethos of perfection.

In 1908 the market for Rolls-Royce cars widened throughout the British Empire when the Ghost won a huge trial – Bombay to Kolhapur in India – climbing to five thousand feet and then winning medals at the Bombay Motor Show. Following this, the Indian princes bought Rolls-Royces by the dozen and, with the aid of the coachmakers, turned many of them into stunning conveyances in an attempt to outshine each other. The maharajas and princes petrollised!

Irrespective of Rolls's remarks at the factory opening about the tradition of the firm, by 1911 there was an assembly line at Rolls-Royce although the workmanship was still sublime. A legacy from Royce, each day one perfect chassis rolled off the production line. Then the coachbuilders worked their subtle craftsmanship to whatever the new owner wished, and the company catalogues blossomed under the artistic public relations genius of Claude Johnson.

And Rolls, in the three years to the end of 1908, all in Rolls-Royce cars, had driven from London to Monte Carlo in record time, won the Tourist Trophy race, driven at Brooklands and in America. What other roads were left untravelled? He was now a gifted amateur, looking in on a professionally run company, which had succeeded in producing 'The Best Car in the World'. His salesmanship, Royce's engineering genius and Johnson's master-planning had, in the final analysis, left him without a proper job to do. It was time to move on – or rather 'up'.

Henry Edmunds and chauffeur Goody.

A Royce chassis.

One of the three Royces.

Another of the three Royces.

Accountant De Looze and Adams in one of the three Royces.

A Royce in Piccadilly heading for the Sideslip Trial.

Charles Stewart Rolls.

Frederick Henry Royce.

A C.S. Rolls & Co. advertisement featuring just Rolls-Royce.

Percy Northey – runner up Tourist Trophy Isle of Man 1905.

Percy Northey and a disconsolate Rolls after Tourist Trophy 1905.

Measuring the fuel for C.S. Rolls's car – Tourist Trophy 1906.

C.S. Rolls with Platford – full throttle Tourist Trophy.

C.S.Rolls with Platford – on the way to victory Tourist Trophy 1906.

C.S. Rolls (wearing Platford's goggles) winning the 1906 Tourist Trophy.

C.S.Rolls in 1906 winning Tourist Trophy car.

AX201 The Silver Ghost and others – Cat and Fiddle.

The "Tatton Bower" catalogue picture.

The Silver Ghost – Scottish Reliability Trial.

1907 Olympia Show – Silver Ghost on the new Rolls-Royce stand.

Rolls and the Wright Brothers in the Silver Ghost.

John Montagu's 'Dragonfly' – a Silver Ghost.

The Derby Factory.

Test track and manoeuvering in France.

The Sedanca de Ville on 40/50 h.p. Rolls-Royce Chassis
Barker's latest production.

BARKER COACHWORK

By Appointment to His Majesty The King

has been world-famous since 1710. At Barker's works over 200 bodies of all types can be seen in course of construction, and your inspection of Barker's exclusive designs and special wood-grain finishing colours is invited

By Appointment to H.R.H. The Prince of Wales

ROLLS-ROYCE CHASSIS—
BARKER BODY
Acknowledged the World's Best Car

BARKER & CO (COACHBUILDERS) LTD

Coachbuilders by Appointment to H.M. The King and to H.R.H. The Prince of Wales

66-69 SOUTH AUDLEY STREET LONDON W1

Rolls-Royce Retailers and Body Specialists

Telephone: Grosvenor 2420

Barker coachwork advertisement.

Everyone who wishes to keep in touch with current affairs should buy The Daily Mail Year Book for 1914. "A treasure house of facts and also a very valuable record of opinion." Now on Sale. Price 6d.

Daily Mail

Daily Circulation SIX Times as Large as That of Any Penny London Morning Journal.

GREATER LONDON EDITION.

WEST LONDON MISTRESSES

THURSDAY, NOVEMBER 20, 1913. LONDON. MANCHESTER. PARIS. ONE HALFPENNY.

THE BEST CAR IN THE WORLD

ROLLS-ROYCE

NOT ONLY THE BEST CAR BUT THE BEST PEOPLE TO DEAL WITH

"I wish particularly to say that your people at Derby have put the chassis in first-class condition, and I consider the charges made by you very reasonable in comparison to what I have had to pay in the past for repairs on other makes of cars, before I had dealings with your firm."

MR. JELLINEK-MERCÉDÈS

states that, in his opinion, the Rolls-Royce is

THE BEST CAR IN EXISTENCE.

"Le plus fini"
"Le plus souple"
"Le plus silencieux"
"Le mieux suspendu"
"La meilleure qui existe"

"J'ai l'honneur de vous informer que j'ai commandé chez-vous le chassis No. 2510E pour mon usage personnel, car je considère que c'est la voiture Rolls-Royce qui est aujourd-hui l'automobile le plus fini, le plus souple, le plus silencieux et le mieux suspendu. En un mot, je considère que la voiture Rolls-Royce est la meilleure voiture qui existe actuellement."

(Signé)
E. J. MERCÉDÈS.

ROLLS-ROYCE, LIMITED, 14-15, CONDUIT STREET, W.

Daily Mail advertisement.

Monte Carlo Rally record attempt.

Monte Carlo run – waiting at Boulogne.

A 1906 Rolls-Royce Heavy Twenty, purchased by the Hon. Mrs May Assheton Harbord.

Chapter Ten

A Pastime with a Purpose

'The basket was about two feet high and four feet long… to me it seemed fragile indeed… the gaps in the wickerwork in the sides and bottom seemed immense and the further we receded from the earth, the larger they seemed to become' – General George Custer 1862

The Montgolfier brothers first flew in 1783. Fourteen months later, in 1785, another Frenchman, Jean Pierre Blanchard, and an American, John Jeffries, set out from Dover and crossed the Channel for the first time and narrowly achieved their destination by jettisoning ballast, including Blanchard's trousers, in order to lighten the craft as it neared the French coast. *Mon Dieu!* Ballooning had come to Britain whether the Island Kingdom wanted it or not. Early British balloonists included Charles Dickens, the poet Percy Bysshe Shelley (a forebear of Rolls's brother-in-law, Sir John Shelley) and Percy's second wife, Mary Shelley, author of Frankenstein. American balloonists included the poet, Edgar Allan Poe and General Custer, cavalry general and Indian fighter, who perished at the Little Big Horn in Montana.

By 1900, by which time Rolls was twenty-three, ballooning was chiefly familiar as a fairground spectacle. Edwardian balloon girl, Dolly Shepherd, was a household name between 1905 and 1910[32]. Dolly, a London waitress, flew regularly from Alexandra Palace and various fairgrounds. She used no balloon basket at all, but hung, fully exposed, from her trapeze, dressed in a blue-trousered flying suit with a jaunty cap and tight lace-up boots to show off her legs. Her only instrumentation was a tiny altimeter, which she wore as a bangle on her left wrist. She would ascend several thousand feet, hanging beneath the

---

32 *Dolly Shepherd was a very handsome girl. Unsurprisingly, she had many male admirers and received several offers of marriage, one of which she accepted. She lived until 1983 and died peacefully at the age of ninety-six. (Richard Holmes, Falling Upwards, William Collins 2013, ISBN No. 978-0-00-738692-5).*

trapeze and then pull a simple release cord and drop back to earth by parachute. She survived at least one substantial fall that left her temporarily paralysed, but continued to thrill crowds all over England.

Before this, the only ballooning of which the public was aware, was the fairground exploits of professional showmen such as the Spencer brothers, Percival and Stanley. They took up passengers at £5 a time, a very substantial sum, but the sort of thing that one would do, even then, on special occasions.

Rolls first flew in 1898. The transfer of his interests from motoring to flying was gradual and he pursued both hobbies simultaneously for many years. His interest was significant for the future of the sport. With his friend Vera Hedges Butler and her father, Frank, and others, it was Rolls who helped to turn ballooning into a fashionable activity and sustain it as an up-market diversion. His charisma helped turn it from circus act to social spectacle and whirl, and the fad among the fashionable lasted for a decade, only passing when powered flight became a reality.

Ballooning was unusual as a sport because women could enjoy and compete in it on equal footing with the men. This arose from the manner in which the 'Aero Club' was formed, in 1901 – up in a balloon. Miss Vera Butler explained how the Aero Club was formed: 'We undertook the venture in the balloon *City of York* (forty-two thousand cubic feet). Rolls came as third passenger, and the balloon was under the control of Stanley Spencer. We remained over London for two hours and we decided to form an Aero Club and the founder members were father (Frank Hedges Butler), Rolls and myself'.

She wrote later, in the *Automobile Club Journal*: 'This Club owes its origin to the private balloon ascent from the Crystal Palace of three well-known pioneer motorists, who thought that to try a voyage through the air rather than on *terra firma* would be a novel and probably delightful sensation, and so, on one beautiful morning, we sailed away to the upper regions'.

She was still enamoured of ballooning some five years later when she told *Motor Car World*: 'Ballooning ranks as one of the most delightful and exhilarating pastimes of the twentieth century, in which women, without loss of dignity or 'mannishness', can share. It has always amused me that whenever I confess to an unalloyed delight in the pastime, people should still regard me as avowing myself endowed with a spirit of foolhardiness and unconventional love of adventure above the average for my sex'.

Women's involvement in ballooning was very much due to Vera. They might only be allowed in the Automobile Club between 3.00 p.m. and 6.00 p.m. and could go nowhere near the Jockey Club or join one of the many golf clubs then springing up, but, inspired by Vera and, later, by May Harbord – both companions of Rolls, ballooning was open to all women if they had the means.

Women were acceptable, however the lower orders were visible by their absence. Ballooning, like polo, was an aristocratic preserve. The names of the balloons reflect something of the Edwardian aristocratic scene in those blissful pre-war years: *Vivienne, Kismet, Nebula, Thistledown, Enchantress* and *L'Esperence*. Frank Hedges Butler's balloon was called *Dolce Far Niente* (he had a houseboat of the same name) – 'Sweet Idleness'. Early flights were made from Crystal Palace, Stamford Bridge, the Ranelagh Club, Regents Park, Aldershot, Wandsworth Gas Works and later at Hurlingham where, incidentally, the first rules of polo were drawn up in the 1870s. Laurence Meynell[33] described ballooning as 'yachting of the skies' and, although enthusiasts did not need as much money as for a yacht, the sport was not cheap – even when using a shared Club balloon. A four-person car cost around £160 – perhaps eighty times as much today – and the balloon envelope cost around £90. Gas for a day's flight was £4 10s, then there was £3 for inflation. One wonders if that was why the ever-parsimonious Rolls commissioned two of the smallest balloons ever made, the *Imp* at seventeen thousand five hundred cubic feet and the even smaller *Midget*.

Rolls's ballooning log records a hundred and seventy-three flights between 1898 and 1910[34], including thirty-five flights in 1906 and fifty-two flights in 1907, an average of one a week in the latter year. He shared costs with his fellow fliers but, even so, an average balloon flight cost about £8 (£700 today), once the cost of the gas, filling the balloon, transporting it to point of landing back to

33 *Laurence Meynell – 'Rolls, Man of Speed'.*

34 *Rolls's balloon log contains one item, which was not a balloon flight at all, but his four minute maiden flight with Wilbur Wright on 8th October, 1908. He, Major Baden-Powell, Griffith Brewer and Frank Hedges Butler, were all flown separately on that day, and their impressions are contained in Appendix 2.*

the station, repairs and miscellaneous tips were taken into account. Fifty-two balloon flights in one year would have cost £35,000 in today's terms. His interest in ballooning was never entirely frivolous however. From his point of view, balloon flights drew well-to-do sightseers and, since both pilots and passengers were well-off, there was always the possibility that they might be persuaded to buy an up-market car – or a Rolls-Royce in the later years. An average balloon flight was two to three hours, long enough for Rolls's smooth and entirely enjoyable sales patter, linked as it was with social gossip of the day to make it's mark.

The sport grew rapidly as the *Evening News* reported on its tenth anniversary: 'From the original membership, the Royal Aero Club has now grown until it has one thousand five hundred members. More than that, it is the acknowledged authority, not only in connection with ballooning, but with aviation, and can boast being the Jockey Club of the Air. Its tenth anniversary sees not only dirigibles, but the aeroplane in active use for scouting purposes at army manoeuvres, and the future presents possibilities which all, save a very few, would have scoffed at, when the Club was founded. Probably there is no body in the world that has seen so great an advance in the sport, which it was founded to promote'.

Ballooning had a charm and a technique all its own. A typical basket was four feet square with room for three passengers. Rolls's fellow Cambridge student and balloonist, John Moore-Brabazon (later Lord Brabazon of Tara) described a typical launch: 'You got into the balloon and took many bags of ballast – fine sand – with you. You then asked everybody to take the hands off the car so to speak, weighed yourself slowly and took bag after bag out of the balloon until you were just able to rise. When that point was reached and everybody had let go, you went slowly, majestically up in the air. It was a most curious experience; there was no noise, no draughts, no movement of any sort. Naturally you had to follow with a map where you were going, with whatever wind there was, and you never went up in a strong wind, about 30mph was quite enough.

But once up in the air you felt nothing of the wind, you could hear sounds, the barking of dogs and trains close by – these came up quite clearly, but apart from these, you were alone in the sky, a wonderful sensation'. Then, wistfully, Brabazon added: 'The only handicap of course, you could not smoke because the gas was just above you (forty thousand cubic feet of coal gas), and it would have made it dangerous.

The drill, when you came down, was to throw out a grapnel, which was meant to anchor itself in a field or hedge and pull you up while you valved, i.e. let the gas out of the balloon'.

A ripping valve was invented later, which was a split in the balloon covered by a panel of fabric, which could be pulled away to let out a lot of gas quickly. When you had a ripping valve, you might have thrown a bag of ballast to slow down the descent. When you hit the ground, the balloon, which was in a big net, expanded, but the gap made by the ripping valve meant all the gas escaped very quickly, perhaps in twenty seconds – so there was never any chance of being dragged.'

There was a fee for sewing up a balloon if the ripping valve was used, so predictably Rolls very rarely used the valve, and diarised his criticism of other balloonists. Brabazon continued:

'Once down on the ground you looked for a local farmer or landowner or carter to take your balloon to the nearest station and he was tipped five shillings. With good luck and planning, you could be home for dinner'.

Misunderstandings between wealthy balloonists and the locals were not unusual. On one occasion a balloon crew interrogated, for some minutes, a scarecrow without significant success.

On another occasion, Frank Hedges Butler got lost in the dark while navigating a balloon from London to Brighton. 'At about 2.00 a.m., just as the first larks started singing to us, we dropped, thoroughly mystified as to our whereabouts, into a rookery close to a house. The rooks, startled out of their sleep by the sudden advent of our great car amongst their nests, made an extraordinary clamour. We halloed very quickly, but with our noise and increasing cawing of the rooks, a gentleman put his head out of the bedroom window. Judge his surprise to see us sitting in the top of his tree, with the great balloon towering above'. A conversation of this sort ensued. 'Good gracious, who are you?' 'Balloonists, resting'. Where are we?' 'Twelve miles from Brighton, going south. Are you stuck?' 'Oh no, we are very happy. You don't mind us sitting here in the top of your tree do you?''No, not at all. Goodnight'. And then the window banged, and I think he was soon snoring, but the rooks didn't settle down so quickly'.

Brabazon again: 'To go up in a balloon is the only way to go into the air like a gentleman. The peace and quiet of it all must be experienced to be appreciated, but I doubt whether it is as much now (writing in 1956) as it was then because of all these high tension inter-connecting cables running across England. It will be a ghastly thing to run into one and I should be terrified of them… sometimes you caught a balance on the trailing rope, the rope might wrap itself round a telegraph wire, hold you for a moment and then quietly unwrap itself. I don't say that I have never broken a glass of a greenhouse, but I never did more damage than that'.

The women balloonists were also, no doubt, part of the attraction. In 1906, Rolls flew several times with the Argentinian-born, Miss Hilda Krabbe, who later married Brabazon. That same year, he found a long-term ballooning partner in the elegant form of the Honourable Mrs. May Assheton Harbord, widow of the Australian businessman, Arthur Blackwood, and second wife of Captain Edward Assheton Harbord, son of the fifth Baron Suffield. Rolls and May first flew together on the maiden flight of Butler's Gordon Bennett balloon race entry, *City of London*. In total they flew together sixty-six times. She became a Rolls-Royce devotee and, over the years, bought three cars: two Twenties and a Thirty. Rolls and Brabazon encouraged a firm called 'Short Brothers', which, as the fashion grew, developed production facilities for balloons and then moved to the production of military-use balloons and early aircraft as the decade ended and continental tensions began to increase. For last minute excursions, Short brothers could get a balloon ready in an hour, if a Club member wanted one.

On good days ballooning was enchanting. Rolls again: 'With Mrs. Harbord in *Midget*, passed over a good part of London at four hundred feet, keeping perfect equilibrium just above the houses'. He recorded flying over St. Paul's, the twin towers of Crystal Palace, Brooklands and the round tower of Windsor Castle at various times.

There were balloon distance-races, with as many as fourteen balloons taking part in the British events, the limiting factor being the time it took to fill the balloons. Rolls invented Hare 'n' Hounds racing. Previously, motor cars had chased a balloon – first one to find the winner – but in Hare 'n' Hounds a number of balloons would follow Rolls's tiny *Imp* and try and land near it. The nearest was declared the winner.

Rolls had adapted a 70hp Rolls-Royce, with a suitable basket for a carefully folded balloon envelope. He could thus retrieve his balloon at the end of the day avoiding carters' costs, tips and other expenses.

Rolls's records of those carefree days have survived: It is July 17th, 1909 at Hurlingham, and the main event is the Rolls Trophy. The sun is shining, the race is due to start at 3.30 p.m.

The runners and riders are:-

1	Owner	Mrs. John Dunville	Balloon – *La Mascotte*
2	Owner	R. H. Barrington Kennett	Balloon – *The Comet*
3	Owner	Ernest L. Bucknall	Balloon – *Enchantress*
4	Owner	The Hon. Mrs. Assheton Harbord	Balloon – *Valkyrie*
5	Owner	Baroness Von Heeckeren	Balloon – *L'Esperence*
6	Owner	A. M. Singer	Balloon – *Satellite*
7	Owner	C. A. Moreing	Balloon – *Thistledown*

The Hare balloon, *Imp*, and balloon numbers 2, 3 and 6, are piloted by their owners. John Dunville is driving the family car No. 1, May Harbord has trusted her steed to Mr. Pollock and Baroness Von Heeckeren, hers to old hand, Griffith Brewer; Mr. Moreing his No. 7 steed to Major Baden-Powell – who is naturally well prepared. The balloons are in the paddock – one might almost paint numbers or smiley faces on their roundnesses. The band of the Royal Horse Guards (the Blues) is in full swing, with music by Schumann and from the Mikado and other hits of the day, soon to be followed by the Hurlingham Club Orchestra, with a programme of Dvorak, Saint-Saens and Brahms.

Sharp at three-thirty they're off. Parasols go up to protect the ladies on the lawn, from clouds of ballast sand. Mrs. Harbord looks elegant 'in a large brimmed, flat crowned, brown hat, trimmed with hydrangeas and green tulle, a dainty white muslin blouse and a cream sage skirt'.

Dunville is first away (wasn't he unlucky in last year's Gordon Bennett race?)[35], and Rolls's *Imp* disappears out of sight, carrying black and white streamers for ease of identification. Rolls cannot make interim stops, but the chasers can, if they overshoot. The previous year, the press, covering the event, had been carried in AX201, the original Silver Ghost, supplied by Claude Johnson, and the Ghost followed the race to its conclusion near Arundel, but where will the Imp finish today?

Not so far, Rolls flies *Imp* for the two hours specified and starts to descend at six o'clock, landing twelve minutes later at the Carpenters Arms at Wickford in Essex, which still exists today. He lands without difficulty. Will it be Dunville in La Mascotte or Pollock in Valkyrie, old hands from the 1908 Gordon Bennett race, who will find him first? Who knows?

Pollock lands seventy yards from Rolls. May Harbord, his balloon's owner, would like to have landed closer and have they beaten the Baroness and Griffith Brewer? Surely seventy yards should be good enough, but no, *Satellite*, a balloon with no tracking device other than Mortimer Singer, the sewing machine magnate, aboard, comes through just before the post to land a mere seventeen yards from the *Imp* – a worthy winner. And so to dinner or tea or something stronger as the case may be.

Rolls was one of three British contestants in the September 1906 Gordon Bennett balloon race, launched from the Tuileries Gardens in Paris and which took place the weekend after his Isle of Man TT victory. Each national team could enter three balloons and Rolls competed in *Britannia* with Colonel Capper. Frank Hedges Butler flew another Short Brothers balloon and Professor Huntingdon was the third team member in *Zephyr*. No one knew which way the wind would blow and so the contestants had visas and passports for various countries,

---

35 *In 1908, the British entry, Banshee, was robbed, in many balloonists' view, of the Gordon Bennett Trophy. The balloon was flown by Messrs. Pollock and Dunville, and it was thought that the winning Swiss balloon should have been disqualified. This came down in the sea off the coast of Norway and was rescued by a steamer. It was argued, however, that the rule, as to the necessity for coming down on dry land, was passed after the entries had been sent in. On this slender pretext, which did not exactly appeal to the British mind, the prize was presented to the Swiss.*

including France, Germany, Austria and Russia, also a questionnaire in several languages so that they could ask where they were and where was the nearest railway station! As it happened, the wind blew them across England. An American, Lieutenant Frank Lahm of the United States Army, had the good fortune to be blown over land throughout and finished furthest away at Fylingdales in Yorkshire.

Of the British team, Hedges Butler failed to reach England, Professor Huntingdon landed in Kent and Rolls was blown slightly to the right of Lahm and, rather than come down in the North Sea, which was dangerous, brought his balloon down in Norfolk between Sandringham and the sea. He was lampooned in the press for seeking to maximise publicity for Rolls-Royce by not reporting in for over twenty-four hours – which was by no means beyond him. He claimed that the reason he took so long to report in was that there was no telegraph office in the vicinity of where he landed.

Balloon accidents were uncommon. During the Rolls era, few, if any, socialite balloonists had major accidents. Rolls, Hedges Butler, Brabazon, Griffith Brewer and Mrs. Harbord made hundreds of flights between them without serious consequences, but there were moments. Rolls once flew as high as eleven thousand two hundred feet in a race across France from Brussels, travelling for twelve hours at 12mph and another twelve hours at 30mph before coming down in the Landes region of France. On another occasion, he recorded descending from six thousand feet at the rate of seven hundred and fifty feet a minute and on another occasion – the Butler Trophy Race – he recorded in his log book:

'Descent, violent storm, rain, squall and thunder – Wimbledon Common – endeavoured to effect temporary landing to get away from the thunderstorms, but caught by violent squall, and after passing through some trees had to rip. Race won by Colonel Capper'.

Griffith Brewer described a serious near miss in thundery conditions. He had decided not to start, deeming the conditions too dangerous, and when asked by May Harbord for his balloon, because Rolls had torn hers, had said no:

'Rolls went up with very little lift and, as the balloons entered the wind, the bottom of his car brushed against the top of May Harbord's balloon, *Nebula*… this cut the top of the net and fabric so that the gas poured out, while Rolls's car (basket) pulled free and saved those in the car from asphyxiation. These things happen so quickly that they (the occupants of Rolls's balloon basket) probably did not appreciate the risks they had run'.

Brewer, almost a professional amongst amateurs, recognised the danger of going up in a thunderstorm. He forestalled any further entreaties by May Harbord by pulling the rip cord and letting out all the gas. Hedges Butler, another competitor in the race, described their fear of the lightning and how they covered up their picnic knives (an essential piece of kit in a Hedges Butler balloon) as a precaution. Brewer's fear of thunderstorms was vindicated a few years later when several balloons were hit by lightning in a Gordon Bennett race in America, some of their occupants suffering death and injury.

Rolls knew that the sport had little scientific or technical purpose in itself beyond his immediate business interests. Although the dangers were relatively slight, his flight logbook contained barometric drawings and his very substantial number of flights gave him insight into the vagaries of air pockets and other traps, which would endanger early aviators.

Rolls and Frank Hedges Butler had their differences over who founded the Aero Club and, almost certainly, over Frank's daughter, Vera, but they remained on good terms. They shared their one hundredth flight in 1908 (they had engineered it so they would reach their centuries together) not in a balloon but in a dirigible airship, *Ville De Paris,* a vehicle whose flight destination could be planned and controlled, with consequential military and commercial passenger-carrying possibilities. May Harbord and Lieutenant Frank Lahm (Gordon Bennett winner, 1906) were also on the flight. Rolls took his place behind the navigating bridge and watched the trimming of the ship, how ballast was discharged both at the bow and the stern, to balance the vehicle before it lifted. He described how…'forty men were needed to get the two hundred foot airship ready for flight, as it emerged ominously from the hangar', and how … 'the captain shouted, 'slow ahead', communicating by telegraph with the engine room… this was something worth living for. The conquest of the air… she moved as gracefully and as easily as a bird. Upwards and downwards to right and to left, however the navigator chose to guide her. She swooped and curved with incredible swiftness and accuracy'.

Ville de Paris headed for the French capital at 40mph. Later, to the Imperial Defence Committee, Rolls described the military implications when the airship passed over a fort. He mused on what mayhem that could be caused by a bomb. He described the difference in sensation: 'The dirigible is driven through the air – the balloon glides peacefully, and seems still'. The leviathan was a little more difficult to land than a balloon, but this was achieved with the aid of a gigantic trailing rope grasped by many helpers on the ground. Rolls ended his description on a note of rhapsody: 'The next morning the whole experience seemed like a dream, and it is hard to believe that we had not merely been reading a story by Jules Verne or H. G. Wells'.

Later Rolls gave detailed briefings as an expert witness to the Imperial Defence Committee on military aeronautical policy. He said quite clearly that bombs could be dropped from dirigibles and could cause mayhem.

Rolls had seen the future and was captivated but he was, however, quick to see the many ways that such a vehicle could find itself in difficulty in contrast to an ordinary balloon, and he was vindicated almost immediately when, within a week, another French balloon, *Patrie*, broke free from its moorings and drifted over Wales and Northern Island, crewless, before disappearing forever into the Atlantic, at a cost of £12,000 (£1 million today).

The private owner of *Ville de Paris* gave her to the French military days after this, so Rolls, Hedges Butler and the others were fortunate to have flown when they did.

Chapter Eleven

Fast and Flying Ladies

Charles Stewart Rolls was tall, handsome and one of the most eligible men in England. He was a national celebrity by 1900 through his continental racing, his letters to the press and his winning the Gold Medal in the Thousand Mile Trial. At twenty-two he was the best-known motorist in the country. He had a generous allowance, with the prospect of a future fortune by inheritance from Lord Llangattock, he had access to a London home at South Lodge, and his membership of the Automobile Club of Great Britain and Ireland gave him access to rich and powerful men and to the rising stars of the Edwardian motoring age.

Despite these manifold advantages, he remained aloof and was somewhat shy, and he was very focussed on what he wanted to achieve. In addition, he was perhaps too clever and insufficiently interested in the aristocratic gossip of the period to flutter many ladies' hearts. He had been used to a male environment until university, (apart from his sister), and it would not have been surprising if he had struggled to form relationships with members of the fair sex. Indeed, why hurry? It was normal for men to marry much later in life than nowadays. He had time to achieve and then to settle down later.

He was a gentleman and very discreet. It was undoubtedly a man's world in Edwardian times. It seems remarkable that at that time women could not vote. The Suffragette movement only began in 1872 – five years before Rolls's birth and, by coincidence, the year of birth of Emily Davidson, who perished under the hooves of King George V's horse, Anmer, to draw attention to the cause of women's suffrage during the 1913 Epsom Derby.

The world of the Automobile Club of Great Britain and Ireland and of motoring was also a man's world – but not exclusively. Women were involved from the start. Bertha Benz, the wife of Karl, who built the world's first practicable automobile powered by an internal combustion engine, invested in her fiancé's business before their marriage. She became frustrated by his inability to market his new invention – so, on 5th August 1886, she borrowed the car. With her teenage sons, Richard and Eugène, as passengers, she drove Karl's precious, newly-constructed

Patent Motorwagen from Mannheim to Pforzheim (in the Black Forest), a one-way trip of sixty-six miles. It took from dawn to dusk. She stopped at a city pharmacy in Wiesloch to purchase fuel, and, somewhere en route, inveigled a blacksmith to mend a chain. She fixed the brakes and used a long, straight hairpin to clean a fuel pipe[36] and she insulated a wire with one of her garters. On arrival at Pforzheim, she telegraphed her husband and calmly drove back the next day, achieving nationwide publicity, as she had intended[37].

Britain has its own doughty female motorists. In 1899, Baroness Campbell de Laurentz became the first woman to own and drive her own car and, four years later, became President of the Ladies Automobile Club of Great Britain to which Rolls gave a talk on more than one occasion.

The Thousand Mile Trial of April 1900 brought Rolls into contact with three lady motorists. Two were spoken for, but the third caught his eye.

Mrs. Louise Bazalgette was a friend of Henry Hewetson, a tea importer turned car dealer, who imported Benz cars into Britain. She had possibly driven with Hewetson in the 1896 Emancipation Run – they were certainly photographed together – and she had been involved in automobilism from the earliest of days. In that same year, the *Daily Mail* had reported: 'Lady automobilists are increasing rapidly. The longest run so far, made by an English lady, has been achieved by Mrs. Bazalgette, who drove the other day from her London home in Portland Square to Southampton'. Her private Trial entry in 1900 – A25 – was a 3hp Benz Ideal and cost £175. She drove untroubled for most of the Trial and won a silver medal and a bracelet (A.C.G.B.I. Thousand Mile Trial Report).

Another female entrant was Mary Kennard, the Victorian novelist and automobilism enthusiast. She listed her favourite pastimes as 'driving a 40hp Napier, a De Dion voiturettte and a 15hp Darracq or a motorcycle'. A very sporty lady, she wrote popular novels for the young, with hunting and other gung-ho titles such as 'Killed in the Open', 'Glorious Gallop' and 'Hunting Girl', acquiring the nickname 'Diana of Fiction' after the Roman goddess of hunting. She wrote in

---

36 *Thus coining the phrase 'Hairpin Benz'.*

37 *This redoubtable lady lived until aged ninety-five, dying in 1944, and her triumphant trundle can be followed today as the Bertha Benz Memorial Route celebrates her historic day out.*

1896 'A Guide to Lady Cyclists' and was at home mending punctures – a frequent occurrence for early automobilists.,and appropriately wrote one novel entitled 'The Motoring Maniac.'

She lived in Northamptonshire with her magistrate husband, and having sportingly lent their newly-acquired Napier car to Selwyn Edge for the Trial, she followed in her De Dion as a spectator. It overturned in Lincoln, although she was unhurt. Mrs. Kennard was an early contributor to *Car Illustrated*. She said there were two sorts of drivers.

'Writing from personal experience, I have been out with gentlemen, who performed the most surprising tours de force and yet not enjoyed a tranquil minute; hairbreadth escapes, foolhardy tricks and not a wont of judgement not only kept the occupants in a state of perpetual apprehension, but effectively destroyed pleasure. With others, it is just the reverse and you never had a bad moment. They give rise to a sense of absolute trust'.

She was a friend of Rolls. Her description of an outing with him gives a precious glimpse of how he then appeared to those around him: 'Heaved a heavy sigh of regret and packed my bag and decided to wait and see what the morrow would bring forth. For once the fates were kind. About one o'clock, Mr. Rolls most kindly called round and asked if I would go with him on his flying 12hp Panhard of Thousand Mile fame. I jumped at the offer. At ten minutes to two Mr. Rolls left London, steering the car splendidly through the greasy streets, and with a master in the art of motoring at the helm, even the fear of sideslip soon vanished. Such a consummate driver inspires his passenger with absolute confidence, even when travelling at a rate of something over 40mph!

The car herself was a revelation, so smooth, so steady, so speedy and vibrationless. She romped up the steepest hills in a fashion, which made one positively scornful of gradients, apart to inspire apprehension on an ordinary vehicle, but alas the puncture theme pursued us. Twice we were brought to a standstill owing to cruel nails over an inch in length, and a terrible jolt necessitated a repair to the brake rod. Off with his mackintosh, on with his boiler suit and in a second Mr. Rolls was lying flat on his back under the car, his head reposing gracefully in the mud.

At this juncture, a dear, old, white-haired dame came tottering by. For a few seconds she eyed the prostrate motorist with undisguised concern, then unable to restrain her sympathy, she turned to me: 'Dear, oh dear', she said. 'Is that poor thing lying crushed there beneath the wheels?' I tried to calm her by the assurance that the poor thing was not quite in the plight she imagined and murmured something about brake repairs, but she was not content and shaking her hoary head she asked with kind solicitude 'if a cup of tea would be of any service?' It was difficult to see any connection between the tea and the brake, but we were much touched by her offer. The rural population seemed everywhere kindly disposed towards motoring. Steady rain and furious winds accompanied us both to and from Peterborough'.

The third lady trialist, who drew the attention of the young, elegant Rolls, was Frank Hedges Butler's daughter, Vera. Rolls and Butler were good friends and committee members at the A.C.G.B.I., and Vera attended social functions and used the Club at the times when the ladies were permitted to do so. Her father was Treasurer.

Vera had inherited her father's adventurous spirit and she was no fool. She passed examinations at Cambridge in 1895 and during a school vacation at age fifteen, she made the ascent of Mont Blanc (15,781 feet) with her father and guides, sleeping two nights at ten thousand feet above sea level. She was also a good swimmer too and once saved a school friend from drowning. Having studied three years in Paris, she saw the Paris-Marseilles 1896 automobile race with her father, as it passed through Beaune, and she drove with him throughout the Thousand Mile Trial. She obtained the first lady's certificate to drive a car in France, drove from Paris to London and back, and, on the return journey, became the first lady to be fined for driving above the speed limit.

Rolls and Vera were in danger of becoming an item. In September 1901 a planned motoring holiday in Scotland for them and Frank was postponed after Vera's Renault caught fire. Vera organised a balloon flight – her first, Rolls's second – as compensation. The trio took to the air and over champagne and the city of London, resolved to start an aero club, inspired by the recent success of French-based Brazilian balloonist, Santos-Dumont, in flying round the Eiffel Tower.

The young couple's love of adventure perhaps encouraged Frank Hedges Butler to hope for something more permanent. Rolls and Vera were certainly together alone some time later when they were involved in a highly-publicised road traffic accident, although this may have marked a turning point in their relationship.

They were returning from Barnet Fair when it appears that Rolls was run down by one Mr. Ahern, who might just have tried it on for compensation, given Rolls's celebrity status. There are two sides to every story, but the *Holloway Press* took delight in mocking the aristocratic C. S. Rolls.

'Touching the Fair, it seems almost poetic justice that the Honourable C. S. Rolls, who is one of the leading lights in the cult of the automobile, should have come to grief in spite of all his efforts to avert a collision by turning his motor car into a hedge to avoid a horse and trap. Mr. Rolls was not hurt, beyond a slight shaking. The horse seems to have come off worse with a cut on the leg from its arch-enemy, the motor car. Did the horse object to the motor visiting the old horse fair and decide on a collision as an appropriate and forcible hint to such things to keep away in future?'

Mr. Ahern's story was somewhat more detailed. He said in an interview with our representative: 'I knew nothing about the collision for about twenty-five minutes and then I thought I was in hospital. My son was unconscious for some hours.

As to the stolen property, a mob collected round the vehicle and after they finished helping us, there was not much left but the wreck of the car, the injured horse and my trap and myself. The whip, the rugs, £11 in money all belonging to me had been taken off and even the lamps of the trap were missing'.

The Barnet horse fair, which harked back to Elizabethan times, was traditionally fairly riotous. Mr. Ahern may have been the worse for wear and was letting his horse take him home. Rolls drank very seldom and then sparingly, and an extract of the *Automobile Journal*, 11th September, 1902, may represent a more credible version of events:

'Reading the contents of some of the evening journals on Saturday last, one would have imagined that a well-known member of the Club, the Hon. C. S. Rolls, had met with a most terrible accident and what is now so outrageous, is that all the garbled versions seemed to put all the fault at the door of the motorist and motor.

The poor horse and its driver posed as badly injured innocents, run into unawares'.

There is another side to the tale. Greatly to the surprise of Mr. Rolls's many friends, he put in an appearance at the Crystal Palace during the evening. From what we can gather of the actual facts, the vehicle in question was drawn by a fast trotting horse, not only without lights, but also using the wrong side of the road. What a terrible outcry there would have been against a motor car driver, who would have dared to commit such a multiplicity of sins against the rules of the road'.

Whether Rolls was in the right or otherwise, we are left to wonder whether he was solicitous enough of Vera because, about two months later, they ballooned together for the last time (excluding one trip, with Frank Hedges Butler in Paris in December 1903). Sadly, their relationship, if it was such, cooled and ended. Rolls's papers contain a cutting of the announcement of her wedding to a Captain Nichol in 1904.

It was several years before Rolls, apparently, entered any other significant relationship but various other remarkable women crossed his path in the meantime. He competed twice against the most extraordinary sportswoman of his time, the Frenchwoman, Camille du Gast.

Marie Marthe Camille Desinge du Gast, also known as Camille Crespin du Gast, married Jules Crespin at twenty-two and was a rich widow seven years later in 1897. Her father-in-law, Jacques Crespin had founded a department store in Paris in 1856. The subsequent owner, Georges Dufayel had taken it over later and popularised the sale of furniture by instalment and catalogue. At one time there were three million customers buying from Dufayel, and after her husband's death, Camille found herself a major shareholder and a very wealthy widow.

Marie Marthe was a balloonist, fencer, tobogganist, skier, rifle and pistol shot, horsewoman, concert pianist and singer. In 1902 she became nationally notorious after it was alleged, during a family court battle, that she posed naked for a master picture, 'La Femme du Masque'. In 1905, together with balloonatic and fellow countryman, Louis Capazza, she jumped out of a balloon at two thousand feet, and landed safely to the relief of her daughter – who thus had time to arrange for her mother to be assassinated in 1910 so she could inherit.

The attempt failed. This confirmed her wisdom in using her maiden name in sporting contests rather than her married name, Crespin, or her connection with the department store 'Dufayel'. She finished thirty-third in the Paris/Berlin race in 1901, the only lady finisher, after twenty-five hours driving but, as a woman, was refused entry for the 1902 New York/ San Francisco race.

Undeterred, and accompanied by her patrician mechanic and admirer, Prince du Sagan, she drove her white, Number 29, De Dietrich in the 'Race to Death', Paris/Madrid, 1903. She was not part of the official De Dietrich team of Barrow, Jarrott and Stead, but was driving a lighter De Dietrich car, which she had purchased herself to give herself a chance of a highly-placed finish. The cars started at one minute intervals. Jarrott was first to start and third to arrive at Tours on the first leg after Louis Renault (Number 3) and Werner (Number 14) driving a 90hp Mercedes. Werner was to crash and luckily escape major injury a few miles later.

Then Jarrott's team mate, Yorkshireman Stead arrived complaining bitterly about the crowds of unruly spectators, who were increasing the danger to themselves and the drivers.

After Libourn, Stead duelled for several miles, side by side with another competitor, Salleron, driving a Mors, and eventually they collided. Stead's car overturned, trapping him in the driver's seat but Camille, in car No.29, arrived moments later. She stopped, without hesitation, to assist. With some spectators and her mechanic they lifted Stead's car off him; then she personally bandaged Stead, made him as comfortable as possible and removed his dead mechanic and debris from the road before continuing. She continued as fast as ever to Bordeaux but dropped from eighth to seventy-seventh place overall. Charles Jarrott paid public tribute to her later for her prompt and spirited action, which undoubtedly, he said, saved Stead's life,although costing her a much higher place in the race.

Following the race, the German Benz team offered her a works drive in the 1903 Gordon Bennett race to be held in Ireland, but the sports ruling body, the Automobile Club de France had by then banned women drivers and she gave up the sport. She had, in any event, by this time and by dint of her own personality and wealth, become the only woman official of the Automobile Club de France.

Camille took up power boat racing and raced unsuccessfully against Selwyn Edge in Monaco. She then won an epic race from Algiers to Toulon via Minorca in her own boat, *Camille*. All six other boats in the race sank, hers sank too, although it was the last to do so. She was pulled from the sea, victorious but unconscious, having as captain been the last to go down with her ship. The *New York Times* reported: 'Madame du Gast… has sent 10,000 francs to the sailor, who jumped into the sea from the cruiser, Kleber (an escort vessel) and rescued her during the storm that scattered all the racing boats'. She was declared the winner because she had taken her boat closest to the Toulon finish.

In later life, this extraordinary woman explored Morocco on horseback and was later commissioned by the French government to carry out research work there. She published travel narratives and served as President to the French equivalent of the R.S.P.C.A. and as President of the League of Women's Rights. She established centres for orphans and disadvantaged children and impoverished women and, during her spare time, she bred and exhibited Orloff horses. She is described as: 'An elegant, handsome woman[38], with an imposing and nonchalant beauty. Her wealth, her magnetism, her independence and her gallantry were often the talk of the town, and her totally unprejudiced attitude was often to attract the jealousy of the (all male) motor sports authorities'. She died in occupied Paris in 1942 aged seventy-four.

Male hostility to women drivers has long festered – ever since a Parisian journalist reported on the occasion of the very first successful driving test, passed by a Parisian noblewoman, the Duchess d'Uzes in April 1898: 'It would be wise not to entertain any ideas of taking the family out for a drive'. The Duchess d'Uzes was also the first woman to be booked for speeding – by a man presumably.

No one suffered more from this chauvinism and male superiority than Dorothy Levitt, England's first female motoring superstar, who achieved fame the hard way. She was dependent on Rolls's great rival, the Australian Selwyn Edge who was her Svengali – she worked for him, she drove his cars and his boats, did his bidding and was almost certainly his mistress for several years. Yet

38 *'Fast Ladies – Female Racing Drivers' – Jean Francois Bousanquet (Veloce Books 2007).*

he forbade her to compete in the 1905 TT race, although Mors had offered her a car, because he did not want her to succeed to the detriment of the cars that he sold and hoped to publicise at the race.

Edge vouchsafed for Dorothy's driving ability, but the Brooklands Automobile Racing Club[39] would not allow her to drive at Brooklands, even though a ladies' race had been held there in 1908, shortly after the track opened. She in her turn acknowledged Mrs. Edge as a fine driver in her only book *The Woman and the Car*, although Edge never mentions her in his own memoir *My Motoring Reminiscences,* written many years later – even though at one time she was as well-known as him for her motoring successes in hill climbs and trials.

She joined the Napier company as a temp and appears to have been picked out for her physical beauty: 'Selwyn Edge, director of Napier... spotted Miss Levitt amongst his staff, a beautiful secretary with long legs and eyes like pools'. In a bid to promote his cars – Edge decided she should take part in a race, though first he had to teach her to drive. She surpassed his expectations by winning her class in the 1903 Southport Speed Trial, and proved such a good driver, she was taken on by De Dion for a major publicity stunt.' In fact, it was one of Edge's salesman who taught Dorothy to drive, ungallantly complaining that it was his day off and that Dorothy 'smelt of scent and wore large bracelets, silk stockings and innumerable petticoats'.

She competed everywhere. In 1903 she drove a Gladiator from Glasgow to London. She took part in the Southport Speed Trial. She won a powerboat race in Cowes, and was prosecuted for speeding in Hyde Park[40]. When stopped, she allegedly said: 'She would like to drive over every policeman and wished she had run over the sergeant and killed him'. She was fined double that of any other defendant the day the case came to Court.

She helped Edge to steer his speedboat to win the first British International Harmsworth Trophy in Cork in 1903, and she drove a Napier speedboat to

---

39 *Brooklands Automobile Racing Club – Formed in 1906, licensed by the Automobile Club, its first committee included Montagu, Northcliffe and Julian Orde (A.C.G.B.I. Secretary) from 'The Birth of Brooklands' – Roger Bird.*

40 *The Penny Illustrated Paper and Illustrated Times, 17th November, 1906.*

victory at Cowes, where she was congratulated in person by Edward VII. Later that year, she won two more major victories at Trouville in France against all male competition. She was permitted to race men on water but never on land.

In 1904 Dorothy successfully completed a Thousand Mile Trial in Hereford, winning a silver medal. The other competitors, all of them male, disliked her Pomeranian dog, Dodo, and they all sported doggy mascots on one day of the trial. Dorothy allegedly purchased dog biscuits the following day. She then embarked the longest drive by a woman at that time. She drove a De Dion Bouton from London to Liverpool and back in two days, the outward leg from Great Marlborough Street in the capital to the Adelphi Hotel in Liverpool, a distance of two hundred and five miles, taking eleven hours.

1905 saw her drive a powerful 80hp Napier at the Blackpool Speed Trials, thus proving that a dainty but determined female could drive big cars, and she drove an even bigger Mors, 100hp, at the 1906 Blackpool Speed Trials. 'The Fair Entrant' achieved 91 mph and earned the soubriquet 'The Fastest Girl on Earth'. In fact the Fair Entrant was a tremendous asset to the Napier marque and earned publicity that even Claude Johnson could not match for Rolls-Royce. Johnson could hardly compete with lines such as this on 'the little drawer' (the glove compartment) from *The Woman and the Car*: 'the secret of the dainty motoriste… the following articles are what I advise you to have. A pair of clean gloves, an extra handkerchief, a clean veil, a powder puff (unless you despise them), hairpins… a hand mirror and some chocolates are very soothing sometimes'.

Dorothy is credited with inventing the driving mirror, which was not fitted as standard to cars for another decade. 'You'll find it useful to have it handy, not for strictly personal use, but occasionally to hold up to see what is behind you… without losing your forward way and without releasing your grip on the steering wheel'.

One of her final triumphs was to win a gold medal in the Herkomer[41] Trophy Race in 1905 in Frankfurt. She ran first of all the ladies in all the competitions and fourth overall in the trial out of a hundred and seventy-two competitors, forty-two of them with cars with bigger engines than her 60hp, six-cylinder Napier. In the same event the following year, she won the Prince Heinrich Trophy.

Though an amateur, Dorothy collected prize money and plaques and was presumably paid well by Napier. She lived well and mixed with the great and not so good of her day – she undoubtedly met Charles Rolls, who makes a passing reference to her in his diaries, and she certainly chased balloons by car for the Hare 'n' Hound races in which he would have competed. A bohemian with the confidence of the well-to-do, either inherited or acquired, her private life was flamboyant but very discreet, like many of that era, including Charles Rolls. Her 1909 book, *The Woman and the Car*, was snappy, easy to understand and mirrored her no-nonsense personality. She was a good shot as well as horsewoman. If driving alone, she advised: 'It might be advisable to carry a small revolver. I have an automatic Colt and find it very easy to handle', and, on running out of petrol: 'It's unpleasant to be stranded on the road, miles from anywhere, minus petrol. The petrol tank is… under the seat, lift the cushions, unscrew the cap and peep in – if it is dark, it will be necessary to hold a piece of stick to see how much petrol there is… It is perhaps unnecessary for me to warn you not to take a light near the petrol tank…'

Dorothy gave many lectures to women, urging them to take up motoring (and presumably to buy Edge's cars). She started to learn to fly and then, suddenly, she disappeared, without warning, from public gaze. It was probably illness that forced her to give up her whirling lifestyle.

---

41 *The Herkomer Trophy Race was the most important international trial held in Europe each year and involved several hill climbs and speed events, in addition to the usual long-distance aspect of the Trial, when each car had to carry an official observer and cover a set distance within the time allowed. Dorothy and her Napier finished without any penalties, which did much to increase the prestige of women drivers in Germany. She also did her bit for British fashion by appearing at the prize-giving wearing a stunning outfit she had designed specially for the occasion – 'Fast Women' – John Bullock (Robson Books, published 2002).*

Dorothy Levitt contributed to the glamorous image of motoring. Cars were becoming more reliable, the playthings of the better off. Travelogue novels such as *The Lightning Conductor*[42] became popular. Lord Lane, the hero of *The Lightning Conductor*, drives Molly Randolph, a wealthy young American beauty, round France and Italy and on to Capri and Sicily in a Napier, while pretending to be a chauffeur. This is motoring without the breakdowns. The heroine rejoices how 'all the impressions follow each other like flickering pictures in a cinematograph, and then with one flicker one is out again on the broad, white road, with the flying trees spinning by on either hand and the white filmy clouds floating in an azure sky. It is only in a motor car that you will get all these sensations. In a train you are in a box; on a motor you are in a chariot of fire with the whole heavens open above you'. One can scarcely countenance a London cabbie today 'too-tooing a fanfaronade on the horn'.

By 1902, John Douglas-Scott-Montagu, Second Baron Montagu of Beaulieu, equalled Rolls as the best known motorist in Britain. That year he launched *Car Illustrated*, which was upmarket and lavishly produced and added further to the glamour of the era. It's first cover ('The Car makes its curtsey to the public', 1902) showed King Edward VII being driven by Montagu. *Car Illustrated's* offices overlooked Piccadilly Circus with its 1893 statue of Eros. In 1906 a tube station opened. It was the place to be.

Cis Montagu (Lady Cecilia Kerr), the first wife of John, drove with him on the Thousand Mile Trial and contributed significantly, with humour and fashion, to motoring's appeal to women readers. By 1902 Cis and John had been married thirteen years and had their differences. He was extrovert and restless by nature; she was sensitive, humorous and artistic. They disagreed over the family car and she exploited their differences in droll articles that supplemented her regular 'Costumes and Chatter' feature: 'It's no good talking to Jack (Montagu), the only response to my query as to how long this misery (driving) was going to last was a grunt, don't talk to the man at the wheel, so after that I lapsed into silence'. And, describing Jack's early driving: 'It was rather the other way because Jack became too sure of himself (he is apt to get conceited I fear), drove too quickly round a

---

42 *'The Lightning Conductor' (C. N. & A. M. Williamson 1902).*

corner and as he is not too used to steering, collided with the opposite bank. The next thing I knew was that I was lying in most undignified and unbecoming position in the top of the hedge with the breath nearly knocked out of me. Jack himself had fallen on his side and got all cut about the head, but luckily he was free of the motor, which was also on its side, blazing away furiously.' And a month later: ' I was rather excited for Jack let me have my first drive in the car. He said it wouldn't matter much if I broke it up for he had ordered a new one. The only bother would be if I broke myself for this would be expensive in doctor's bills, not to speak of the daily creature comforts Jack would miss... What fun it would be to see the faces of my friends when I turn up at their doors driving my own car'.

She kept the story going into July: 'I had a terrible blow yesterday. Jack told me he was getting tired of his car and that he had made up his mind to sell it and get a new one, which would go at a higher speed, this – when I flatter myself I'm becoming a more or less proficient driver – is very trying.

To make matters worse, Jack says he cannot think of allowing me to even try and drive the new one. He says that women seldom keep their heads when they get into a tight place and I should most probably ruin the car.

I feel as if I could sit down and have a good cry like a disappointed child: it is annoying. The only thing to do is try and save up my pocket money and buy a car for myself; but what with the cost of frocks and hats, not to speak of bazaars and various other calls of Society nowadays, I don't see a chance of buying a car until I am over eighty. I shall have to make it up to concede giving in to all his little foibles for a time and then perhaps I shall wheedle him into giving me one. Meanwhile, I shall have no scruples whatever in driving our present car at any pace'.

And then, finally, a few weeks later: 'Jack is a brick. He has not sold the car, but he has given it to me. I am in seventh heaven at the moment... the only drawback is that Jack and I cannot share the chauffeur, so I shall have to economise in frocks and get a man, which will be better for the car and myself'.

Lady Montagu was the first lady of the 'Little Kingdom in the Forest', as the Beaulieu estate was called. She was good fun and was tolerant of her husband's projects and absences in London, first in the Commons, then for *Car Illustrated* and then in the Lords. While 'tolerant' might be too strong a word, she survived his famous lover, Eleanor Velasco Thornton, by four years with grace and fortitude.

Eleanor Velasco Thornton has a particular place in Rolls's story since she was very probably the model for the Rolls-Royce car mascot, 'The Spirit of Ecstasy', sometimes known as the 'Flying Lady', designed by sculptor Charles Sykes. Rolls-Royce and Johnson had become concerned at the inappropriate mascots that adorned some of their cars. Johnson, with his artistic bent, sought to find something tasteful and special. Sykes, Montagu and Eleanor had the occasional outing in Montagu's Rolls-Royce,named Dragonfly, and on one of the trips, the concept of the famous mascot was conceived. 'Thorn' – as Eleanor was known to Montagu – was sculpted by Sykes in a revealing, yet tasteful, floating costume. The Flying Lady was born, although detractors referred to her as 'Nelly in her Nightie'.

Born in South London, and christened 'Nelly', Eleanor Velasco Thornton first became Claude Johnson's secretary at the Automobile Club. She was intelligent, ambitious, attractive, emancipated and stylish, and she captivated Montagu, leaving the Automobile Club to work for him when Johnson left the Club in late 1903 to join C. S. Rolls & Co. *The Car Illustrated* and the Club were the heart of motordom, and Montagu's lifestyle was frenetic. No wonder he strayed – Eleanor was his personal assistant, confidante and mistress for over a decade.

There was much discretion, but eventually Lady Cis Montagu had to know about John and Eleanor, and she reluctantly accepted the situation. She had borne with patience and strength of character the fact that she had but one child early in her marriage, her daughter, Helen. Helen was a disappointment both to herself and John because she took to the stage, and especially to John as she was not a son. A second daughter, Elizabeth, was born in 1909, but still no son to continue the lineage.

In 1915, John took Eleanor on a voyage to Aden, on his way on military service to India. Cis wrote to her husband: 'I am glad Miss Thornton is going to Aden. She will be away for quite a long time'. Eleanor never returned. The *S.S. Persia*, carrying John and Eleanor, was torpedoed off Crete in 1915. The explosion 'rocked the ship, splitting her deck open and filling the main saloon… with smoke, steam, fragments of broken crockery and the stench of gun cotton and TNT[43]'.

---

43 *John Montagu of Beaulieu 1866-1929 by Paul Tritton (Golden Eagle 1985).*

Charles Rolls did not fly at Brooklands, as Aero Club members flew elsewhere, nor did he race there albeit he drove a Rolls-Royce in the parade on the opening day. The parade was led by Ethel Locke King to whom all motoring sportsmen are forever grateful, as she risked everything to realise a dream.

Ethel Locke King's name is synonymous with Brooklands, a two and three-quarter mile track at Weybridge, Surrey, the first purpose-built racetrack in Britain. Her prudent father-in-law had left her the equivalent of £35 million, but Ethel and her husband, Hugh, a qualified barrister, who never practised, were determined to spend it. Having first bought a hotel in Egypt and lost money on it, Hugh saw circuit racing in Italy and asked why there were no British cars on the circuit. He was told that Britain did not have a track on which to develop them.

On their return to England the couple met Lord Northcliffe and Julian Orde, the Secretary of the R.A.C. (as it was soon to become) who by that time had succeeded Claude Johnson. Hugh also enlisted the support of Selwyn Edge[44] and Charles Jarrott. It was to be a circular banked track, containing two hundred thousand tons of concrete. Concrete could be laid in sections whereas asphalt or tarmac would have been difficult to lay on the angled banking. Hugh and Ethel expected the project would cost some £1.3 million at today's values but this turned out to be a substantial under-estimate. A contract was finally agreed at almost £4 million and it has been estimated that the final contract cost the equivalent of £50 million in today's money.

Planning was not needed in those halcyon days otherwise their dream would not have come to fruition. Some of the Locke King's farm-workers were invited to clear the site, but in time between five hundred and two thousand men worked

---

44 *Eleven days after the opening ceremony on 26th June, but before the first racing, Selwyn Edge booked the track and set his twenty-four hour record of one thousand five hundred and eighty-one miles and one thousand three hundred and ten yards in twenty-four hours, averaging 65mph. He had to change some twenty-four tyres, six on the front and eighteen on the back. The other two Napiers, which accompanied him to relieve the monotony, covered slightly less miles, but the trio achieved a more than satisfactory coup for the Napier marque.*
The total prize money for the six races on the opening day was stunning – some £15,000 – equivalent to well over £1 million today.

on the construction. There were problems with payment. The contractor took a charge on some of the farmland, which he eventually had to sell. And there was opposition. A local action group averred: 'No good can possibly come of such an institution… upon which (track) a fiendish motor car can indulge in its wicked lust for speed to the utmost. Here, the merry motor may pursue his career of compromise of destruction unchecked'. Compromise was necessary over the use of an access road and the siting of the main entrance. Despite these problems, the circuit, with banking on one end as high as twenty-nine feet and, at the other, twenty-two feet, was completed in just over six months and the total project, including site clearing, was completed in ten months.

The opening, on 17th June, 1907, was a grand affair with the first racing scheduled for early July. Selwyn Edge recalled: 'After the ceremony an inspection of the course was made by all present. Mr. and Mrs. Locke King led the way in their 70hp Itala, followed by Rolls in a Rolls-Royce, J. E. Hutton in his 80hp Berliet, the Duke of Westminster, Lord Lonsdale and many others.

There was no attempt to indulge in speed work until Mrs. Locke King, who was driving, let her car out a little; Lord Lonsdale gave chase and within a few minutes we were all tearing round the track as hard as we could go. There were about sixty, all rushing along for dear life.

I do not know what speed we were going, but suddenly there appeared Warwick Wright on his racing Darracq. He passed us all as if we were standing still, and we heard afterwards he had touched 85mph'.

Meanwhile, the contractor was still owed £25,000 and the inheritance from Ethel's father-in-law had run out, but Ethel had managed to persuade her own (also very wealthy) side of the family, including her father, Sir Thomas Gore-Browne, former governor of Tasmania, to rally round. She was a very determined and supportive wife and she undoubtedly deserves her place in motoring history as the 'Mother of Brooklands'.

Attitudes to women drivers were mixed in those early days. Rolls thought they should drive; Johnson thought they should not. They were an idiosyncratic bunch. Fined for speeding in 1904, the Duchess of Manchester was accused of doing 25mph. She replied: 'There must be something deceptive about the roads in Slough'. Lily Langtry, semi-official mistress of Bertie, the Prince of Wales, later

Edward VII, could manage a 'good mouth-filling oath', to quote Shakespeare. On one occasion 'when an impious male hand was laid on Lily Langtry's immaculate Wolseley, her face 'convulsed with rage' and she seemed to be about to resort to violence, but instead 'she expressed herself in language not even a lady of her great personality could use and get away with'. Lily was out-muscled by the Empress of China, who became a convert to automobilism and bought no less than nine cars in one order. Three were bright imperial yellow with blue and silver dragons painted on them, the curtains were also of yellow and the seats were red.

Domestic motoring could be complex. One lady, writing to the letters page of the *Graphic* in 1905, following an article scribbled by Lady Greville, responded: 'Sir, I think it would be more sensible of you to ask should ladies scribble? If Lady Violet Greville, instead of scribbling in the public press, devoted herself to an occupation more fitting for a woman, I should today be driving my motor car; I think that driving an automobile is far better than penning twaddle.

And now to explain. My husband had agreed to let me take up motoring and he was about to buy me a duck of a little car, until his eyes lighted on the words written by Lady Greville. Now he holds the firm conviction that ladies should not drive motor cars. I'm well nigh heartbroken at the loss of the car, and my dear toy terrier, sharing my grief, so sympathetically, will die of it – Yours truly, a disgruntled wife'.

And, finally, more disconcertedly, a letter from America regaled about absentmindedness and its result: 'It is related that two couples of Indiana lovers, who forgot that an automobile and a horse are not exactly the same, had a most exciting experience… last week. The machine plunged down an eight foot declivity and tore down several yards of rail fence as a result of leaving the automobile to guide itself, the driver having his hands otherwise employed.

An instant later, an irate farmer appeared on the scene and at the point of a shotgun ordered the young people to rebuild the fence, which they did as meekly as possible' (*Automobile Topics*).

Charles Rolls's female companion in the last years of his life was the Honourable Mrs. May Assheton Harbord. She had started ballooning in 1906 and made over a hundred flights, four across the Channel, and was the first lady to obtain an aeronauts certificate in Britain. She was also very attractive, the widow of an Australian, and had married into the aristocracy. Her second husband was Captain Edward Harbord, second son of Baron Suffield, K.C.B., P.C. She wed him in April 1905 when she was thirty-seven. She had spent time in India, presumably as her father, James McNab Cunningham, was Surgeon General, the most senior medic in the armed services. Married or not, she spent a lot of time with Rolls, going to concerts with him at the Queen's Hall in London, flying with him in the dirigible, *Ville de Paris*, and travelling with him to France for meetings with the Wright brothers. She also supported him in business and bought a Rolls-Royce Heavy Twenty at an early stage in its development and then two other Rolls-Royce cars. An ardent motorist, she drove from London to John O'Groats in nine days, and, using the same car, covered eight thousand miles in three months without a mechanical fault.

If they were a couple, Rolls and May Harbord were extraordinarily discreet. But Rolls, nine years younger than her, was able to relax in her company and, because she was married, he felt under no pressure in the relationship. They ballooned with all the leading exponents of the sport and one of May's balloons was called *Valkyrie*, which, in Norse mythology, means a lover of heroes and other mortals – a sign of their status or merely a wish?

Ladies who flew other than in balloons were few in the early years of powered flight because it was extremely dangerous. Ethel Berg, the American wife of Hart O'Berg, an associate of the Wright brothers, was the first woman to fly in an aeroplane on 7th October, 1908, the day before Wilbur Wright piloted the British quartet of Griffith Brewer, C. S. Rolls, Frank Hedges Butler and Major Baden-Powell . There is a picture of Mrs. Berg in the *Illustrated London News* of 24th October, 1908, sitting next to Wilbur Wright.

Katherine Wright, more at ease in company than her famous but somewhat shy and introverted brothers, flew twice as a passenger in 1909. She was awarded the Légion d'Honneur, a rare honour for an American woman, but one that she so richly deserved for the emotional support she had given to her extraordinary brothers.

Santos-Dumont dirigible.

First balloon Flight – C.S. Rolls, Vera and Frank Hedges Butler.

C.S. Rolls's small balloon – Midget 1907.

C.S. Rolls's small balloon – The Imp 1908.

Start of the Gordon Bennett Race Tuileries Paris.

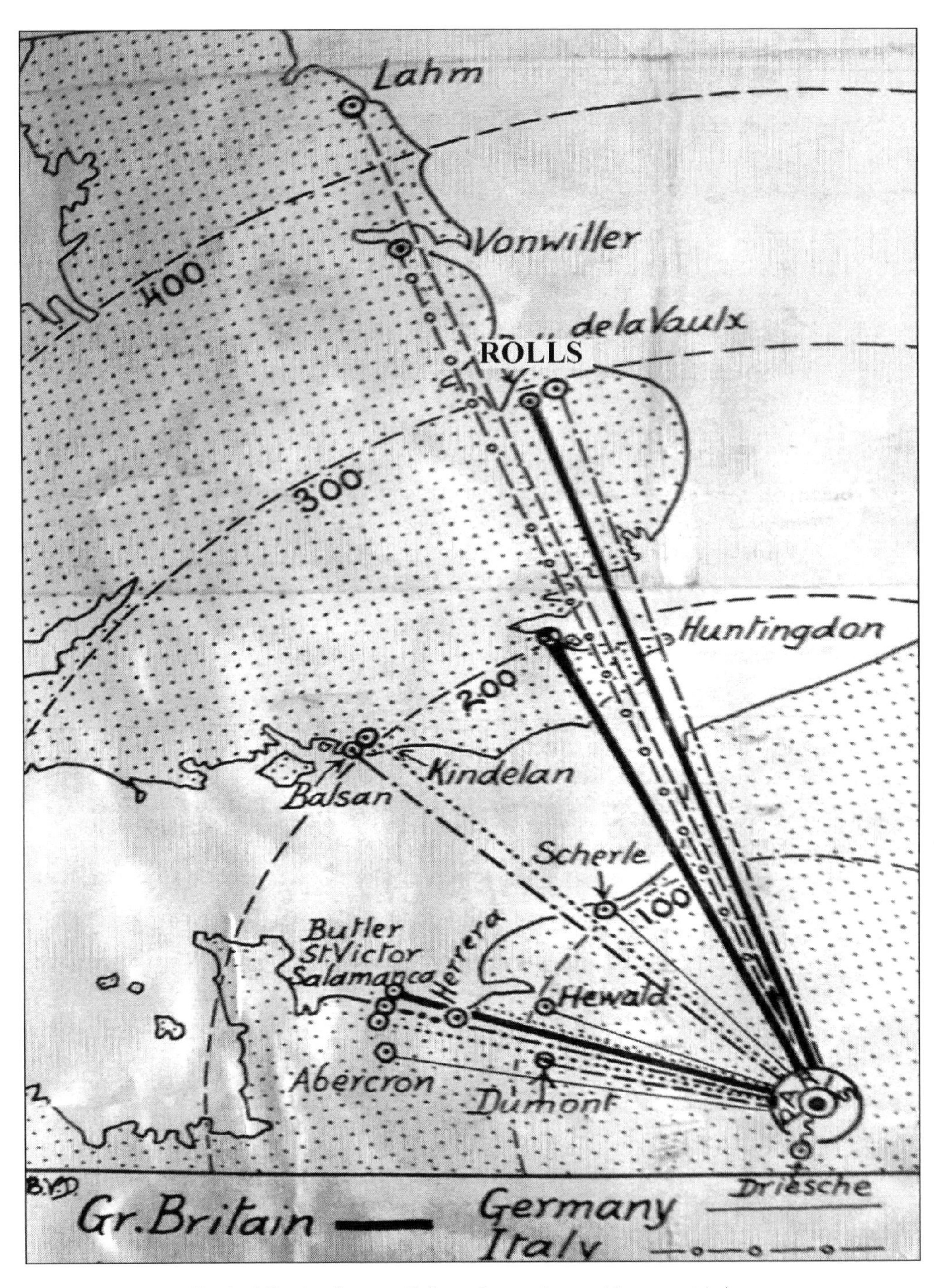

Track of Gordon Bennett Balloon Race winner – Lieutenant Lahm.

Dirigible Ville de Paris.

C.S. Rolls and the Hon. Mrs May Assheton Harbord.

C.S. Rolls, May Harbord and Baroness Von Heeckeren.

C.S. Rolls's balloon car with H.J. Mulliner.

. . FOURTH . .

BALLOON CONTEST

ORGANISED BY THE AERO CLUB OF THE UNITED KINGDOM.

"HARE AND HOUNDS" RACE,

Saturday, July 17th, 1909,

at 3.30 p.m.

Cup presented by the Hon. C. S. ROLLS.

"HARE"—Hon. C. S. ROLLS. BALLOON—"IMP."

LIST OF COMPETITORS.

COMPETITOR.	BALLOON.	PILOT.
1. Mrs. John Dunville ...	**La Mascotte** ..	John Dunville
2. B. H. Barrington Kennett	**The Comet**	B. H. Barrington Kennett
3. Ernest C. Bucknall	**Enchantress** ...	Ernest C. Bucknall 3
4. Hon. Mrs. Assheton Harbord	**Valkyrie**	C. F. Pollock 1
5. Baroness Von Heeckeren	**L'Esperance**... ...	Griffith Brewer 2
6. A. M. Singer... ...	**Satellite** ...	A. M. Singer 9
7. C. A. Moreing ...	**Thistledown** ...	Major Baden-Powell

The Club Balloon "Aero Club IV." will follow the Race, in charge of Major Sir A. Bannerman, Bart., R.E.

Hare and Hounds – Rolls Trophy – Hurlingham July 1909.

Miss Vera Hedges Butler.

Mrs Mary Kennard.

Bertha Benz.

Madame Camille du Gast.

Madame Camille du Gast.

Lady Cis Montagu.

The Spirit of Ecstasy.

Eleanor Thornton.

Eleanor Velasco Thornton, P.A. to John Montagu, Publisher.

Dorothy Levitt beating John Montagu at Blackpool.

The Hon. Mrs May Assheton Harbord.

A brave early flying lady… who is she?

Dunhill Motorities – a passion for fashion.

Chapter Twelve

A New Horizon

> ***The sensation of flight was delightful and novel and the fact of accomplishing what several eminent scientists had 'proved' impossible gave an added satisfaction...***
>
> *C. S. Rolls, The Times, 1908*

Rolls's late 1906 visit to America for the New York Motor Show was an undoubted success. He sold some cars, set up an agency and flattened the locals in a five mile car race. Crucially, he met the Wright brothers whom he had invited to London earlier in the year as guests of the Aero Club although they had declined, and Colonel Capper, his companion in the 1906 Gordon Bennett balloon race, also met them. Rolls did not see the brothers fly on this occasion – they did not fly at all, anywhere, between October 1905 and August 1908, which only added to their mystique. Some people doubted their achievements but Rolls was fully convinced; he spoke to several eyewitnesses and wrote to *Ballooning and Aeronautic Magazine* upon his return: 'I was quite convinced and perfectly satisfied that they had obtained in flight more than had been published in the newspapers'.

Early flying experiments started in the nineteenth century and the Wrights paid close attention to their predecessors. Sir George Cayley is regarded as the first pioneer. One of his key assertions was that to achieve longitudinal stability the engine had to be in the centre of a flying machine. The Wright brothers, who were self-taught, chose not to do this and achieved flight by their own separate ideas and their tenacity and by constant practice.

Among other early pioneers were Englishman, Percy Pilcher and a German, Otto Lilienthal, who both paid with their lives in early flying accidents and whose notes the Wrights absorbed. Sir Hiram Maxim was also involved in development, but gave up after spending $100,000, a huge sum at the time. An early mentor of the Wrights was the American Octave Chanute who defined the state of flying in 1894 in a book, *Progress of Flying Machines.*

By 1900 Rolls was already avidly following developments. Ever the publicist, he told the Evening News in November 1901, after his first balloon flight with Frank Hedges Butler and daughter, Vera, that powered flight would be achieved: 'If aerial navigation is ever to become practical, and if we are to have aerial conveyances to run in all weathers, if we expect to cross oceans without ploughing through them, to skim over the land without resting on it or burrowing into it, the aeroplane is the most practical and dependable conveyance'. His remarks were visionary because this was before the Wrights flew their first powered flight in December 1903 (although they had experimented with gliding earlier).

Rolls was in at the very start of organised aeronautics in Britain. He was a founder member of the Royal Aero Club – at first all balloonists. Its objects included 'the encouragement of aerial locomotion in all its forms… to encourage the study of aeronautics and develop the science connected therewith'. He was also a member of the quite separate Aeronautical Society of which Maxim was one-time chairman, and it was through the Aeronautical Society (Royal patronage came later) that Rolls probably first heard officially of the Wright brothers' progress. The Wrights went public on their experiments in 1901 in Chicago in an address to its Society of Engineers.

Who could fail to be inspired by these two daring and unusual inventors who became so inextricably intertwined with Rolls's own flying career and his ultimate end at Bournemouth? Wilbur and Orville, the 'Bishop's Boys' as they were known, were born in 1867 and 1871 respectively, the 'Bishop' being because their father was bishop in an American sect. They didn't go to college, but read widely and avidly and seem to have been born with greasy fingers. They loved tinkering and they liked to make their hobbies pay. Early schoolboy ventures had included selling bones to a fertilizer factory, building a miniature primitive chewing-gum factory and, prophetically, making kites for their schoolmates. They built a lathe, organised a circus parade, and Wilbur built a device for folding the weekly issue of the local church magazine so they didn't have to fold them all by hand. And they started a printing press, something they may later have regretted given the local press's disbelief in their achievements.

In 1892, at age twenty-one, Orville bought a bicycle, and with the advent of Dunlop's pneumatic tyres, the brothers realised the potential of cycling and set up their own shop in their home town, Dayton, Ohio, making sales and providing service and, later, constructing their own brand of cycle. When the first cars appeared they fleetingly considered the possibilities, but stuck to cycles. By then, they had been given a toy helicopter invented by a Frenchman, a present from their father. It flew under its own power to a height higher than it took off and it was this that first made them think about gliding and powered flight. They read everything they could obtain, writing to the American Smithsonian Institute to ask for any material it had.

The brothers were inspired by the fact that Percy Pilcher had made a glide of two hundred feet and that Otto Lilienthal had spent more than five hours in the air in total, albeit over a large number of flights. They read that Lilienthal had been killed moving about in the glider to maintain balance and that there had to be some arrangement whereby the wings could be warped at will, one turned up slightly and one turned down, so as to present them at different angles to the air – the forerunner of aeroplane flaps. In 1899 they built a biplane kite with a five-foot wingspan.

Their bicycle business was seasonal and, in autumn, when inclement weather arrived, there was less demand for cycles and repairs so they could spend more time on their experiments. They wrote to the American meteorological authorities and found a good place to fly at the aptly named Kitty Hawk in North Carolina. Wilbur went there in September 1900 taking the unassembled glider with him. Kitty Hawk was a huge area of sandy dunes, and, mindful of what happened to Pilcher and Lilienthal, the Wrights conducted their glides at twenty feet above the soft sand.

Back in Dayton they were regarded as two sober-living devoted brothers who managed a successful business although with a quirky interest in experimentation. Neither of them was married nor intended to be, Wilbur once admitting that he could not cope with both a wife and an aeroplane. On Kitty Hawk they lived in a tent. Kitty Hawk was remote and could only be reached by boat and they had nothing to spend their money on and once they were there they just worked and thought. They made friends with the Taits, the leading citizens in a tiny nearby hamlet where Bill Tait had been postmaster, occasionally staying with them at the start and ends of their visits, and assembled their first kite with the aid of Mrs. Tait's sewing machine. In 1900 at Kitty Hawk, they assembled a glider (according to biographer, Fred Kelly[45]) that weighed fifty-two pounds and had a wingspan of seventeen-and-a-half feet. The total lifting area was one hundred and sixty-five feet and they achieved just two minutes of actual gliding with one of them aboard.

Back in Dayton, they had read Octave Chanute's treatise on flying theory. He visited them, which gave them more credibility, and he became a friend and long-term mentor. He was a respected, practical engineer, having had senior involvement in the construction of the Kansas City Bridge and some of Chicago's stockyards, and from him they acquired substantial theoretical knowledge of aerodynamics.

Summer of 1901 at Kitty Hawk saw a glide of over a hundred yards but the brothers had hoped for better and were discouraged. Luckily Chanute persuaded them to carry on, and that year, at Chanute's insistence, Wilbur addressed the Society of Engineers in Chicago, giving very full information without keeping anything back. He pointed out that in his view the whole business of being able to balance a machine of any kind in the air depended on one thing: getting the centre of pressure to coincide with the centre of gravity. The brothers built a small wind tunnel, which was rectangular in shape with an opening of sixteen inches square and a length of six feet. Wind was blown into the device by a fan. Knowledge of airflow was vital and the Wright brothers were the first men in the world to compile tables of figures from which one might conceivably design an aeroplane that could fly. It helped that Orville was a very fine, if self-taught, mathematician.

In Autumn 1902, on their third visit to Kitty Hawk, and with a new thirty-two wingspan glider, they made over a thousand glides. They added a tail fixed in vertical veins, intended to balance any difference in the resistance of the wing tips. Their longest glide this time was over two hundred yards and some of the glides were against winds of up to 36mph.

---

45 *'The Wright Brothers' – Fred C. Kelly, 1943 (Dover Publications, Inc.).*

The brothers applied for patents in March 1903 with full drawings and specifications, and now they were ready to add a motor to achieve powered flight. Unable to find a suitable motor because motor manufacturers fought shy of assisting a so-called flying machine built by two crazy cycle-shop owners, the brothers built their own – in less than eight months. It weighed one hundred and seventy pounds, developing 16hp. To reduce the danger of the engine falling on the pilot (as it nearly did for Moore-Brabazon in later years), it was placed on the lower wing, a little to the right of centre. The pilot would ride flying flat as on the glider, but to the left of centre to balance the weight.

Their next problem was a propeller. Little or no data was available so they popped down to the local library and discovered to their surprise that less was known about propellers than they had supposed. They experimented. At one point one brother visited a joinery factory looking for suitable material and came across strange, almost-circular wooden circles which, on enquiry, he discovered were – toilet seats.

They knew that propellers would drive boats but propellers to drive an aeroplane would need to be much more precise. They thought and argued and thought some more and they came up with the answer – two propellers. They were conscious that the torque of a single propellor rotating one way will tend to curl the aeroplane the opposite way, so they deliberately introduced two props rotating in counter directions in order to cancel out this effect. Thus from the single engine the two chain drives were direct to one propellor, but 'crossed' to the other.

That September 1903 they set off again for Kitty Hawk. A storm had damaged their workshop but they repaired it and then assembled their new machine. It took a month. This was followed by bad weather and when Chanute came to witness the launch he had to leave again after further weather delays. With hindsight this dealt a bad blow to their credibility because Chanute would have made a formidable and respected eyewitness. The brothers used the delay to construct a timing device to measure time in the air and distance travelled.

Next, one of the components was faulty and Orville had to return to Dayton for a replacement and, while there, he learned that a rival, a Professor Langley, had failed to launch a full-size, rigid machine. Langley's machine had taken off from a floating scaffold and fallen into the Potomac River. The U.S. government, which had financed the project, had refused to sanction any reconstruction or further funding. Previously models had been flown, but the first real trial failed. Orville could be forgiven for feeling a sense of relief at the news – relief, which must have turned to frustration later when the Smithsonian Museum in Washington displayed Professor Langley's machine, labelling it the first machine to fly[46].

It was late November 1903 when Orville returned to Kitty Hawk and the brothers were ready. Sadly Chanute had gone home. The Wrights put up a pre-arranged signal on their tents to attract people from the nearby Kitty Hawk village. They needed help to get the machine to the launch site, a quarter of a mile away on the hillside. The glider and engine together weighed some 750 pounds and was moved to the launch by laying a track and then re-laying it, as the plane proceeded on its way. Thanks to their six helpers, they gained six witnesses.

They tossed for who went first. Each brother weighed about 140 pounds. Wilbur's first powered flight lasted just three and a half seconds... he pulled the stick back too hard... stalled and crashed .After a three day delay for repairs, Orville's second flight was six hundred and fifteen feet, Wilbur's next flight, the third, was fifteen seconds and two hundred feet – and Orville's second attempt, the fourth of the day, was a stunning flight of fifty-nine seconds and eight hundred and fifty-two feet. It was the 17th December, 1903, and powered flight was a reality even if, after those first four extraordinary flights, a gust of wind turned the plane over and damaged it so badly that it was never used again.

Orville sent a telegram to his father: 'Success! Four flights, Thursday morning. All against twenty-one mile wind, started from level with engine power alone, average speed through the air thirty-one miles, the longest flight fifty-nine seconds. Inform Press. Home Christmas – Orville Wright'.

Back home in Dayton, Bishop Wright refused to let the press see the telegraph because he wanted to announce the flight properly, but someone leaked the

---

46 *America would not grant the Wrights their legitimate claim to be the first to fly. Because of this astonishing American establishment reaction, the original Wright machine reposed in the London Science Museum for twenty-five years.*

story in a garbled version, and a description of a three mile flight ended up on editorial desks and they refused to believe it. Inaccuracy killed the story. The editor of the *Dayton Journal*, when told by Lorin, older brother to Orville and Wilbur, that his brothers had actually flown for fifty-nine seconds, said: 'Fifty-nine seconds eh? If it had been for fifty-nine minutes, it might have been a story'.

Rolls may have seen the confused newspaper reports of the 1903 flights or perhaps he corresponded with the Wrights or his American contacts through the Aero Club of America, but by April 1904 he was borrowing the Albert Hall (!), together with his friend, Moore-Brabazon, where they flew home-made gliders from balconies and watched them glide to the floor of the Hall, measuring the angle of descent.

Meanwhile in America, the Wrights were building Flyer Two. Having been largely ignored by the American press, they just got on with it and, unlike Professor Langley, they used their own, not government, money. The fact that they still had cash in the bank after the December 1903 success was a tribute to their business acumen and frugality. Another American professor, Professor Newcombe, demonstrated with unassailable logic why man could not fly and two obscure bicycle makers, who had not even been to college, were attempting just that, it was risible. But not to everyone – members of the Cabot family, a legendary American dynasty, asked the brothers if their device could fly freight. The opportunities presented by powered flight were obvious – if only to a few astute businessmen.

The 1904 plane was going to weigh nine hundred pounds. The brothers changed the spars and were allowed the use of a field known as Huffman Prairie, just eight miles from Dayton, where they built a shed. They could have it for free said Mr. Huffman, if they drove his cows to a safe place and did not run them over. The field could be seen clearly from two roads and a railway line. There was no intent on secrecy. That May, they even had an open day for the Press but everything went wrong. The wind was too strong to fly and even when they sought to demonstrate their plane on the track, the engines failed to perform. The assembled journalists returned to their editors empty handed and muttering.

By this time the brothers were using a derrick with a falling weight as a launch vehicle. Rolls later used the same method in his own early attempts. It comprised a three-quarter-ton weight falling some sixteen feet, with ropes and pulleys to launch the plane along the rail. What happened when it got to the end of the launch rail was down to chance and the pilot's skill. That year it took them fifty flights until they achieved a flight of sixty-one seconds, only two seconds more than the 1903 best mark.

Despite the slow going and despite many setbacks, by September 1905 there was substantial progress, but the brothers were still being ignored by the press. The City Editor of the *Daily News* in Dayton received various requests from people who had driven past the field or passed it on the train, and who had seen the aeroplane aloft and wanted to know why there was nothing in the paper. Editor Kumler tried to explain himself. 'Well,' he said on one occasion, 'we just didn't believe it – if you remember at the time the Wright brothers were being terribly secretive.' 'You mean they were secretive about the fact they were flying over an open field?' 'I guess,' admitted Kumler, 'we were just plain dumb'.

One reason for his attitude was that the plane circled above the field at only ten to fifteen feet for safety. Rolls broke his neck from perhaps forty feet but the Wrights seldom flew above fifty feet – and they lived longer. A second factor was the nature of their flights, which was circular. Flying from point to point would have meant moving the launch track. Landing wheels would come later, there were more important technical issues to be overcome in those early years. Their quiet modest methodology worked well technically but it worked against them publicity-wise.

The following year, 1905, things began to move more rapidly. That September they flew eleven miles in eighteen minutes and twelve miles in twenty minutes (on the 29th). On 4th October they flew twenty-four miles (the width of the English Channel) in thirty-eight minutes.

The complacency and lack of interest of the press never ceased to amaze them. Frank Tunison, who had made the 'fifty-nine second' jibe about the Kitty Hawk flight, made no reference to them at all, being reluctant to admit past mistakes.

Luther Beard was Managing Editor of the *Dayton Journal*, and he knew the Wrights as advertisers and local businessmen and used to chat to them – but initially he was too polite to ask about their flying. Presumably he thought their behaviour was eccentric, which it was. They didn't mention it either, so Beard decided that the fact that a flying machine could be flown under perfect control in circles for over half an hour didn't amount to anything.

Gradually Beard began to ring Orville up.

'Done anything of special interest lately?'
'Today one of us flew for five minutes.'
'Where did you go?'
'Oh, round the field'
'I see, okay, well keep in touch.'

Unbelievable – but true.

But it was the interest of a beekeeper, an Amos Root who eventually pollinated the word and sent the details to the *Scientific American* of some sixty witnesses who had seen the flights. He told a Sunday School class back in March 1904 about the Wrights, and in 1905 his magazine, *Gleanings in Bee Culture*, reported: 'These brothers have probably not even a faint glimpse of what their discovery is going to bring to the children of men. No one living can guess what is coming along this line, much better than anyone living can conjecture the final outcome of Columbus's experiment when he pushed off through the trackless water. Possibly we may be able to fly over the North Pole…'

Bees are a kind of flying machine, if smaller even than Alphonse Penaud's toy helicopter that had inspired the Wrights, and thus a beekeeper magazine from Modina first reported successful powered flight into the disbelieving public domain.

In December 1906, the *Scientific American* finally, after much procrastination, acknowledged the work of the Wright brothers: 'In all the history of invention, there's probably no parallel to the unostentatious – quiet might be a better word – manner in which the Wright brothers of Dayton, Ohio ushered into the world their epoch-making invention of the first successful aeroplane flying machine'.

The continuing disinterest of both the American and the French authorities, over several years, in the work of the Wrights has no place in the Rolls' story, save that even after the intervention of President Theodore Roosevelt, after he had been sent a copy of the *Scientific American*, America still failed to capitalise on the flying start the Wright brothers had given the Americans in aviation.

The French, however, were more receptive to technological advance, and the Wrights used France as their European base and to train early pilots. The French themselves were major innovators and perhaps stalled the Wrights in the hope that one of their own would come up with a superior product. However, apart from Santos-Dumont, a French-based Brazilian, who flew in Paris, there were few advances in aviation technology in France in the four years after the 17th December, 1903 flight. Santos-Dumont had flown round the Eiffel Tower in 1900, but only in a balloon.

As patriotic Americans, the Wright brothers wanted their own country and government to develop their invention and offered them a world monopoly on all patents and on all their secrets relating to the aeroplane. They described their achievements in a letter to their Member of Congress for Dayton, one Mr. R. M. Nevin, at the beginning of 1905:

Dear Mr. Nevin,

'A series of aeronautical experiments, upon which we have been engaged for the past five years, has ended in the production of a flying machine of a type fitted for practical use. It not only flies through the air at high speed, but it also lands without being wrecked.

During 1904, one hundred and five flights were made at our experimental station on the Huffman Prairie, east of the city; and though our experience of handling the machine has been too short to give any high degree of skill, we nevertheless succeeded, towards the end of the season, of making two flights of five minutes each in which we flew round and round the field until a distance of three miles had been covered at a speed of 35mph. The first of these record flights was made on November 9th and the second on December 1st, the hundredth flight of the season.

The numerous flights in straight lines and circles over S shaped courses in calms and in winds have made it quite certain that flying has been brought to a point where it could be made of quite practical use in various ways, one of which is that of scouting and carrying messages in time of war.

If the latter features are of interest to our own government, we should be pleased to take up the matter either on a basis of providing machines of agreed specification, at a contract price, or of furnishing all the scientific and practical information we have accumulated in these years of experimenting, together with a license to use our patents; thus putting the government in a position to operate on its own account. If you find it convenient to ascertain whether this is a subject of interest to our own government, it would oblige us greatly as early information on this point will enable us in making our plans for the future.

Respectfully yours, Orville and Wilbur Wright'.

A representative forwarded the letter to the Secretary of War who handed it over to the Board of Ordnance who put it in their crank file. They had received many proposals concerning flying machines and had stopped looking at them.

The Congressman never contacted the brothers, never investigated their claim, indeed the whole of the U.S. government establishment was described by Chanute as 'a bunch of asses'. Maybe the local Congressman spoke to the local Press, but his lack of interest was at least disappointing and at worst, negligent.

The government replied in a letter that was almost a template for some computer-generated verbiage today. It said that the government would not provide funds for air and airplane development but the Wrights were not asking for funds, they had savings in the bank and funded their experiments themselves. The letter also said that no help would be given until a working plane had been developed; the Wrights' letter had said that they had built a plane.

British response was no better. Colonel Capper, Superintendent of the Royal Aero Establishment and a ballooning chum of Rolls, had met the Wrights and had suggested that they write to the U.K. government. Two years of letters got precisely nowhere and the blind ignorance of authority was again in evidence. The Wrights employed an American agent, one C. F. Flint, who in spring 1907 received the following rebuff from the Admiralty: 'The Admiralty are of the opinion that they (aeroplanes) could not be of any practical use to the naval services'. And from the War Office: 'The War Office is not disposed to enter into relations, at present, with any manufacturer of airplanes'.

Presumably cavalry would be better.

At this point, Rolls, free of all racing and looking to the future, offered to be the Wrights' advocate but the Wrights appointed an American, Mr. Berg. Not to be rebuffed, Rolls persisted about buying a plane from them and acquiring the U.K. patents. He was sure that with his father or Lord Northcliffe or with his contacts in the Army, he could open the right doors for the American inventors.

The Wrights were relatively unsophisticated businessmen, and they perhaps thought that, as with America, the British including Rolls, were stringing them along, and this was true to some extent because, by 1906, the Army were building 'British Army Aeroplane No. 1'. It was based on the Wright principles. Their test flyer was an American, Colonel Cody.

Despite Rolls's efforts, nothing happened and Rolls must have been very disheartened. He could not get hold of a plane and would not do so until 1st October, 1909. And the Wrights too continued to be frustrated. They had a flying machine, proven from the end of 1904, but no government was prepared to make them a firm, sensible offer – and all this at a time when the powerful Lord Northcliffe, via the *Daily Mail* and following Santos-Dumont's brief flights in Paris, was thundering, about the fact that Britain 'was no longer an island'. *War in the Air* was published by H. G. Wells in 1908, well in advance of Blériot's triumphant flight across the Channel, Wells describing vividly how aeroplanes could be used in warfare for bombing, reconnaissance and other military duties but officialdom continued to move slowly.

Wilbur Wright lived in Europe for six months in order to promote the plane. He had a plane crated and shipped across but it was still uncrated at the end of his visit. Rolls and he met more than once, and Rolls remained well-informed on developments. By now Europe was catching up, and, as with his motoring activities, Rolls chose not to have all his eggs in one Wright basket, understandably perhaps since the Wrights had failed to choose him as their British agent. He considered buying a plane of the Voisin type that Moore-Brabazon eventually bought. Later he bought a Sommer, powered by a Gnome engine.

Rolls was now a salaried director of Rolls-Royce Ltd. Although he would receive a future share of the profits, he had sold C. S. Rolls & Co. only in exchange for shares in Rolls-Royce Ltd., not cash. He did not thus have unlimited finance and the new company, due to reorganisation and sorting out bad debts inherited, was not yet very profitable. Rolls-Royce also had an ambitious financial plan that included moving to a new purpose-built factory in Derby.

His father, Lord Llangattock, may not have been keen to help. He was getting older. Although Rolls-Royce had financed the T.T. success, car development and the various costs, including new tooling and the proposed move to Derby would almost have certainly precluded dividends or advances to its own directors. Rolls was keen to get a plane and he had asked Wilbur Wright in June 1908 when Wilbur wrote to Orville: 'He (Rolls) did not propose to buy one himself, but thought he would get a wealthy friend to buy it and let him run it'.

At this stage, Rolls was perhaps hoping to persuade the Wrights to assign the U.K. manufacturing rights to him and then he could approach Rolls-Royce with firm proposals. He still did not have the funds himself, and it is not impossible that he approached Lord Northcliffe. Northcliffe, as a wealthy patriot but also with an eye to the advertising and news potential of aviation, had already put up a huge aeroplane prize, £10,000, for a flight from London to Manchester. The Brooklands Committee had also put up a prize – for the first plane to make a single circuit of the track without touching the ground, a distance of two and three-quarter miles. The track had opened in 1907 for motor racing, but had hangarage available and had been used for various early flying experiments.

Rolls may even have asked Northcliffe to buy the Wright brothers' patents and to finance the whole enterprise, but Johnson, who was closer to Northcliffe than Rolls, would have been against any such idea. The Shorts' factory could have built the airframes, but if Rolls was looking to get Rolls-Royce to build the engines, this would have put more pressure on Royce's health – and Johnson wanted to protect Royce and for him to concentrate solely on the development of the 'Best Car in the World'. Claremont and Edmunds (both still directors of Glover), together with Royce and Johnson, had realised the remarkable potential of their six-cylinder Silver Ghost, and Johnson was still very much the guardian of Royce's frail health and was determined that Rolls-Royce would not diversify. Rolls's aviation ambitions were stuck as a consequence of these various factors and, anyway, the Wrights decided not to have a British company at all and to continue to operate out of France, so that was that.

Meanwhile, czarist Russia had joined England and France in a three-way *étente*, international tension towards Germany was rising – maybe even the War Office/

Admiralty myopia would disappear. Montagu's biography[47] mentions Charles Rolls attended the Rheims Air Show in 1909 and hints 'mysteriously' that he was maintaining a watching brief on behalf of the British government. He probably was, he had given evidence to Lord Esher's Imperial Committee Defence[48], which made recommendations on a coherent aviation policy concerning both planes and airships in December 1908. The sub-committee asked Rolls for a 'rough idea' of the current state of development, and Rolls gave them more than just a rough idea. His evidence was brilliant, drawing on his practical experience of ballooning, airships and aeroplanes in the United States and Europe. During this period he had made well over a hundred balloon flights and had flown for over an hour, just weeks before his evidence to the committee, on the huge French airship, *Ville de Paris*, and in October 1908 had flown for the first time with Wilbur Wright.

Committee Chairman, Lord Esher was interested.

> 'What is your view as to the accuracy with which explosives can be dropped?'
> *'They have been trying a good many experiments in France…'*
>
> 'Can you give us details…?'
> *'No, I cannot, except what I picked up generally by conversation with them. I know they are learning that business a great deal and that they occasionally send men off with sealed orders, which they open when they get up (in the air), to go to a certain place and blow up an imaginary fort, take photographs there and come back again. They have been doing these things with very satisfactory results, and coming back and delivering their reports in a very short time'.*

---

47 *'Rolls of Rolls-Royce' – Montagu of Beaulieu (Cassell 1966).*

48 *Lord Esher recognised Rolls as a catalyst through his work in aviation in late 1910 after his death; a separate arm of the services was needed. After two more years of bureaucracy, the Royal Flying Corps was born – the forerunner of the Royal Air Force – a fitting tribute to Rolls's vision. Had he lived, he would certainly have been credited in no small part with its foundation.*

Before his appearance before the Committee, in his capacity as an Aero Club member, Rolls had entertained the Vice-President of the French Aero Club, a captain of the French-Army Balloon Department and a Monsieur Lebaudy, constructor of two large military airships. Rolls was very well-informed. He told the Committee that, firstly, the utility of an aeroplane would be enormous for military purposes and, secondly, that the government should buy a Wright Flyer for £1,000 and a Lebaudy-type airship, two proven successful machines. Subsequently the Committee decided to stop the funding of the current English-Army plane at Farnborough and to continue airship development and agreed 'that advantage should be taken of private enterprise in the form of aviation'. This was quite a plaudit to Rolls and perhaps, with hindsight, unwise because it meant effectively abandoning English aero development to rely on an American one, which subsequently proved to be excellent, but with longitudinal stability problems which were discovered and appreciated only later. Rolls left the Committee with his considered opinion that an airship attack on London or on dockyards was not only feasible, but likely in the event of war.

The first Zeppelin attack on England took place in 1915.

Rolls's expertise and credibility was such that the government acceded to Rolls's offer to put his Wright plane at their disposal and placed officers under him for instruction. Some instruction did indeed take place up until the date of the Bournemouth accident.

The fact that he had not yet got a plane or could fly seems to have been of secondary importance.

Meanwhile across the Atlantic the Wright brothers continued to be baffled by the inability of four major governments – America, Britain, France and now Germany – to buy their technology. It was as if the diplomats and the Press, in all four countries, were colluding against them, none wishing to look foolish for making a wrong decision. In extreme frustration, the Wrights even eschewed their status as serious innovators and held talks in London with Barnum and Bailey, circus proprietors, about flying for them within an enclosure with an admission charge!

But at last, things were about to change. Several American newspapers, although not having seen powered flight, had strongly taken up the Wrights' case. The *New York Globe* thundered: 'It will be worth to the world almost any number of millions of dollars, and will certainly revolutionise warfare, possibly the transportation of passengers; and open to easy access, regions hitherto inaccessible except for the most daring pioneers and would, in short, be probably the most epoch-making invention in the history of civilisation'.

Eventually it was James Gordon Bennett, whose father had been the patron of Henry Stanley, a philanthropist and sponsor of balloon, car and power boat races, who broke the deadlock. Bennett was a flamboyant New York millionaire, who owned part of the *New York Herald* and had helped finance an early transatlantic telegraph cable. Since he spent a lot of time in Paris, he decided that the Americans had to rid themselves of their doubts or they would look very foolish, especially in France. He arranged for pressmen and a photographer to visit the Wrights and get first-hand confirmation of their achievements.

Bennett's press mission bordered on farce or a Keystone Cops movie. He sent one of his top men, a Mr. Newton, to Kitty Hawk alongside a reporter from the *New York American*, a reporter from Lord Northcliffe's *Daily Mail*, and a photographer. They did not ask the Wrights if they could come because they thought they might be refused or else the brothers would live up to their undeserved reputation for being secretive and refuse to fly.

The reporters decided to hide in the woods with field glasses, this meant a short walk to a wharf on Roanoke Island, a five mile trip in a sailing boat to Hammonds Bay across the Sound, and then a walk of about a mile or so over the sand to a place where they could secrete themselves. Provided with food, water, field glasses and cameras they set out at four o'clock every morning from 11th May to 14th May to keep their vigil. Hour after hour they fought mosquitoes and wood ticks and sometimes were drenched by rain, but to their astonishment they several times witnessed human-powered flight.

Newton of the *New York Herald* described the action: 'The propeller blades continued to flash in the sun and then the machine rose obligingly in the air. First it came directly towards us so that we did not know how fast it was going except that it appeared to be increasing rapidly in size as it approached. In the excitement of the first flight, men trained to observe details in all sets of circumstances forgot their cameras, forgot their watches, forgot everything but this aerial monster chattering over our heads'.

The flights they witnessed were under full control, carrying two men and each lasted at least three minutes. Newton's diary predicted, quite correctly, that Congress would one day raise a monument to the Wrights. But, back home again, something went wrong with Newton's *New York Herald* report. It went astray and Newton was temporarily suspended.

In London the *Daily Mail* carried an exclusive. In America, the *New York American* – owned by William Randolph Hurst – ran the story, an American exclusive, much to Gordon Bennett's chagrin. Perhaps because the two reports were not simultaneous, some were convinced but others remained sceptical. Some weeks later, Newton sent his article to another leading magazine which sent it back unpublished: 'While your manuscript has been read with much interest, it does not seem to qualify either as fact or fiction'.

All the time that the journalists had been hiding and perspiring, the Wrights had realised that they were being observed. They would have given permission, they said, they could not have stopped it anyway. When they had first been told by the Kitty Hawk life-saving crew just how many visitors had come, they had decided it would be a good joke on the mysterious observers, whoever they were, simply to ignore them. The Wrights were asked later what they would have done if the correspondents had come out of hiding to watch, and Orville said: 'We had to go ahead, we wouldn't be delayed with our work, there was far too much to do at the time'.

Orville then went to Fort Myer, and on the 3rd September, 1908 flew in front of a thousand people, including Theodore Roosevelt's son. The crowd went crazy. Hard-headed businessmen crowded round Wright with tears running down their cheeks. The following day, many thousands gathered and Orville flew three miles. Professor Newcombe, having already proved that flying was impossible, was asked by a reporter whether passenger planes would be the next step. 'No,' said Newcombe, 'because no plane could ever carry the weight of anyone beside the pilot'.

On 9th September Orville circled the field fifty-seven times and then, in a separate flight, remained airborne for over an hour. The flights finally ended on 17th September when tragedy struck. Orville had taken off with a passenger, a West Point graduate by the name of Lieutenant Selfridge. Once airborne, Orville 'heard or felt a light tapping in the rear part of the machine' and thought it was in the chain drive. A hurried glance revealed nothing wrong but he decided to shut off the power and descend. Hardly had he decided this when two big thumps shook the machine violently and the machine swerved to the right. He proceeded to shut off the motor but directly ahead was a gully filled with small trees – a dangerous landing spot – so he decided on a half circle to the left in order to land on the parade ground. He discovered that the tail was inoperative. By twisting the wings to give the greatest possible resistance to the left wing, he succeeded in turning the machine until it faced directly into the field. In this manoeuvre the machine descended about one-third of the way towards the ground without any further indication of serious trouble and Orville moved the lever to straighten the wing tips to proceed straight ahead.

The plane suddenly turned down in front. At just fifty feet it was heading almost directly towards the ground even though the front elevator was turned to its limit. At about twenty-five feet the machine began to right itself and if there had been another twenty feet to go, or possibly even ten feet, it might have landed safely, but the recovery of the control came too late. They hit the ground with such impact that Lieutenant Selfridge was fatally injured and died a few hours later. His skull had been fractured by a blow against one of the wooden uprights. Miraculously, Orville, at first believed to have been perhaps fatally hurt, escaped with what appeared to be an injured leg and four broken ribs. He never lost consciousness and his first concern was about Selfridge.

Lieutenant Selfridge thus became the first passenger to be killed in a plane crash but at least he disproved the ever-opinionated Professor Newcombe – planes could carry passengers. The flight made front page news if for all the wrong reasons, and, in America at least, powered flight was at last believable and believed in.

Two weeks later Orville again, and for all time, established the bicycle brothers' immortality, making spectacular flights, witnessed by millions of people, over New York. One flight was over Governor's Island and a second from Governor's Island round the Statue of Liberty and back again, all of which was extremely brave in the light of the Fort Myer accident. A week later he flew twenty-one miles from

Governor's Island up the Hudson River, beyond the statue of the Civil War General and American President, Ulysses Grant, and back again. Practical as ever, he had taken the precaution of buying a red canoe, which he roped to the lower part of the plane, the idea being that if anything went wrong with the plane, the canoe might possibly serve as a buoy or pontoon to keep the machine afloat. Fortunately the insurance was not needed, and the seaplane idea was never put to the test.

America was conquered. The American government agreed a price of $25,000 and gave them a $5,000 bonus as well. Wilbur prepared to conquer Europe where the press still doubted; memorably the brothers were described as 'flyers or liars'. He had uncrated the 1907 plane from Le Havre and was billeted at the Bollée establishment near Le Mans, now home of the famous 24-Hour Race. Bollée offered hangar facilities and Wilbur found open ground at Auvours and started flying demonstrations. He was out of practice, not having flown since May and had scalded his hand badly. The opening flight was delayed a few days, and a cruel French headline read: 'Le Bluff continué'.

He got on with it, working the same hours as the Bollée factory workers and quickly earning their trust and respect. The launching derrick was built on 8th August, and soon the flight was ready to go before the press from Paris, Aero Club de France members and hundreds of other onlookers. He flew gently from the launching rail at a height of thirty-five feet for one minute thirty-five seconds. The crowd went wild and, on landing, Wilbur fought off excited French pressmen and others wishing to bestow the formal accolade of kissing him on both cheeks. French reaction was now *'cet homme à conquer l'air il n'est pas bluffeur'*. He followed up his triumph with a week's flying demonstrations on the site of Auvours, ten miles away. It became, while it lasted, the greatest show on earth; Parisians would drive down or take the train to witness the flights, which drew important visitors from all over Europe.

That September, Wright flew forty miles in an hour and a half. At an Aero Club Paris dinner in his honour, the unassuming American was not expected to make a speech, but he managed a few words: 'I know of only one bird, the parrot, that talks, and it can't fly very high!'

Mr. Dickin, an English-born correspondent from the *New York Herald* became the first Englishman to fly. In the Paris edition of 6th October, 1908, he was impressed: 'If only some of our people in England could see or imagine what Mr. Wright is doing, I am certain it will give them a terrible shock.

The conquest of the air by any nation means more than the average man is willing to admit or even think about. That Wilbur Wright is in a position of a power which controls the fate of nations is beyond dispute'.

The hour of the believers had arrived: H. G. Wells felt vindicated, Lord Esher was concerned about his nation's defence and Northcliffe, Montagu and Rolls were more than a little smug.

Rolls had been quick off the mark, ordering a Wright Flyer in September 1908, a month after the Wrights' world-wide successes. Shorts were to make the first six airframes under licence from the French company formed by the Wrights – the plane to be known as a Short-Wright – but it took them until June 1909 to make the first plane because the engines by Bollée were delayed. Rolls only received his plane at the end of September 1909.

The following week, Rolls was in France to attend an international roads conference as a Royal Automobile Club delegate. He went with John Montagu and gave a paper on road surfaces, his last significant contribution to motoring. He managed to secure a flight with Wilbur Wright on the 8th October. Reputedly Wilbur said: 'I think I'll take you up today', and they flew for some four and a half minutes at a height of about fifty feet, covering three and a half miles at an airspeed of forty miles an hour. Sitting next to Wilbur, who wore an ordinary cap, Rolls looked as though he was out for a jaunt or off to his club in high collar, necktie and breast-pocket handkerchief. Rolls thus became the third Englishman to fly after Griffith Brewer and Dickin and he was quick to write about his experience in the Automotor Journal: 'There is nothing as fascinating or exhilarating as flying. It gives one an entirely new sense of life… the fact of accomplishing what several eminent scientists had proved impossible gives also an added satisfaction… and then almost reverently… Flying is a fresh gift from the Creator, the greatest treasure yet given to Man'.

His full reaction, and those of Griffith Brewer and Frank Hedges Butler, who were passengers with Wright on the same day, are recalled in Appendix 2.

Nowhere is Rolls recorded as being a particularly religious man but perhaps he had found his new religion.

Chapter Thirteen
Flying and Dying

Flight is freedom in its purest form,
To dance with the clouds which follow a storm;
To roll and glide, to wheel and spin,
To feel the joy that swells within.
To leave the earth with its troubles and fly,
And know the warmth of the clear spring sky;
Then back to earth at the end of the day,
Released from the tensions which melted away.
Should my end come while I am in flight,
Whether brightest day or darkest night;
Spare me no pity and shrug off the pain,
Secure in the knowledge that I'd do it again.
For each of us is created to die,
And within me I know I was born to fly.
(Gary Claude Stoker 1951)

Rolls continued to sell cars and continued to be very good at it but his attention was now elsewhere. In France, Louis Blériot's factory was turning out significant quantities of planes.

Governments were waking up to the strategic importance of aviation, and in Britain who better to develop a similar innovative, light-weight, reliable engine than Henry Royce?

However, at the time, the majority of the Board were opposed or neutral towards any engagement with aviation, even though allowed in the Memorandum of Association when the company was founded. As Commercial Managing Director, Johnson, for one, was opposed to diversification. They were onto a winner with their development of six-cylinder cars, the Silver Ghost in particular, so why risk all on a new venture? Johnson also opposed diversification because it would increase the strain on Royce.

Despite this, Rolls twice tried to bounce the company into aero engine development and twice used some of the London engineering capability without Board permission: once on work for a projected Dunne aeroplane, never fully developed and subsequently scrapped by Lord Esher's Defence Committee, and once to develop gearing for the Gamma airship, another government project. Claremont found out about Rolls's rather devious attempts and was very unhappy, but Rolls was not entirely isolated and, despite the opposition of the Board, Henry Royce's engineering curiosity had been piqued and he was complicit with Rolls on work on the Gamma airship project. They also discussed the problems of light-weight, yet reliable, aero engines.

At the same February 1909 Board meeting Rolls submitted a proposal that the company acquire the Wrights' patents. He had a close balloonatic friend, Griffith Brewer, a patent agent, who was aware of the Wrights' U.K. patents. The pace of these various discussions was frantic. According to Rolls's diary, there were eleven Rolls-Royce Board meetings in 1909 – one a month excluding August, at least one in July to be held at the Imperial in Regent Street and another marked for Manchester, although Rolls never attended the Manchester meeting. He went to France three days earlier and it is likely that he knew his aviation proposals were going to be turned down and also that he was going to get his knuckles rapped over the Gamma affair.

The Wrights had promised Rolls, when he flew with them, that they would arrange for him to be trained in France by the Comte de Lambert, their best pupil in that country[49], but this never happened and, because of a delay in delivery of the French-Wright plane that Rolls ordered in 1908, Rolls made his frustrations known when the Wrights visited England with their sister in Spring 1909. The Wrights were typically blunt: 'Buy a glider and learn the same way we did' they told him. Rolls ordered a glider from Shorts that May and it was delivered within two months[50]. Meanwhile, he waited impatiently for his plane. His diary, for a few weeks of the summer 1909, includes the following entries:-

49 *Gordon Bruce, 'Charlie Rolls – Pioneer Aviator' (Rolls-Royce Heritage Trust 1990).*

50 *ibid.*

June	Shostakovich concert, Albert Hall
30th June	Rolls-Royce Board
3rd July	Lady Jenner, 3.30 p.m. – 7.00 p.m
7th July	Lady Riddell, 65 Eaton Place
9th July	Rolls-Royce Board
10th July	Butler Cup, Ballooning at Hurlingham
24th July	Lady Jenner, 3.30 p.m. – 7.00 p.m
25th July	(Blériot flew the Channel)
30th-31st July	Sheppey (presumably gliding)
1st-2nd August	Sheppey
9th August	Leave East Cowes
16th August	Wrights at Pau
27th August	(Rolls's thirty-second birthday)
30th August	Shorts (glider trials)

The diaries present a brief insight into the hectic life of thirty-one year old Rolls at that time. Two Board meetings in a week were unusual, (one was probably an alternate date), but the many car-selling appointments, the ballooning, the start of the glider trials, the Wrights' visit and the inspection of the first airplane (minus engine, yet to be delivered) at Shorts, were typical of the pace of his life. One might also speculate on his two weekend appointments with Lady Jenner.

Rolls started gliding trials on 30th July, 1909. On the 2nd August he flew for twenty-five seconds and made a flat landing. He ordered that the wing-warping control be connected and other adjustments, including a rudder, be fitted.

During this same period, he entertained both Orville and Wilbur Wright, and their sister, Katherine, who had joined them in France. She was three years younger than Rolls, but far more at ease in social situations than her notoriously shy brothers. The French newspapers were fascinated by what they saw as the human side of the Wrights, and the contrast between the brothers and their attractive sister to whom Rolls was obviously drawn.

Rolls found time to observe the flying exhibition in Rheims. He was always cautious, but his reaction to the displays there may have made him impatient.

According to Montagu[51], Rheims and its surrounding district was suffering a champagne slump. The price of champagne had fallen to five shillings a bottle for the best, half a crown for the ordinary – whatever that was. (No other booze was available and a well-known motoring critic, Henry Knox, had to drive elsewhere for whisky.) The city fathers had first wanted a Grand Prix motor race to attract visitors to their town but the French and German car makers had not been interested and neither had the Automobile Club de France, so they settled on a flying exhibition and discovered crowds of a hundred thousand daily could be drawn by the air racing and displays.

The inaugural Gordon Bennett Air Race at Rheims was won by an American, Glenn Curtiss, in a race over twenty kilometres. A close second was Louis Blériot, much to the chagrin of the French. That chagrin that was mollified as their national hero flew the fastest lap. Champagne corks popped and the drought in demand was over. To keep things in perspective, the 47mph that Curtiss achieved in the air that day must have felt pedestrian to him. In 1907 he had driven his own-design 40hp motorcycle at 136mph to become the 'fastest man on earth', a record that stood until 1930[52].

Two native Englishmen, both resident in France, won prizes. Henri Farman took the passenger carrying prize. Hubert Latham, who had nearly pipped Blériot to be first to fly the Channel, reached an altitude of five hundred and eight feet to win the Air Show's equivalent of the high jump. None of this was without risk, they were all very brave men.

Rolls could but sit and watch. He lamented that all twenty-three aircraft flying at Rheims were French made. The Prime Minister, David Lloyd George, who also attended, echoed his thoughts: 'Flying machines are no longer toys and dreams. They are an established fact… I feel, as a Britisher, rather ashamed that we are so completely out of it'. Had H. G. Wells been with them, the seven planes aloft at one time would have vindicated his Jules Verne vision of two years earlier in *War*

---

51 *Lord Montagu, Rolls of Rolls-Royce, (Cassell 1966).*

52 *4th July, 1908, Independence Day, Glenn Curtiss flew five thousand and eighty feet to win the Scientific American Trophy and its $2,500 prize.*

Two years later in June 1910, Curtiss provided a simulated bombing demonstration for the U.S. Navy.

in the Air. Wells saw the dangers. After Blériot's Channel triumph of 25th July, he wrote scathingly about Britain's inability to defend itself against aerial invasion, and of the smug, unrealistic complacency of a nation that relied on its naval fleet to combat any new menace.

Rolls acquired his first powered plane, a two-seater Short-Wright No. 1, in October 1909. He returned home from Rheims to find it almost ready save for the Bollée engine, which was delivered shortly afterwards. The plane was a two-seater version of the machine that the Wrights had flown round Huffman Prairie in 1905. On that occasion it had been launched off a rail with the aid of a weight and catapult. The catapult had now been dispensed with, and the Bollée engine alone provided the power for take off.

Two weeks earlier, Eugene Lefebvre, chief pilot for the French-Wright company, had been killed flying. *Car Illustrated* had reported: 'Monsieur Lefebvre was testing two of the new Wright planes built in France, and when flying with one of them, at a height of about twenty to thirty feet, the machine suddenly tilted forward and came to the ground with a crash, mortally injuring the pilot, who expired a few minutes later from a fractured skull.

The reason for the machine suddenly dipping forward has not yet been ascertained, but it is thought that this was, in all probability due to the breaking of a propeller blade'.

Early flying was incredibly dangerous. Rolls made two short hops in his new plane. The first flight ended in him 'going up with a wallop and down with a thud'. The plane rose thirty feet almost vertically, stalled and fell from that height, smashing the starboard wing and each of the two propellers. During the autumn and winter of 1909, there was significant correspondence between the Wrights and Rolls. 'Your smash' wrote Orville on the 21st December, 'was due to insufficient flying speed'.

Selwyn Edge, the Australian racer, no mean risk-taker himself, wrote scathingly to the press in October 1909: 'In my opinion there has been a great deal of nonsense written and talked about the airplane business. The present position of the airplane, as we know today, is simple.

If one sold one hundred to one hundred customers and these customers seriously started to fly, using the machines anywhere except over the most carefully prepared grounds, and with the machines themselves in most perfect condition, I consider that at least half of one's customers would die within three months of the machine being delivered to them. While the possession of the airplane is such as it is – namely that if it requires an exceedingly careful and expert pilot to fly it at all and a most exceptional person to fly it safely – there is no serious commercial business in airplanes.

It may be, within a few months or even days, that a satisfactory solution would be brought before the public, but at the moment all those that are known publicly would very quickly deplete ones list of customers, if they were sold in large quanitities to the average person. There may be many purposes for which the risks are well worthwhile taking, but the ordinary person, who buys an apparatus, does not want to purchase with it, the exceedingly grave risk of a funeral.

By all means let those who have money to spare to experiment with the airplane, try and force it to the front in this new science, but do not let us humbug ourselves in believing that one can sell airplanes like bicycles or motor cars, lest one was perfectly callous of the many people to whom it would be little short of manslaughter to supply an airplane to, as at present made'.

Edge's cynicism notwithstanding, two British air shows took place that October 1909, both on the same weekend (which was foolish of someone). The Aero Club, approved Blackpool for an official meeting but not the other meeting at Doncaster. Rolls, delayed by the tardy delivery of his plane, could not compete in either. At Blackpool, Henri Farman flew forty-seven miles and won £2,000 although *Car Illustrated* described the action as uninspiring, partially due to adverse weather.

Rolls meanwhile commenced powered flight, living and making his base at Sheppey. He ate little and survived mainly on milk puddings – his eating habits were always unorthodox. The work was hard. In four days he made thirty-five launches. Each time the Flyer, which landed on skids, had to be dragged back to the launching rail, which then had to be repositioned before the next take off. Rolls's recorded his progress in copious notes, so illegible as to be almost meaningless to anyone else.

By the 22nd October he had flown two hundred and fifty yards. His progress was rapid and, on 1st November, he won £25 for Sir David Salomons's trophy for a quarter-mile out-and-back flight. This was actually by courtesy of Moore-Brabazon. Brabazon had pipped Rolls by being the first to fly a circular mile in Short-Wright No. 2 and had won a £1,000 prize from the *Daily Mail* for that achievement. Rather than antagonise his friend by winning £25 for Salomons's quarter-mile out-and-back cup as well, Brabazon delayed so that Rolls could win the trophy instead[53]. Three days later Rolls flew a circular one mile flight so the two men remained neck and neck in terms of flying achievement.

Moore-Brabazon (later Lord Brabazon) had learned to fly in France. Possibly Brabazon had fewer commitments that October and thereby progressed fractionally faster than Rolls. Or maybe Brabazon was merely braver or more foolhardy – later, at seventy years of age, he was still tobogganning the Cresta Run at St. Moritz. Rolls, unlike Brabazon, was entirely self-taught. Rolls had not mastered the banked turns and this was the cause of most of his smashes. He did not master the art until shown by the Comte de Lambert, who was to have taught Rolls the previous autumn, but had not done so. Brabazon had, in fact, been taught in France by Lambert.

In the first half of 1909 Frank McLean, another early flyer, purchased Stone Pitts Farm at Eastchurch on the Isle of Sheppey. He gave the use of the ground to members of the Aero Club for a nominal rent of one shilling a year. The first aircraft to land there, on the 20th November 1909, was a Short-Wright Flyer piloted by Rolls. Harold Ingleton, son of the previous owner, described the efforts of the well-heeled gentleman adventurers, including some serving army officers who flew from there: 'Nobody ever thought they would get off the ground long enough to get any distance. They were treated rather like people would be treated today, if they started to practise with wings attached to their arms and were determined to fly to the moon. We humoured them and at the same time earned an honest shilling out of it. If I had known these men were making history, I would have paid more attention to their doings, but as it was, we became used

53 *Years later, Rolls's sister, Georgiana, indeed gave the Salomons Trophy back to Brabazon as a gesture in thanking him for his fine sportsmanship years before.*

to their capers and crashes'. The risks were great, and also perhaps the ridicule, but so were some of the incentives. Lord Northcliffe was offering £10,000 for a London to Manchester flight with two refuelling stops. This would create an instant millionaire at today's values.

In those days, winter flying was not normally an option but, in late November 1909, Rolls flew the four miles from Leysdown, on the Sheppey coastline, to the new flying ground at Eastchurch. He landed halfway to adjust his elevator, causing some concern as to his safety. A fortnight later, he tilted on to a wing tip and repairs took two weeks. On 21st December he flew fifteen miles from the Shorts' facility at Leysdown to Eastchurch, a flight which won the attention of the national press. He ended the year with a flight of fifty-five minutes at Eastchurch and then a further flight of twenty minutes with fellow aviator, Cecil Grace, the longest passenger flight in England so far. He had joined a very select band of distance fliers: Wilbur and Orville Wright, Curtiss (twelve miles in the Gordon Bennett), Roger Sommer (two and a half hours), Hubert Latham (ninety-six and a half miles) and Henri Farman (one hundred miles plus).

His year end flight gave him the longest day's flying in the United Kingdom – longer than American, Colonel Cody's forty mile flight in September 1909 in British Army Aeroplane No. 1. Rolls was the first licensed civil aviator to train in the United Kingdom and held U.K. Pilot Licence No. 2, Brabazon holding Pilot Licence No. 1 – which went with his cherished car number plate, FLY 1.

At the start of 1910, Blériot, Voisin, Farman and the Wrights had manufactured and sold some four hundred planes between them. The Press were speculating, would the Prince of Motoring become Monarch of the Air, but Rolls himself was also wondering whether the name of Rolls might become synonymous with quality airframes, and whether he could then approach Rolls-Royce to make the engines and become their biggest customer? A second self-made fortune seemed there for the taking. Rolls's diary notes a meeting with the *Financial Times* (founded 1888). Was he looking for backers? He was well placed. He was in a position to approach Northcliffe or Briggs at Rolls-Royce or Lord Llangattock.

In March 1910, he purchased a second powered plane, a French-Wright Flyer, with a Bollée engine, originally ordered in September 1908, and then a Sommer Farman with a Gnome 7 cylinder, 60hp engine. Also that March, he bought an aircraft, Short No. 3, but there is no evidence that it flew and he advertised it for sale in May 1910. The Wrights built him two other machines but, due to the difficulties experienced in importing the French-Wright, they were obliged to sell them elsewhere, hence the delay in Rolls obtaining his plane, a delay which was thirteen months from the initial order to its delivery at the end of September 1909.

Rolls might have achieved a flight of an hour, but take offs, landings, turns and descents were (and still are) the most troublesome areas in aviation, as turns, corners or braking are for cars. What troubled Rolls was that the elevator required too much stick force. Orville could not identify the problem, and over the next three months suggested a lower lever for the elevator, fractioning the control lever and fitting a tail plane. Rolls was convinced that the centre of gravity was misplaced and added balance weights – bars weighing a few pounds, as a stop gap. This added to the overall weight and inefficiency.

Learned analysis, in later years of this generation of Wrights' planes, has shown that the centre of gravity was too far towards the rear (aft), which caused the machine to be unstable longitudinally, giving rise to undulating flight. Rolls was instinctively correct in trying to move the centre of gravity forward, but in correspondence the Wrights disagreed with him. Rolls grumbled to the Wrights and Orville gave him a £50 discount for his trouble, thus reducing the plane cost to £950. This did not prevent Rolls from selling it (Short-Wright No. 1) to the Army a few months later for the full £1,000, equivalent of what he first paid for it… still a smooth operator.

As a result of the Wrights' 'correspondence course', the English-built Short-Wright No. 1 was ready for the new season with a fixed horizontal tail of approved Wright design and manufacture, mounted behind the rudders on its own set of longerons. Rolls reported the tail plane had been entirely successful in correcting the problems of the machine's undulating flight. He also gave ground instruction on the plane, at Farnborough, to the Army in mid-June 1910, mere weeks before his crash.

Rolls was, by now, so taken up with flying that he resigned from the Royal Automobile Club. He had served for more than a decade, chairing many meetings. He also asked Rolls-Royce to relieve him of some duties. They did so willingly, but chose not to finalise things – he might be their aviation engineering consultant should they ever, eventually, diversify.

In April 1910 Rolls reluctantly took delivery of his French-Wright aeroplane. Two earlier planes had been made to his specification, but sold on to somebody else. He nearly rejected the aircraft, but Comte de Lambert, who had tested the machine, persuaded him to accept it, and it was in this machine that Rolls flew at Nice, crossed the Channel and finally flew at Bournemouth.

Rolls subsequently bought the last Short-Wright flyer No. 6 in March 1910 to replace the model sold to the Army. Within days he had flown it to one thousand feet and twenty-six miles round the Isle of Sheppey. This was, reported on the 24th March in the Times, the longest, straight, cross-country flight in England up to that time. His confidence was sky-high; he was ready to fly the Channel. He promptly advertised No. 6 for sale, having taken delivery of the much-delayed French-Wright and its better engine.

When the flying season began in early 1910, it was probably the switching of planes and the fact that he had not flown at night, which kept Rolls out of the race for the London to Manchester prize. £10,000 was an enormous sum in 1910, perhaps a million pounds today, and Rolls can scarcely have been unaware, but was not ready. The race between the winning Frenchman, Louis Paulhan, and Claude Grahame-White in April, 1910 captured the popular imagination. Tens of thousands watched the planes at take off and landing. The interim landings, allowed under the *Daily Mail* rules, brought passenger flight out of the realms of fantasy into probable reality.

In a lighter vein, flying was creating a stir in Ireland caused by no less a person than Harry Ferguson, whose name later became synonymous with the Fergie and other tractors.

He had a monoplane, and in April 1910 had managed a flight of a mile then in June he flew two and a half miles in preparation for the first aviation event in Ireland, at Newcastle, thirty miles south of Belfast. His flying was to be the centrepiece of a 'Grand Aerial Display and Sports Meeting', which eventually took place in summer 1910. This brought special excursion trains into the town in droves. Ferguson supervised the assembly of his monoplane on a hotel lawn. Prevailing south winds caused turbulence and were of little help. On one attempt, Ferguson crashed from a height of ten feet, smashing the propeller and the wheel. He tried again and exactly the same happened, and spectators on hand jeered their hero. The offer of a prize of £100 for a successful flight was left open for a month, during which time Ferguson was subject to much ribaldry, according to his biographer, Colin Fraser. He consumed three propellers, three wheels, two wings and yards of stays, and it was remarkable that he did not break his neck.

He had, however, previously been called the Mad Mechanic of Belfast, so he was fairly thick-skinned.

People wrote him sarcastic letters. One was addressed to H. Ferguson, Esquire, Aviator on the Ground and another to Lord Swank Ferguson, Bluff Aviator.

The first said: 'Who said he could fly? Who can't fly? Who shouldn't have said he could fly? Who ought to sell his aeroplane and buy a kite? Who are we sick of? Harry Ferguson'.

Another article ended with the words: 'He's not done it yet. On the first day the wind was too high, on the second the barometer was too low, on the third he could not find his flying boots and on the fourth, conditions were unfavourable and so on, but today everything seems favourable and it was reported that the wizard of the skies was getting up'. Subsequently a huge crowd collected in the paddock and an enthusiast threw his cap into the air. 'With a grave face, the aviator stepped forward: 'Gentlemen', he announced, 'I regret to state that owing to a member of the crowd having just thrown his cap up and disturbed the air currents, there will be no flights today'. Only in Ireland!

However, on 8th August, Ferguson flew three miles over the town of Newcastle and was carried back shoulder high to a dinner to collect his prize money of £100.

Legend has it that, despite several near misses and mishaps, it was his wife who prevailed upon the tractor magnate to stick to tractors![54] Nevertheless, he was one of the first British flyers, although the accolade of the first all-British powered flight went to A. V. Roe, who flew a tri-plane on Walthamstow marshes in July 1909. This was three months earlier than Rolls and Moore-Brabazon.

---

54 *'Tractor Pioneer – The Life of Harry Ferguson', Colin Fraser (Ohio University Press 1973).*

Rolls was moving towards his own aeroplane manufacture. It emerges from his extensive correspondence with the Wrights that he was happy to manufacture aircraft in Europe, incorporating their designs and his own, to sell in the United States, and he wanted their permission and co-operation. However, his faith in the Wrights' ideas was not blind, as evidenced by his Sommer Farman purchase – in the summer of 1910, there was a growing body of opinion that the Wrights' design was a dead end[55] and that the future lay in the Sommer Farman, which was a derivative of the *Voisin*, the plane originally chosen by Brabazon.

Rolls quietly considered the problems of the Wright planes about which he had learned so much. Something was wrong. Balancing weights could not possibly be right. He started his own designs, working from scratch, but he needed partners. He approached the Short brothers. He had brought them to the front of ballooning technology when the sport became fashionable and they owed him. Not only that, but Rolls, together with Griffith Brewer, had been instrumental in their involvement in the Wrights' development of their wares in England.

There is a picture of the founding fathers of the British aircraft industry in Muswell Manor on the Isle of Sheppey. It shows almost all the pioneers of aviation together for the one and only time. They include Oswald and Eustace Short and also Horace, their brother, a man with a head much larger than normal, the result of a childhood illness, which left him disfigured, but which may have explained his deification in the South Pacific. Once Oswald and Eugene realised that the aircraft industry was going to be exciting and profitable, they urged Horace to leave where he was working and join them. Versions of the story included Horace's capture by cannibals and being worshipped as their King in the South Pacific, his trekking on foot across South America and driving off blood-thirsty bandits from his silver mine in Mexico. Horace lived life to the full or had a very vivid imagination.

By April 1910, Rolls felt ready for aerial competition. He had missed the London to Manchester bonanza, won by Louis Paulhan, but had sorted out his planes. He

---

55 *No Wright Flyer featured in the first six finishers in the October 1910 Gordon Bennett race, which was held at Belmont Park, New York, U.S.A., following Curtiss's victory at Rheims. Rolls's crash had added to the doubts about the Flyer's safety.*

was renting four thousand square feet of space in two hangars at Eastchurch. He had modified Short-Wright 1 and sold it, bought Short-Wright No. 6 and had this as back-up to the French-Wright and had the Sommer Farman in reserve. He had owned several cars simultaneously in the past, but four or five planes in quick succession, including the glider, an RPG4...it was a lot to learn about. His diary for 1910 includes aero meetings in Wolverhampton (June), Bournemouth (July), Lanark (August), Cardiff (August) and Southend (August). He seldom attended Rolls-Royce Board meetings; his business post was sent to South Lodge and the telegraph address – Aerolls – reflected his all-consuming interest in aviation.

He decided to compete at Nice and dispatched the Short-Wright 6 by rail – but the French railways lost it. Ever cautious, he had also sent the new French-Wright, but it took until 16th April to bring it to a competition-ready state, which included adding a tail locally, not approved by either Wright or the Shorts. 'I am ashamed to go out without one, owing to the way the machine bucks about' Rolls told the Wrights. Was he was pushing too hard?

Despite the belated start, he won some £240 in prize money at Nice and set a record for over-sea flying – more than fifty miles of which thirty-two were non-stop, more than enough to cross the Channel. He grumbled at the Wrights about the starting rails and so wheels were to be fitted before the next meeting scheduled for Wolverhampton. Despite the newness of the plane, he entered the competition for the altitude prize and flew at seven hundred and fifty feet although this was far less than the winner's two thousand feet.

After Nice, the French-Wright went to Paris for an overhaul and was then shipped back to England, to Dover where Rolls had the Channel crossing in his sights. He was spurred on by the second successful Channel crossing by Jacques de Lesseps, whose father had supervised the construction of the Suez Canal. Rolls greeted him on arrival in England, and probably decided to attempt the first crossing from England to France immediately because it was rumoured that de Lesseps meant to try a double crossing very shortly. Rolls was ready by the 21st May, but was delayed by bad weather and mechanical problems. He kept a low profile away from the expectant press, who drifted away after a few days, so relieving the pressure to perform.

Thus few were present at 6.30 p.m. on the 2nd June, 1910 when Rolls took off for France. He wore a life jacket and the French-Wright had flotation buoys fitted and a fixed tail plane. He flew from Dover to Sangatte in France and back in ninety-five minutes, dropping a message wrapped around a coin with a ribbon attached, which read: 'Greetings to the Auto Club of France… Dropped from a Wright aeroplane crossing from England to France. C. S. Rolls, June 1910. P.S. *Vive L' Éntente*'. He dropped two identical greetings just in case any were lost.

The three notes indicated Rolls probably only intended a one-way crossing and his support team also expected this. After flying a few hundred yards into France, he decided that conditions were good so flew back to his starting point in Dover. He flew at a height of eight hundred feet, completed a victory circle of Dover Castle and landed in an army flying field. A large crowd saw him return. He later joked: 'It is the only time I have succeeded in taking ten gallons of fuel in and out of France without paying duty'.

Rolls was a national hero overnight. The new king, King George V, sent a congratulatory telegram: 'The Queen and I heartily congratulate you on your splendid Cross-Channel flight – George R.I.' Rolls received awards from both the Aero Club of England and the Aero Club of France. Statues were subsequently raised in Monmouth and Dover, and a waxwork was started in Madame Tussauds. *Motor* magazine chortled, 'Britannia Rolls the Waves' and a cartoon appeared in *John Bull* magazine. The magazine congratulated him: 'Well done my boy – you have given us the lift we sadly needed'. *Flight Magazine* boasted that he was not a competitor for the sake of 'merely winning souvenirs' and that his crossing was without 'the smallest monetary inducement'. Rolls might have been forgiven some irritation on reading this. His flying activities were costing him a fortune – £300,000 at today's prices in the six months to 1910 alone, and he was by nature rather miserly.

The French-Wright was taken to Rolls's new London base at Hounslow and Rolls next flew at Hurlingham where he had a minor accident when avoiding some trees, and a repair kit had to be sent from France. The damage was made good and a wheeled undercarriage fitted days later, in time for the Wolverhampton show at Dunstall Park, organised solely for British aviators by the newly-formed Midland Auto Club. Wolverhampton was spoilt by the weather. The *Car Magazine* reported: 'Strong winds and rain storms almost every day brought disappointment after disappointment, but it is pleasing to record that the spectators behaved in a manner that could only have been described as ideal. During the five days the crowds numbered between five and ten thousand people, but on Saturday, from three o'clock onwards, there were about fifteen thousand, and throughout the week there was no suggestion of the crowds becoming unruly. The wind was blowing 25mph-30mph. Saturday was really the great day – presumably the only day of good weather.

The Hon. C. S. Rolls on his Wright biplane won Lord Plymouth's Trophy for the fastest three circuits with fourteen minutes thirteen seconds.'

Rolls's next aviation meeting was scheduled for the 11th to 16th July, 1910, at Bournemouth, on an airfield at Christchurch, to the east of the resort. It was to be part of the town's centenary celebrations. Edward VII had died two months earlier; mourning was now over and Bournemouth was expectant. A French director was appointed to give the event some Gallic polish. There were to be masked balls, concerts conducted by luminaries such as Edward Germain (later Sir Edward) and Sir Edward Elgar with performers such as Dame Clara Butt – she of 'Land of Hope and Glory'. The band of the Coldstream Guards was booked.

The handsome Hampshire seaside resort was *'en fête'* for a fortnight. There were prizes for the best decorated hotels and houses. Everyone was involved. A motorised battle of flowers was planned, with the Lady Mayoress of London on hand to present the prizes. The Mayor summoned five hundred of the town's hoteliers to warn them against profiteering. Cooper & Co., gents outfitters, offered commemorative ties for one shilling and sixpence, and the *Bournemouth Graphic* advertised a powerful solar and terrestrial telescope at half a guinea to view both Halley's Comet and the Bournemouth aviators. Even Frank Hedges Butler, bon viveur and adventurer, must have been gleefully rubbing his hands together. His London vintners business had two out of town branches – one in Brighton and the other… in Bournemouth.

The second week was to be devoted to the air show, a flying fiesta that had attracted all the great fliers of the day from the United Kingdom, Europe and America. John, now Lord Montagu, was Chairman of the Aviation Committee for the event, and the present Lord Montagu can still recall that his father's 1899 Daimler was on prominent display.

The programme profiled all the best-known fliers and, in the light of subsequent events, what seems slightly ghoulish was the listing in the programme of the fliers, who had died up to the date of the meeting, pioneers such as Lilienthal and Pilcher and the unfortunate Lieutenant Selfridge, who had died flying with Orville Wright in America. Six fliers had indeed been killed in 1910, including the celebrated Frenchman, Léon Delagrange[56].

Among the participants were Louis Paulhan, who had won Lord Northcliffe's London to Manchester £10,000 prize in April at the expense of Claude Grahame-White, another entrant. Two former racing drivers, who had taken to the air, were Louis Wagner, a former Darracq motor racing driver – and Jean Christiaens. Past successful flyers included the French national hero, Blériot, and Glenn Curtiss, who had won the 1909 Rheims Gordon Bennett race.

W. E. McArdle and his partner, J. Armstrong Drexel, were almost local, operating a flying school at an aerodrome close to Beaulieu, and McArdle had flown their Blériot plane some twenty-eight miles to the Bournemouth meeting.

Attending as both flyers and manufacturers were Anglo-Frenchman, Henri Farman and Roger Sommer, manufacturer of planes of the same name. Hubert Latham was another popular entrant, missing out so closely in his attempt to be the first to fly the Channel days before Blériot.

There were half a dozen other participants, but although the event programme optimistically included Wilbur Wright as being in attendance – perhaps to add to the gate – the maestro did not participate.

Meanwhile, the newspapers reported another mouth-watering prize from Northcliffe's deep pocket – £10,000 for the first flyer to complete a one thousand mile circuit, encompassing London, Harrogate, Newcastle, Edinburgh, Stirling, Glasgow, Carlisle, Manchester, Bristol, Exeter, Newport, Isle of Wight, Brighton, Tunbridge Wells and returning to London. This would have been the gossip of

---

56 *Delagrange, President of the Aero Club de France, made a sensational flight in a storm at Doncaster the previous October, establishing a world record flight at that time of a monoplane in England of six miles.*

the day amongst the twenty or so aviators present – Louis Paulhan had made £1 million flying from London to Manchester, who would be next to hit the jackpot?

Rolls made five flights on the first day of the meeting, 11th July – the first three of them being, a test flight, a slow speed flight and a speed flight. He flew at nine hundred and seventy feet in the height contest – won by Drexel at nineteen hundred and fifty feet – but a lack of response from the controls worried him. He went no higher and landed. He put the hiccup as down to a gust of wind but it should have served as a warning. His final flight on the first day was in the speed category, and the day ended with him £100 richer from a slow speed contest.

Author, Gordon Bruce, has kindly permitted me to quote verbatim the configuration of Rolls's Bournemouth aeroplane from his book, *Charlie Rolls – Pioneer Aviator.*

'Initially Rolls entered his Short-Wright for the Meeting, with the Sommer as reserve, but he took the French-Wright after deciding to improve pitch control by substituting a French moving tailplane for the original Wright-approved, fixed tailplane, whose sole purpose of which had been to improve stability.

In the new configuration, the tailplane moved in harmony with the forward elevator thus giving leverage, both forward and aft; the modification had been developed without the Wrights' approval by the French-Wright Company and the Comte de Lambert and Rolls saw the device in April 1910.

The French-built moving tailplane was delivered to Bournemouth immediately before the meeting – and if a telegram from Rolls to the chauffeur, Smith, is read literally, a new elevator was also supplied.

On Sunday, 10th July the tailplane was fitted to the outriggers, previously used for the fixed tailplane; there was some difficulty in rigging it, and Rolls telegraphed to France asking for advice; the reply, timed 6.30 p.m. on Monday, 11th July, advised zero incidence on both tailplane and elevator, but that fine adjustment was not important'. A note in Rolls's Memorandum Book, 'Sell tail', probably refers to the discarded fixed tailplane.

On the standard Wright Flyer, the pilot's feet rested on a footrest, pitch was controlled by the left-hand lever connected to the canard elevator while both roll and yaw were controlled by the right-hand lever connected to the warping wing tips and the rudder.

Wilbur and Orville had their own distinctive arrangements for the right-hand lever; Rolls used the Wilbur system, but tried to obtain drawings of the Orville system.

A first photograph shows Rolls's French-Wright at Bournemouth after modification; the standard push-pull rod controlling the canard elevator from the left-hand lever and the newly installed push-pull rod operating the moving tailplane are both clearly visible.

A second photograph shows the tail of a French-Wright (but not Rolls's) modified in the same way; in plan view the outriggers, carrying the hinges of the moving tailplane, are not more than thirty inches apart in order to clear the discs of the pusher propellers so that over five feet of the span is unsupported outboard of each hinge.

A third photograph shows Rolls's French-Wright at Bournemouth in its final configuration, with the moving tailplane mounted on four outriggers surrounding the two booms carrying the rudders'.

Friends and acquaintances of the author, including a senior scheduled airline pilot, who holds a helicopter licence, and a veteran pilot who still trains airline captains in a simulator, have shuddered when they reviewed these pages. Rolls was a very talented and brave man – they all were, but when does bravery, except in wartime, become foolhardy. The angle of descent of a scheduled airliner is three degrees, for a dive-bomber fifteen to twenty degrees. Rolls's angle of descent was some thirty-five degrees to forty degrees.

Rolls was noted for his caution. He had 'wonderful hands', but was self-taught and had but a few months experience.

The engines hardly ever seemed a problem – it was the structure, the centre of gravity of the plane, for which there had been no drawings to start with, a fact which, in itself, horrified Short Brothers, when they started to manufacture to the Wright design. Rolls told a reporter before Bournemouth: 'All good engineering calls for casualties, so why not? It was once my ambition to arrive at the Golden Gate on wheels, not wings'. Had Rolls a premonition? Did he care? He had a long-term friendship with the wealthy May Harbord. He had the prospect of a massive future inheritance, the world was at his feet, so why would he take an unnecessary risk?

You could get into the event for two bob – for the cheap seats. The best seats – next to the Music Lawn – were fifteen shillings or one pound (£80 today). The Press Box was to the left of the main grandstand. Motors could be parked in the first class enclosure for ten shillings – uniformed chauffeur included – car parks further out were but two shillings.

The course was like a lopsided rectangle, as the topside was about four hundred and sixty yards, the bottom side three hundred and sixty yards and the sides about three hundred and four hundred and fifty yards respectively – a lap total of almost a mile.

If the Judges' Box is perceived to be slightly left of centre of the rectangle, the posh seats were at eight and nine o'clock respectively, the Trade and Automobile sheds were at ten, the hangars at eleven and the cheap seats at twelve o'clock. To the right the Solent stretched away to the Isle of Wight.

Rolls had also found time, while staying in the Christchurch area of Bournemouth, to send a message to the balloon factory at Farnborough authorising the sale of the Short-Wright glider.

On the following day, 12th July, saw a wind estimated at 15mph-20mph. A motoring magazine correspondent recorded gusts of up to 25mph, a lusty six on the Beaufort Scale. The wind was blowing towards the first class grandstand.

A principal feature of the day was an alighting contest in which a circle and bullseye had been marked on the ground halfway between the first-class grandstand barriers and the Judges' Box, which were some one hundred and twenty yards apart. The rules stated: 'Competitors must stop past the barrier in flight with their engines entirely stopped and on passing this line are at liberty to come to the ground before or on arriving at the target' (Royal Aero Club 1910 programme).

From contemporary photographs taken, the grandstand seems to have stood at least forty feet high and the Judges' Box slightly less. On a still day the Alighting Contest was perhaps reasonable, but on a windy day it was foolhardy. If it was the Aero Club that had set the rules, had they allowed for bad weather? It may have been up to the competitors to compete, but in golfing parlance, the pin was in the worst possible place. Dickson in his Farman alighted within a few feet of the bullseye in practice a day before, but he was not in competition, and conditions were then far calmer.

Nevertheless Rolls had the first attempt and got within twenty-six yards (for which he was posthumously awarded £25). Mr. Bertram Dickson wrecked his plane, and Grahame-White, after one attempt, thought it dangerous to continue. He protested to the judges that, with two crashes already, they should defer the event to the next day in the hope of calmer weather, and Audemars, Dickson, and Grahame-White himself had crashed in France in a similar event a few weeks earlier. The judges refused, the competitors could either fly or opt out. At this point, Frenchman, Edouard Audemars, who had already crashed, walked over to Rolls and urged him to leave any further attempts until the afternoon. It was an all-day contest on a long day in midsummer, and the competitors were allowed unlimited attempts until early evening, so why hurry?

Rolls inexplicably opted to try again, and this was uncharacteristic. *The Aero* reported a few days later (20th July): 'Rolls was always noted for the extreme care he took to guard against accidents, never taking unnecessary risks while flying, and always making sure, before starting, that everything about his machine was in perfect working order, but here we have him attempting one single dangerous feat, with one new piece of mechanism, and all his previous caution is of no more avail than if he had been one of the most reckless pilots'.

It appears that on his second attempt Rolls decided on a different tactic. He decided to meet the wind head on and touch down in the direction of the grandstand. He shook hands with Sir Thomas Lipton, and with a smile then took off at about 12.30 p.m. *Motoring Magazine* takes up the sequence of events:

'In little more than two minutes he had curved over nearly half the aerodrome inside the far pylons and was making the necessary turn behind the line of grandstands.

This was the only way open to him since he had decided to face the wind in the completion of his pre-alighting manoeuvre.

He turned gracefully and well, apparently under perfect control, at a height of some one hundred feet and brought his aeroplane round over the R.A.C. end of the stand (just adjacent to the hangars) and above the heads of those in the enclosure until it was making directly towards the point at which he aimed. Standing vertically below him (presumably in the Press stand, left of the grandstand), I instinctively realised he was keeping too high for a comfortable finishing angle. His altitude above the barrier may have been seventy feet, I believe Rolls had refrained from making an earlier alteration to the angle of descent while he was still over the enclosure and between the lines of the grandstand and the barrier, wholly out of splendid consideration for the spectators below him'.

As soon as Rolls was over the aerodrome proper, apparently he realised his mistake and started to descend sharply to achieve his angle to target'.

The correspondent continued: 'There was a sickening snap. Some part or parts of the tailplane had given way, just inside the line of the barrier – witnesses, who had a profile view, say a failure of some kind had already occurred when the biplane was over the barrier, but there was no evidence of it in the flight when viewed from below. An involuntary spasm of the nerves went through ones system and there was a thud. Rolls was down under our very eyes – it seemed but a few paces away'.

Aero Magazine continues the story:

'Then came poor Rolls. Seeing what had happened to the others, he came downwind after a left-hand turn, turned left again over the top of the stands and came on dead against the wind. When just clear of the stand, he began to dive and went over the barriers and only some forty feet over the heads of the people and evidently going to hit the ground a long way short of the target. I described yesterday the operation of the new tail of his machine. Now this tail is pivoted along its centre line and coupled to the elevator so when the back edge of the elevator falls, the front edge of the tail does the same and the front of the machine goes skyward.

Per contra, when the rear of the elevator rises, the front of the tail rises and the two acting just in the same way as the body of a swimmer, who hollows or arches his back according to whether he wishes to rise to the surface or dive under it.

Now Rolls, finding his descent too steep, pulled back his elevator lever to bring the machine's head up and make her glide further out from the enclosure. As he did so, it naturally tipped down the front edge of the tail, thus presenting almost a flat surface to the wind which pressure would, if all had gone well, have forced the machine down and the head up.

However, when the whole force of the wind came on this one surface, with its four light supports, it was asked to lift up the biplane elevator and double its area, which is carried on the main skids of the machine.

There was a large crack of broken woodwork and the tail collapsed. The wind apparently got hold of the biplane elevator, turned down to a sharper angle than ever and dived vertically for the remaining twenty feet or so.

If there had been two hundred feet instead of twenty feet, Rolls might have picked her up on the elevators alone, but he was diving at much more than his usual angle and trusting too much to his new tail, which failed him at the moment of greatest need. As it was, the elevators hit the ground vertically, crumpled up, the machine turning a somersault over them'.

Air correspondent, Harry Harper, said: 'There was a silence. The crowd seemed numb and the spell was broken only when ambulancemen ran to the wreck'. Rolls was evidently thrown clear and was not badly marked or disfigured. He survived a few seconds, but despite the efforts of two doctors giving him artificial respiration and resuscitation by ether, a minute after the arrival of the first doctor, Charles Stewart Rolls – the Prince of Motoring, national hero and heir apparent to the crown of British aviation, was dead.

The Wright Brothers gliding experiments – a picture.

The Wright Brothers gliding experiments – a photograph.

The first substantial powered flight – 17th December 1903.

Octave Chanute – an early mentor of the Wrights.

Orville Wrights's crash – the death of Lieutenant Selfridge.

The Fathers of Aviation at Muswell Manor.

A Blériot airplane.

C.S. Rolls preparing to fly the Channel.

C.S. Rolls airborne for France 1910.

Return over Dover – double crossing triumph.

Well done my boy- you have given us the lift we sadly needed.

C.S. Rolls on a launching rail.

C.S. Rolls preparing to fly.

C.S. Rolls receiving tuition from Wilbur Wright.

The Wrights flying at Pau – dawn of a new era.

Wolverhampton Flying Week.

J.T.C. Moore-Brabazon – 'Pigs really can fly'.

C.S. Rolls at Bournemouth.

Christiaens about to fly and crash.

Rolls preparing to take off at Bournemouth.

His modified French-Wright tailplane.

The Hon. C.S. Rolls in the air at Bournemouth.

Rolls's final flight… and finally

Rolls's Nemesis.

Chapter Fourteen

Aftermath

Eight months after his first powered flight, Rolls flew the Channel to France and back, returning over Dover Castle, and became a national hero. Six weeks later he became the first Englishman to die in an air crash. Thousands in Bournemouth saw his end at close quarters.

The cult of personality is not as today but the whole nation mourned. His body was returned, first to South Lodge in London and then by train to Monmouth where hundreds stood silently on the platform as the coffin was removed. Lord Llangattock's diary records: 'Funeral at Llangattock, great number of people, but saddest day of our lives'. The old man never really recovered from the death of his youngest son.

Rolls's funeral service, held at St. Cadoc's Church, Llangattock, near the family seat, was a massive, sombre yet dignified affair, made even more so by 'Peals of thunder and flakes of lightning on a scale as though orchestrated by Rolls's beloved Wagner'[57].

Further memorial services were held in London, Derby and at Eastchurch. The strands of Rolls's life, which he had kept separate – his London social and ballooning life, his motoring activities and his fatal obsession with flying – were brought together at last. In London, in the society in which Rolls moved, at concerts, in ballooning, publishing and gentlemen's clubs and, belatedly, in the corridors of military power, the loss of such a dynamic force for change and innovation was widely regretted.

In Derby, the quiet, dignified and enormously capable Henry Royce, car maker, wept openly at the service for his friend. At Eastchurch, the intrepid fliers, emerging from their sheds, bungalows and tents, mourned a flier, who, like them, had pursued a dream that many said was unachievable. Less attractively, indeed somewhat cynically, a waxwork that had been prepared by Madame Tussauds, following Rolls's Channel flight, went on public display the day after the funeral at Hendre.

---

57 *'Charlie Rolls, Pioneer Aviator – Gordon Bruce (Rolls-Royce Heritage Trust 1990).*

Moore-Brabazon, Rolls's fellow student at Cambridge and fellow flyer at Eastchurch, gave up flying after Rolls's death. He was prevailed upon to do so by his wife, who had ballooned with Rolls. She was expecting Brabazon's first child, and he gave up not only to fulfil her wishes but because 'the loss of so dear a friend had sickened me'. Brabazon had come to see flying as 'a sort of circus in which the private man had no place'. He only flew again following the outbreak of the Great War.

An article in the *Globe* of 23rd July, 1910 echoed similar thoughts: 'The world at large had not recovered from the Bournemouth catastrophe, when news came through from Cologne of a distressing accident to a dirigible balloon when five people were killed. The general feeling has gradually crystallised into belief that a science, which may be of immense material advantage to the human race, should not be cheapened by an intrusion of the circus element'.

At Monmouth, a statue proposed to celebrate his Channel flight became a memorial and is now a place of pilgrimage for Rolls-Royce enthusiasts from around the world. The unveiling was attended by thousands, who overflowed the town square. Rolls is portrayed quizzically holding a model of his biplane aloft and examining it closely, as he would have done, for faults and potential improvements. The inscription reads:

'Erected by public subscription in the memory of the Honourable Charles Stewart Rolls, third son of Lord and Lady Llangattock, as a tribute of his great achievements in motoring, ballooning and aviation. He was a pioneer in both scientific and practical motoring and aviation and the first to fly across the Channel from England to France and back without landing. He lost his life by the wrecking of his aeroplane at Bournemouth on July 12th, 1910. His death caused world-wide regret and deep national sorrow'.

Nearby, the Monmouth Museum stands quietly, containing wonderful photographs of the Hendre and of Rolls's motoring, ballooning and flying deeds.

There are other memorials. The employees at Rolls-Royce contributed to a memorial plaque for their Social Club, and much later a marble bust was commissioned and placed in the Marble Hall at Rolls-Royce, Derby. There is a monument at Dover, unveiled in April 1912 by the Duke of Argyll in the presence of Lord and Lady Llangattock, Rolls's sister, Lady Shelley, and her husband, Sir John Shelley.

Unveiling the statue, the Duke congratulated the sculptor, Lady Kathleen Scott[58], on the way in which she had portrayed his dear friend, Charles Rolls. He referred to the quiet reticence of Rolls and the modesty with which he carried out his pioneering work.

Soon after the unveiling, Lady Llangattock lost her husband and, by 1916, Charles's brothers, Henry and John, were dead. The sons were all unmarried and thus the male line of the family ended.

Lady Georgiana Shelley, lived on at South Lodge, surviving until 1961 when she left a fortune of several millions. She was known as the 'Little Old Lady of Old Kent Road' – a hark back to the original cowkeeper, John, who founded the Rolls' family fortune.

There is also a private memorial. It stood in the rose garden at the Hendre until the mid-sixties and was then removed to Rockfield Court in Gwent, the home of the Harding-Rolls, the branch of the Rolls family that succeeded the Llangattocks.

There are other reminders. After Rolls's death, the family established a commemorative coffee room, following their earlier donation of funds to provide a town hall for Bermondsey years before, a further reminder of family ties in Bermondsey, London. One-time Mayor, Henry Fuller Morriss, wrote of Charles and his brother, John, a eulogy entitled *Two Brave Brothers*, the first biography of Charles following his death. Several London place names still echo the Rolls' family connection. Streets and roads named after the family include John, Henry and Alan, while others are named Maria after the family yacht, and two more named after the Monmouthshire rivers, Monnow and Trothy.

On the Isle of Sheppey, a stained glass window, in Eastchurch Parish Church, commemorates the lives of both Rolls and Cecil Grace, who once flew together. Grace disappeared flying over the Channel in 1910, and the window was a gift from the Royal Aero Club and from Rolls's flying friends. A memorial to them was erected in 1955, opposite All Saints Church, Eastchurch.

---

58 *In a rather sad twist and unbeknown to all, Lady Scott's husband, Captain Robert Scott of the Antarctic, had already died on the 29th March, 1912, returning from the South Pole. Lady Scott did not hear of this until almost a year later.*

On the seventy-fifth anniversary of Rolls's death: 'In a heap of matchwood aeroplane'[59], a memorial was dedicated at St. Peter's School, Bournemouth, which stands on the former Bournemouth airfield and this was re-dedicated on the centenary of Rolls's death in 2010.

This memorial, in stone and slate, depicts a Wright Flyer and is quietly tucked away, close to the school field boundary. For those who visit it, it is easy to envisage the aeroplane coming in over the school buildings into the bowl, now largely built over, but still with a large playing-field area. How many pupils, one wonders, know about the many achievements of Charlie Rolls?

Perhaps the man who knew Rolls best was Claude Johnson who, in a moving personal tribute, said:

'I am writing on Wednesday, July 13th. Last Friday, July 8th, at ten in the morning, I was standing on the platform of St. Pancras Station waiting for Charlie Rolls, who was to travel with me to Derby to attend a board meeting. I had not seen him for many weeks; in fact not since the death of the late King, who died in May, when he had discussed with me the project of the cross-Channel flight. As I waited he hove in sight. I could see his brown felt hat rising and falling over the heads of lesser folk. His walk was characteristic. At each step he rose buoyantly as if he wished to leave the earth.

As he caught sight of me he displayed one of his great charms, the eager look of gladness, the quick smile showing his teeth, the cheery glint of his big eyes. If one had owed him a grudge, and no one ever did, because they never had cause to, that glance would have secured his immediate pardon.

A bicycle messenger put in his hand a heap of telegrams and letters and during the greater part of the journey there was silence while CSR wrote telegram after telegram and dispatched them at London, Bedford and Kettering.

Then at last, when he had finished reading and answering letters, we fell a-talking. 'Oh, the Channel trip was nothing, just plain, straightforward sailing' said he. 'It was nothing as compared with this aerodrome business, where the corners are sharp, the air's uncertain and at any moment one might find a sea of human heads, instead of a sea of blue water under ones feet. No, I did not fly

---

59 *Laurence Meynell, Rolls, Man of Speed (circa 1950).*

much at Wolverhampton. Oh, my engine was alright, but the weather was bad and I have no intention of risking my neck'.

Then he described to me the sense of the dive downward, with engine stopped and how every part of the plane vibrated, and he spoke with the whole thing, being alone with me, with his heart open for my inspection, with awe. There was not a note of fear, but a realisation that a man could only be a fool, who looked upon an airplane carelessly or light-heartedly.

I must own that after that conversation I was happier about his flight than I had been for months, and yesterday, Tuesday, 12th, I was lunching at a club in the City and was telling two friends of this conversation. No, I said, Charlie has no intention of doing anything foolish or unsafe. I looked upon him as one of the safest airmen of the day. Then we went out into the street. One of our party turned into the Stock Exchange, the other and I jumped into a taxi and two minutes later we were horrified, shocked, assaulted by one of the ghastly posters, which made London a city of pain and anguish to the friends of CSR throughout the day of his death. Only those who knew him intimately can realise the weight of the blow, which fell on his father and mother, when arriving at Bournemouth, they heard their son, Charlie, was gone.

In these past twenty-four hours heaps of memories of our thirteen years of close friendship have presented themselves. Charlie, the man of business, very serious, very earnest. Charlie, at the committee table, separated from his fellow committee men by an impenetrable barrier, beyond which his mind had flown to other things when tedious twaddle was the order of the day, but bright and intelligent, convinced and convincing when a committee man began to move and act. Charlie, the music lover, absorbed in listening to an orchestra pouring out the wealth of music written by the magic pen of Wagner.

Charlie, in 'overalls', tuning up a motor tricycle or struggling with a mighty racing engine, which was behaving like a naughty giant, but had to succumb to his determined and patient treatment. Charlie, driving one of those monsters, calm outside but palpably aflame within with the fires of glory of motion. Charlie, talking thousands of words a minute to a dissatisfied owner.

But the Charlie which one loved beyond all was the 'schoolboy Charlie'. Years of responsibilities never aged or dulled the splendid, boisterous, humorous, frank-hearted schoolboy that lived within the shell of a man. Something would amuse him, the corners of his mouth would twist upwards, his eyes would sparkle and the next moment, his head thrown back, his mouth wide open showing his healthy white teeth, his body contorted with merriment, there would issue from him the heartiest laugh that ever was heard. With the laugh there dropped from him all vestige of self-consciousness, the important or sedateness of his surroundings; care, worry, business did not exist. He was simply and purely the exuberant schoolboy. He would then elaborate the simple little incident, which had aroused his mirth with such extravagance, so whimsically, that in a moment, by the very infectiousness of his gaiety, he had the whole room in a roar. I have seen a deadly, dull dinner turned into a party of light-hearted laughter, when this glorious gaiety was upon him.

Dinner forgotten, the whole table full of people, who had been wiping their tears of mirth from their eyes while Charlie was working up one of his wonderful crescendos of fun. I cannot believe this fountain of laughter has dried up and we shall never hear its refreshing bubbling again.

In the case of sudden death, one's thoughts turn naturally to those to whom the one departed is most dear. Let us forgetting them for one moment, try and realise how Charlie Rolls might have ended his brilliant career and how it did end, and let us draw such comfort as we can. Adventure was his delight, especially adventure which he could discover and illustrate to the world, possibilities in the realms of mechanics of which men had not dreamed. He had genuine admiration for the prosecution of scientific research in laboratories, libraries and observatories. For the revelations of science, which most fascinated him, were the application of energy given motion to vehicles, and if the demonstration involved necessarily some risk as to his own life, it were all the more gladly undertaken.

He had risked his life and on more than one occasion had narrowly escaped losing it in motor racing, but when men began to fly, all who knew CSR knew full well that he would never be satisfied until he had become proficient to the highest possible degree in flight. He knew all the unavoidable risks and gladly met them. I am quite sure that the science and sport so fascinated him, that had he been told his life would most surely end, as it ended yesterday, he would have said, with his gallant smile 'and how could it end better?'

The end may have come sooner than he wished, but I truly believe that is the ending, which he would have chosen.

Sudden death is awful to those who witness it, especially is this so when the cause of death is novel. A fatal fall from an airplane is, at this time, far more awful to contemplate than a fatal fall from a horse.

But for the person to whom death comes suddenly, it may be a happier lot by far than others, which may come to men to whom risky adventure means the height of good living. Imagine, for example, if the fall, which killed Charlie Rolls, had crippled him for life and left him a powerless being, unable to move a limb without the aid of others.

Can one think of a more unhappy existence than that for a man to whom motion was the meaning and reason of living? Who would not have dreaded more than the coming of death, the task of breaking to CSR the news that he would never move arms or legs again?

And so, thinking unselfishly, and only of him who is gone, one is forced to the conclusion that if it were decreed that serious accident should befall him, it is better that death should gather him into his arms as he fell, than he should have suffered the despair of living the half life of the hopelessly and permanently crippled, but this consolation, such is the selfishness of our nature, only dulls a little the pain of our great loss'.

Rolls left about £30,000 in his will, including his Rolls-Royce shares. He had bought two of the original six Wright Flyers, built by Shorts, Nos. 1 and 6. He sold No. 1 to the Army just before his death – at a profit. No. 6, which he acquired as a spare, went back to the makers and was sold on to a fellow flier, Alex Ogilvie. Rolls's Sommer plane was sold privately and survived for many years, but the fate of the experimental RPG glider, developed at Shorts, is not known.

Rolls's balloon car went back to Derby and was dismantled and the chassis moved on. However, T. O. Smith, Rolls's long-term mechanic, both for cars and aeroplanes, burnt the crashed Wright Flyer to avoid it being stripped by ghoulish souvenir hunters. Since this was done at Rolls's request, one must wonder if he had some sort of premonition?

Horace Short examined the Flyer before Smith, and drew his own conclusions as to the cause of the crash, although, in those days, there was never – as today

– any official enquiry. Two proven relics have survived, firstly, an oil filter, which Rolls's long time friend, journalist and fellow Cambridge graduate, Massac Buist, somehow acquired, and, secondly, a propeller tip that was salvaged by Rolls's mechanics and given as a memento to a farmer's son who lived nearby, where Rolls's plane was to have been based for the duration of the Bournemouth meeting. The boy carved from it a World War I fighter model that was acquired by a Rolls-Royce Enthusiasts' Club member, who gave it to the Paulerspury Museum at Towcester where it remains today.

Today, Rolls lies in a grave at St. Cadoc's Church, Llangattock, next to the grave of his father. It is fitting that Lord Llangattock, once described as 'One of the cylinders of Monmouthshire', should rest with his extraordinary son, aviator, balloonist and essential co-founder of Rolls-Royce, the greatest name in British engineering, Charles Stewart Rolls, the one-time Prince of British Motoring,.

Speculation as to what Rolls might have achieved in later life is idle, but fascinating. Would his presence have secured earlier hatching of the Eagle engine – when Henry Royce finally began aero-engine design? Would he, rather than either Alcock and Brown, have been the first to fly the Atlantic in an aeroplane? He would have been just forty-two when they did so in 1919.

Eighteen months after his death, the Royal Flying Corps was formed. Rolls had previously testified to the Imperial Defence Committee and his testimony had been substantial, expert and respected. He thus would have been highly involved in the formation of the Royal Flying Corps.

Would he have flown in the Schneider Trophy? This was an annual three hundred and fifty kilometre air race for seaplanes held between 1913 and 1931. The 1919 race was, in fact, held at Bournemouth, watched by two hundred thousand spectators. Would he have won the race in 1929 in the Supermarine S6, the forerunner of the Spitfire? Would he have seen Sir Frank Whittle's 'Crazy Flying' routine at R.A.F. Hendon's Royal Air Force Display in 1930, and followed Whittle's development of jet propulsion.

As an old man, would Rolls have witnessed the first man in space, Yuri Gagarin, in 1961; by then Rolls would have been eighty-four, and would he have been surprised when Gagarin died just two years later at a similar age – thirty-four – in a mysterious flying accident?

Returning to Rolls-Royce and Rolls's place within it, it was Laurence Meynell[3], who summed up the partnership so elegantly:

'I see two ghosts, Royce, quiet, dignified, enormously capable, the engineer of genius… and the younger man, bubbling over with the zest of energy and movement; fascinated by the idea of speed, impatient of fools, radiant with the excitement and idealism of youth – Charles Stewart Rolls… and I think here was a man born to fortune and, who by his own efforts and the quality of his character, achieved fame. Not many men do as much and no man can do more'.

In short, Charles Stewart Rolls was a man for the times, a man of the times, and a man whose achievements in those times should long be remembered.

Rolls's memorial at Dover.

Two Brave Brothers, Charles and John and their father.

St Cadoc's Church where Rolls is buried.

Memorial at Derby Works.

Memorial on the Bournemouth airfield, now St. Peters School.

The Rolls statue in Monmouth.

The many faces of C.S. Rolls.

Dramatis Personnae

Gordon Bennett

Ernest Claremont

Selwyn Edge

Henry Edmunds

Harry Ferguson

Frank Hedges Butler

Charles Jarrott

Claude Goodman Johnson

John Douglas-Scott-Montagu

Moore-Brabazon, J.T.C.

Alfred Harmsworth (Lord Northcliffe)

Sir Frederick Henry Royce

Sir David Salomons

Frederick Simms

Charles Sykes

Orville and Wilbur Wright

James Gordon Bennett Junior (1841-1918)

James Gordon Bennett Junior was the son of the founder of *The New York Herald*. His father founded that paper in 1835 and it became the chief newspaper in New York much to the chagrin of other newspaper magnates.

Bennett inherited the paper and continued to flourish, adopting a playboy lifestyle, but living most of the time in France. He was flamboyant. As early as 1877, the trousseau of one early fiancée amounted to $20,000. But he blotted his copybook at a New Year's party, held by her parents, mistaking the fireplace for a toilet (some say a grand piano!) and his engagement to Miss Caroline May was subsequently broken off. He did not marry for a further thirty-seven years.

It was Bennett's father, James Gordon Bennett Senior, who had ordered Henry Morton Stanley to go and find Doctor Livingstone in Africa, giving rise to the famous phrase 'Doctor Livingstone I presume'.

It was Bennett Junior who (finally) ordered one of his journalists to go to Kitty Hawk and verify that the Wrights had achieved powered flight – at a time when the French authorities were alleging that the Wrights had not done what they had claimed.

Like his fellow newspaper tycoon, Alfred Harmsworth, he sponsored international motor, balloon and aeroplane racing. One peculiarity of these contests was that the winning country should host the following year's competition, which caused the 1903 Gordon Bennett motor race to be held in Ireland, following Selwyn Edge's victory in 1902, even though there was a 20mph speed limit in the United Kingdom. This was temporarily suspended for the 1903 Irish event.

Despite his many excesses, Bennett lived until 1918, running his business from his yacht, *The Lysistrata*, in Europe. Whether Gordon Bennett ever met Rolls is unknown, but it is likely that Bennett would have been present at the French Gordon Bennett motor race in 1905, in which Rolls finished in eighth place .

Ernest A. Claremont (1863-1922)

Ernest Alexander Claremont has been described as the quiet hand behind the Rolls-Royce company success. He was the only partner Henry Royce ever had.

The son of a doctor, Claremont was privately educated and attended university but never completed his studies. He became an apprentice and met Henry Edmunds while working in London, and probably met Royce at about the same time at evening classes, where they became equally qualified as electrical engineers. Royce was 'Fred' to Claremont throughout his life, and Claremont was the only man who could get Fred to change his mind if Royce was set on something. Royce thought up ideas, giving vent to his genius, while Claremont paid the wages and ran the administration and sales side of the business. Claremont had an ally in his brother, a London solicitor, who gave sound legal advice as the complexity of the businesses grew.

Royce and Claremont shared accommodation at Cooke Street, Manchester, in the very early days of the business, which they formed in 1884, together with an outside director and the two Punt sisters, who married Claremont and Royce. They rigged up hammocks and cooked their meals in enamelling ovens, the cause of gastric troubles that both suffered from later. In 1888 Claremont bought a house in anticipation of marriage. The business became a limited company in 1894.

Claremont was slight and dapper. He was proud of his appearance and had a barber come in daily. He played tennis and polo, shot and employed a professional wrestling partner/trainer. He cut a gentle dash in Manchester society and night-life. Apparently his wife and her sister abhorred the physical side of life and wanted no children. Claremont was frequently absent from home and had at least one long-term relationship. He and his wife separated in 1906.

In 1900 he became involved in Glovers, the cable makers, becoming Managing Director three years later. He met Edmunds and exchanged shares, Edmunds becoming a shareholder in Royce Ltd and Claremont a shareholder in Glovers. Claremont once locked out the workforce and, in doing so, won a pay battle. The introduction of a mongoose to the works to kill rats was less successful, as not knowing what a mongoose was, one of his workers killed it!

He hedged his bets when the car saga started, spending a lot of time at Glovers and his questioning of the wisdom of the venture is probably the reason he did not attend the historic meeting between Edmunds, Rolls and Royce in 1904.

The story of his ownership of one of the first Royce cars is legendary – 'If the car breaks down, please do not ask a lot of silly questions' was written on a plate attached to his car's dashboard. Indeed Claremont would send a telegram to Royce at the works to announce that the car had stopped at such a place on such a road, where it had been left all night, for the Works to collect.

The car side of Royce Ltd. became Rolls-Royce in early 1906. Royce Ltd. remained an independent business for many years after, with F. H. Royce still fully involved. In early 1907, Rolls-Royce acquired C. S. Rolls & Co. in exchange for shares, negotiated on Rolls's behalf by his father Lord Llangattock while Rolls was away in America. Claremont steered the company through its absorption of C. S. Rolls & Co., and earlier he and Claude Johnson had organised a difficult public flotation in 1906 due to doubts about the car industry at that time. They were bailed out at the last minute, when they were below the minimum subscription, by Arthur Briggs, a satisfied customer, who became a substantial shareholder and director.

Claremont did not move to Derby. His loyalties were split between Royce and Glovers. He went along with the one car decision instigated by Johnson because Royce did not demur, only Rolls being concerned at the policy, and he was vindicated by the very steady rise in the profits of the firm in the Silver Ghost period from 1907 up to the outbreak of the Great War.

He was appreciative of Johnson's albeit commercial concern for Royce: 'I dread the strain on Fred'. Once Royce was away from the factory and only one model was being produced, Claremont was far happier. He later defended the company against a hostile takeover from Max Aitken (later Lord Beaverbrook).

When he died in 1922, his will revealed that he was living in the same house with Clara Jane McKnight, who was at one time his private secretary. He made the same provision for her in his will as with his real wife, whom he never divorced, and left an estate equivalent to £2 million today.

'Apart from his steady hand at Rolls-Royce Ltd[60]., Claremont's greatest contribution to the success of the huge concern was his financial management at Royce Ltd. By building this up into a very large company, he provided the financial strength that supported the early car work ('the two guinea an ounce job')'. That he was, at the early outset, doubtful about the new direction of Rolls-Royce Ltd., is clear. Nevertheless he made it possible and lived to see his first fears wholly dispelled as the company moved into a pre-eminent position.'

Selwyn Francis Edge (1868-1940)

Rolls, Charles Jarrott and Edge represented the pinnacle of Victorian and Edwardian motoring. All three were involved in the motor trade and all saw racing as a way to build a car's reputation.

Selwyn Edge found Napier three or four years before Rolls found Royce, and had the roles been reversed – who knows?

As an Australian, Edge came to London as a child and, by the age of nineteen, he was winning cycle races and managing the Dunlop offices in London. An imposing moustachioed figure, he was well-known for his cycling exploits. One evening in 1899, he, Jarrott and J. W. Stocks were together at the Drury Lane Theatre. Stocks had been persuaded to stay on in London to see the show but had to return to Birmingham for a business appointment the following day. He was due to ride a hundred and ten odd miles back to Birmingham in the dark and Edge and Jarrott agreed to accompany him part of the way – in 18 degrees of frost. They cycled with him for fifty miles, then bade him 'God Speed' and rode back in London, arriving at 7.00 a.m. in time for some much needed breakfast and a hot bath!

He bought his first car when he was twenty-one and went into partnership with Jarrott importing De Dion Bouton cars. With Harvey du Cros, who had bought the Dunlop patents, they went on to form a company to sell Napiers, Gladiators and Clement Panhards.

---

60 *'A Manchester Life with Rolls-Royce and W. T. Glover & Co.- Tom C. Clarke (Hulme Press 1995).*

Edge was runner up to Charlie Rolls in the Thousand Mile Trial driving a four-cylinder Napier borrowed from magistrate, Edward Kennard. He entered the Napier in the Paris/Toulouse race of 1900 and asked Rolls to act as his mechanic. Rolls agreed but only after receiving strict instructions from his mother, Lady Llangattock, 'not to bring his young life to a sudden end'. They retired due to ignition problems. With the help of another high-profile motorist, Montague Napier, acting as his mechanic, he drove in the 1901 Gordon Bennett Cup but was disqualified for having French tyres when the rules demanded that the car be all-British. He put things right the next year when he was the only finisher, and so captured the Cup.

He drove, but fortunately only as an observer in the Race to Death in May 1903 from Paris to Madrid, which was stopped at Bordeaux. All the other cars had to be returned to Paris by train, but Edge was able to retrace the route of the race and saw for himself the horrors that brought an end to inter-city racing. Shortly after, he entered an 80hp Napier in the 1903 Gordon Bennett, but was again disqualified and he fared no better in the 1904 race in Germany.

He promoted, as his protégé, Dorothy Levitt, who became known as the 'Fastest Girl in the World' and they were probably an item at some stage.

In 1907, following the opening of the Brooklands track, Napier entered three cars for a twenty-four hour record attempt, and Edge drove one of them one thousand five hundred and eighty-two miles miles at an average speed of 66 mph. The other two Napier cars did almost as well. The track was lit by lanterns every ten yards or so over the entire two and three-quarter miles of the circuit. In 1922, fifteen years after the epic drive at Brooklands, Edge replicated the feat in a double twelve-hour world record, covering one thousand seven hundred and eighty-two miles at an average speed of 74 mph in two twelve-hour stints on successive days. He was fifty-four years old. He also raced motor boats.

In 1912, he sold his company to Napier for £120,000, about £6 million today. He was not to partake in the motor industry for seven years, but when the restraint was over he started to build up a share in AC Cars, which proved a mistake, because he paid a fortune for it and it collapsed in 1929.

Edge wrote many letters concerning various subjects (including his correspondence regarding the 'Battle of the Cylinders') to the trade press.

He knew there was an opening for British-built cars along the lines of a Panhard. Having been introduced to Montague Napier, he initially drove a Panhard for long distances in order to identify its strengths and weaknesses for Napier. Of Napier himself he said: 'I am now convinced that in Napier I had the good fortune to alight on a motor engineer of outstanding ability. I saw no reason why he should not design and produce a British car, which would be second to none in the world'.

In 1908 Edge wrote to *The Times*: 'The views, which have been so well expressed in your columns with regard to the danger of motor racing, have interested and impressed me greatly. As one who was responsible for most of the racing in this country, I think it might perhaps be my duty, in deference to public feeling, to be the first manufacturer to publicly announce my intention of withdrawing Napier cars from all dangerous competition'. Rolls-Royce had not raced after 1906 despite entering a car for the 1907 Tourist Trophy race. Previously Edge had already written to *The Times*: 'The cost of motor racing is an expensive game of which manufacturers are getting tired'.

There was great rivalry between Napier and Rolls-Royce. By 1911 the Silver Ghost looked better than the Napiers. Napier cars rattled and some people questioned whether it was right to pay more for a Napier than a Rolls-Royce and then drive around with the same radiator on an expensive car as on a Napier lorry or a Napier taxi. Edge and Napier began to have differences. Napier was losing interest in what he was doing and was more interested in his own finances than in those of the company. Napier began to sell cars on his own account. Meanwhile Napier's top designer left to work for Rolls-Royce.

Edge said of the pioneer days: 'They were hard days truly, but their hardness and the overcoming of difficulties produce a feeling of triumph, which is as hard to appreciate today as it is to describe'.

Edge's book, *My Motoring Reminiscences*, has no index, but Edge devotes two pages to C. S. Rolls: 'C. S. Rolls's enthusiasm for everything mechanical and electrical was without limit. Racing, speed and daring was in his very blood for he was one of the first to take up aviation… and only one year after Blériot flew the Channel, Rolls made the double journey from Dover to France and back. Rolls had absolutely no sense of fear or danger whether he was up in a balloon, which was one of his hobbies or in an airplane or driving a racing car.

Rolls was one of the keenest motorists I have ever known and his one thought was the internal combustion engine in one form or another and he was also an excellent motor racing driver, although inclined if anything to be too reckless and never sparing of his car. In the early days he loved to carry out all the repairs to his cars himself. His appearance on such occasions defies description.'

Edge describes a drive by Rolls, St. John Nixon and himself, when they set off to Birmingham one evening in the summer of 1900, when Edge let his new Napier have her head and Rolls's enthusiasm knew no bounds:

'We put up at Towcester for the night, and he anxiously enquired whether Napier and I had any thought of making a car of double the power'.

'Rolls,' he wrote, 'was an exceedingly nice fellow and a great sportsman'.

Following his retirement from the motor industry, Edge farmed for eleven years until his death in 1940.

Henry Edmunds (1853-1927)

Henry Edmunds, son of an ironmonger, was born in Halifax., two years after the Crystal Palace Great Exhibition of 1851, which trumpeted the country's industrial prowess. He was involved in innovation throughout his business career. He met Thomas Edison in America, and on the ship back, regaled passengers with stories of the first talking machine and rigged up a telephone and talked to passengers from either end of the ship.

At an early stage in his life, Edmunds acquired the agency for what became known as the phonograph (later the gramophone), which he demonstrated in the U.K. His business partner, Mr. Sidney Morse, demonstrated it before Queen Victoria in August 1888 at Balmoral. She recorded her voice on a cylinder, although he was told not to exhibit this round the country. No one knows where this cylinder is today. The next recording by a reigning monarch was thirty-five years later by King George V.

Other products with which Edmunds was associated were a non-skidder for motor buses, a detachable wheel rim, a repair kit, a tyre kit, a spare wheel carrier and a carbon-dioxide car inflator.

Henry Edmunds became a director of W. T. Glover, a leading national supplier of cables, in 1886, and over the next three years invested some £6,000 (£600,000 today). The company was substantially involved in Manchester business around the time of completion of the Manchester Ship Canal. This brought Edmunds into contact with Royce Ltd and its electrical products and electric cranes, and around 1899, he became a shareholder in Royce Ltd. and also a director.

An early motoring enthusiast, he bought a Coventry-built Daimler, which he called Rhoda, this being before the advent of car number plates. He took part in the Thousand Mile Trial, became a member of A.C.G.B.I. and presented it with the Automobile Club Hill Climbing Trophy, better known as the Henry Edmunds Hill Climb Trophy, now in the National Motor Museum.

Edmunds also had involvement with Harry Parsons in a company called Parsons Ltd., which continued trading until the current day and was bought by the Chinese in 2007. One of the earlier motoring problems was sideslip, and the Automobile Club (A.C.G.B.I.) arranged for anti-skid trials to address the problem. Fortunately for Edmunds and Henry Royce, the trials were deferred at least twice. By the time they were announced for April/May 1904 Edmunds, by then an investor in Royce Ltd., knew of the new Royce car.

It was Edmunds who persuaded an unenthusiastic Rolls to go north and meet Henry Royce. His persistence and his supply of drawings of the little two-cylinder car were the determining factors.

Parsons' non-skidder tyres had made no great impact in an early trial in France, but certainly did so at the A.C.G.B.I. Sideslip Trial, which included an endurance test over a thousand miles. Each car had an official observer on board to see that no repairs were made (*Automobile Club Journal*). It is thought that Edmunds drove, accompanied by Massac Buist, a Cambridge University colleague of Rolls, and a motoring journalist.

He was in New York when Rolls died: 'While walking near Central Park I heard the newsboy shouting Fatal Accident to Well-Known English Aviator', and then realised that Rolls's plane had crashed at Bournemouth.

Edmunds's last commercial venture, known as the cameograph, proved to be his downfall. It was a photo sculptor and its subjects included Stanley Baldwin, George Bernard Shaw and Mary Pickford. It was not a commercial success. By the time Edmunds died in 1927, his last venture had cost him some £66,000 and most of his personal fortune.

Sadly, his funeral was not attended by anyone from Rolls-Royce; both Claremont and Johnson having died in the previous five years and Royce, by then, was a semi-invalid, living in France. It is possible that none of the remaining Rolls-Royce directors in Derby were aware of the significance to their company of the death of an old man in Hove.

Edmunds enjoyed life to the full and would do almost anything as long as there was some new experience in it. He went on a New York sightseeing trip that included crossing the unfinished Brooklyn Bridge on a workmen's catwalk. He registered a hundred and fifty patents, although none were widely adopted or developed further. Among his friends were: Thomas Edison, Alexander Graham Bell, Henry Royce, Claude Johnson and Charlie Rolls.

He deserves his tribute in motoring history as the Godfather of Rolls-Royce.

Henry George (Harry) Ferguson (1884-1960)

It is little known that Harry Ferguson was the first Briton to build and fly his own aeroplane, ahead of both Rolls and Moore-Brabazon. It was a monoplane, reminiscent of a Blériot with an eight cylinder, air-cooled, 35hp engine, and flew in December 1909.

He worked with his brother in a company called J. B. Ferguson & Co., which sold and serviced motor cars, despite the company being turned down by a bank, which said: 'There is no future for automobiles'.

He attended aviation meetings in Rheims and Blackpool and then decided to build his own aeroplane with the intention of flying the Irish Sea. After many disastrous attempts at Magilligan Strand in Northern Ireland, he flew three miles three weeks after Rolls's death to win a £100 prize. Perhaps mindful of what had happened to Rolls, his wife persuaded him never to fly again. He was quoted as saying: 'The aeroplane sometimes turns a half-somersault after landing or rather falling. Had it not been for the design of the machine, I would have assured that I would have been killed on many different occasions'.

Later in his life, Ferguson was to strike an extraordinary deal with Henry Ford on a joint project for the production of tractors, without the obfuscation of accountants and lawyers, whereby they agreed to co-operate, an understanding that lasted for many years. They had ploughed a furrow each in a field at Deerborn in America and sat down and discussed the deal over a table, taken from the boot of Henry Ford's car.

In 1952 Ferguson agreed to merge his tractor interests with Massey-Harris. He wanted $17 million but Massey-Harris was only prepared to offer $16 million. Negotiations were taking place at the picturesque Lygon Arms at Broadway, Worcestershire. Ferguson said: 'Gentlemen, let's stop haggling about it... In Ireland we have a way of dealing with this... I suggest we toss for it'. Outside in the street, once the consternation amongst the Massey-Harris team had subsided, the toss was made – and Ferguson lost. Ferguson asked for half a crown and they tossed again. Ferguson won. Subsequently the Massey-Harris team had the coin mounted on a silver cigar box inscribed with the words 'A one million dollar coin' and engraved under it 'To our friend and partner, Harry Ferguson... a gallant sportsman!'

Even today, many Welsh hill farmers call their tractors 'Fergies'.

Frank Hedges Butler (1855-1928)

Frank Hedges Butler was born within the sound of Bow Bells in London. His family firm of vintners was founded in 1667, which may have added to his joviality. Part of the family fortune perhaps was based on the following order:-

For the Coronation dinner of His Majesty King George IV:

Sherry and Port	*150 dozen bottles*
Claret	*200 dozen bottles*
Champagne	*100 dozen bottles*
Burgundy	*20 dozen bottles*
Hoch	*50 dozen bottles*
Moselle	*50 dozen bottles*

Some party!

Hedges Butler travelled in Europe and America before the age of twenty-one, visiting Niagara Falls and later travelled to the West Indies, to Venezuela, Italy, Jerusalem, the Dead Sea, India, Ceylon and travelled via Peshawar to the Khyber Pass. His description of the making of port wine in the Douro gives a sense of his love of life:

'As soon as the vat, which holds the equivalent of more than twenty thousand bottles, had been filled with bunches of grapes, twenty men stepped in and began singing and playing guitars and fiddles. They paddled around, gradually sinking lower and lower in the liquid with their naked legs until the whole of the juice was compressed from the fruit. When the performance was at an end, we lunched off a splendid suckling pig, cooked in the earth with wood, the great dish of the Portuguese farmer...'

With his daughter he saw the Paris/Marseilles race pass through the Beaune region of France in 1896. It was their first experience of motoring, and subsequently Hedges Butler purchased a very early Benz that cost him £120, purchased from Henry Hewetson. Motoring was a pleasure:

'What we enjoyed most was pushing the cars up the hills so that when we did go down the other side we had the satisfaction of pleasure well-earned.

We never started without taking provisions in the car to the extent of at least a box of Bath Oliver biscuits and one or two bottles of dry sherry. It was also necessary to have a bag for a night's lodgings because one never knew what time one was going to arrive at the destination. The tramp on the road was a useful individual and many times earned sixpence or more by fetching water from a mile away to put into the car'.

Hedges Butler called his first car *Eve*. He completed the Thousand Mile Trial with his daughter, Vera. In the following year, after a car breakdown, he, Rolls and Vera decided to make an ascent in the balloon *The City of York*. During the two hour flight in the air over London, they decided to form the Aero Club. Claude Johnson was its first secretary. At that time there was no body of oversight for British flying so the Aero Club, by default, became the early British aviation's equivalent of the Jockey Club. The Aero Club issued pilots certificates – Moore-Brabazon had the first, Rolls the second. Hedges Butler in his memoirs[61] described how the opportunity was soon grasped by the committee of the Aero Club, which looked to control the science and sport of all balloons, dirigibles and aeroplanes and so forth which, with the aid of the light petrol engines, seemed certain to become a means of locomotion.

He became a ballooning enthusiast. At one time, he held the record for the longest balloon flight ever, for a flight from London across the Channel to Caen in Normandy in 1902. Although he realised the potential of the new wonder of the age, ballooning was always for the joy of it. On one occasion, ballooning with Charles Rolls: 'We were a merry party and Mr. Rolls, during the voyage, entertained us with tunes on the penny whistle'. Justifying his reputation for bonhomie one Hedges Butler balloon was called 'Dolce far Niente', which translated means 'Sweet Idleness'.

Despite Rolls's association with his daughter Vera, Hedges Butler maintained cordial relations with him as they made many flights together, including that in the Ville de Paris, but there was some dissension as to who should take the credit for forming the Aero Club.

Charles Jarrott (1877-1944)

Charles Jarrott was born in Pimlico, London in the same year as Charles Rolls. Son of a blacksmith, he was at school in London and Cambridge then became articled to a firm of solicitors, but soon gave it up to embrace the motoring movement. He became Britain's most successful continental road racer until his retirement in 1906.

He visited the U.S.A. as a young man, and his considerable talents were recognised by Harvey du Cros, who had bought the Dunlop patents. Jarrott lodged with S. F. Edge, the Australian, and they progressed in racing together.

At the age of twenty-seven he founded Charles Jarrott and Letts, who were agents for the de Dietrich cars, and also for Oldsmobile.

61 *Fifty Years of Travel by Land, Water and Air, Frank Hedges Butler (T. Fisher Unwin 1920).*

Jarrott won a motorcar five mile championship on a de Dion tricycle in 1899, and took part in many events including a match with the famous trotting horse, Gold Ring, which he beat easily. He came tenth in the Paris/Berlin race of 1902 when he drove a 40hp Panhard and finished second in the Circuit de Nord race in 1902. He was a competitor in Paris/Vienna, finishing twelfth in class after many misfortunes. He then won the six lap, three hundred and twenty-one mile Circuit des Ardennes in 1902, averaging 54mph. Weeks later he beat the kilometre record at the Welbeck track, his time being 28.2 seconds or 78mph. He drove a 40hp Napier car in the 1903 Gordon Bennett race and despite having been reported killed, and covered under a white sheet, as if dead, survived!

He started first out of two hundred competitors, in the Race to Death, Paris/ Madrid, and was third of the big cars to arrive in Bordeaux. One of his team mates, Lorraine Barrow, was killed in the race and another, Philip Stead, badly injured.

Later he became manager of the de Dion Bouton and Panhard businesses in the United Kingdom and also Chairman of the Automobile Association.

During World War I he was placed in charge of mechanical transport for the Royal Flying Corps and subsequently the Royal Air Force where he served with distinction.

He then became General Secretary of the Royal Society of St. George. He held this post until his death at the age of sixty-seven.

When he raced at Brooklands, he realised that it was not so much motor racing which appealed to him, but the road. He wrote arguably the best book ever on early motoring (*10 Years of Motor and Motoring 1896-1906*): 'In the memory of those long white roads, with their never-ending fringe of lofty trees flashing by with dazzling rapidity; the roar and stress of the wind intermingled with the hiss and spit of the engine; the flying kilometre stands and the rapidly approaching goal – I long even now for the possibilities of the past and living again of all that I went through. It is all gone and finished; but I would not exchange my memories with any man, whatever his experience and in whatever sport'.

Claude Goodman Johnson (1864-1926)

The extraordinary career of Claude Johnson weaved its way in and out of the life of Charles Rolls, from the time they met in the early days of the A.C.G.B.I. (The Automobile Club) until Rolls's death in 1910.

Following his early success at the Imperial Institute and his imaginative secretaryship of the Automobile Club, it was clear that Johnson was destined for higher things. He created a good social atmosphere in the Club and, despite his modest background, mixed easily with the members. He both drove in and organised the Thousand Mile Trial, an extraordinary feat of administration and endurance. He was thirty-six at the time and into his third year as secretary of the Club that he was to serve for another three years. By this time he had developed a taste for the finer things in life, perhaps as a form of compensation for his home life, which was sad. His first wife lost five children in infancy, only one surviving to adulthood. He married for a second time in later life and had a second daughter.

In 1903 he joined Paris Singer in an electric brougham venture, but soon after, following discussions with his close friend, Alfred Harmsworth, he joined C. S. Rolls & Co. His timing was perfect. This was just a few months before Rolls met Royce. Johnson had the administrative ability to organise Rolls, whose many interests sometimes kept him over-busy.

Having been appointed Commercial Managing Director of Rolls-Royce Ltd. in 1906, under the chairmanship of Ernest Claremont (who had substantial duties elsewhere), Johnson steered the company through a period of substantial growth, until a second tier of superbly qualified engineers, in the mould of Henry Royce, had matured and could take the company forward.

Johnson nicknamed himself 'The Hyphen in Rolls-Royce', and coined the phrase 'Silver Ghost' when the six-cylinder super-car emerged. A cultured man, he enjoyed art and music but also found time to fish for trout and salmon. He spent much of his time with Henry Royce, and conceived the idea that Royce – the principal asset of the company – would be more productive away from the company works, working with his own personal design team around him.

One of Johnson's few failures was that he was unable to dislodge the British Royal family from their allegiance to the Daimler marque, which Johnson christened 'The Unmentionable Car'.

It was Johnson, who threw out the challenge of a non-stop reliability run of fifteen thousand miles, which was effectively an attack on the world record of seven thousand and eighty-nine miles, previously held by Siddeley.

The Rolls-Royce team of drivers drove the Silver Ghost non-stop between London and Glasgow until fifteen thousand miles had been completed. There was one early hiccup around six hundred and sixty-nine miles, then fourteen thousand three hundred and thirty-one miles were covered without any further involuntary stops. Johnson then invited the R.A.C. to strip the car down and recommend the replacement of any worn parts – at a cost of a mere £2 2s 7d (equivalent to £200 today). The monied aristocracy market, which Claude Johnson was aiming for, liked value for money, and this trial proved beyond doubt that the Rolls-Royce was very special – silent, efficient, cost-effective – 'The Best Car in the World'.

It was Johnson who conceived the idea of a Rolls-Royce mascot, 'The Spirit of Ecstasy', after seeing a statue of Nike at the Louvre in Paris. Johnson developed the idea in conjunction with the sculptor, Charles Sykes.

His other achievements included master-minding (with Royce) the move from Manchester to the factory at Derby.

Johnson was in his element with difficult characters, including Alfred Harmsworth (Lord Northcliffe from 1905), with whom he became a close friend. He used Harmsworth's massive media presence to enhance the reputation of Rolls-Royce Ltd.

It was Johnson who probably persuaded Rolls to go to North America in late 1906 to race and see Wilbur Wright. He had the sensitivity to appreciate that Rolls was somewhat disappointed with the company's monumental decision to adopt a one car policy.

He paid a very generous tribute to Charles Rolls, included in the final chapter of this book, and it was as a result of his close friendship with Rudyard Kipling, whom he had met at the Automobile Club, that Kipling wrote a fitting tribute to Johnson: 'To the memory of Claude Johnson, joint founder and Managing

Director of Rolls-Royce Ltd. from its inception in 1906 until the date of his death on April 11th, 1926… He had the imagination to foresee and the energy to meet the needs of his country, both on land and in the air, and his ideals are reflected in all his work'.

Claude Goodman Johnson died of pneumonia in 1926. The man who had organised so many exhibitions and extravaganzas in his life, had the simplest of funerals. He was cremated at Golders Green on the 18th April, 1926. There were no flowers, and only his brother, Basil, later Managing Director of Rolls-Royce, attended.

John Douglas-Scott-Montagu, M.P. Second Baron Montagu of Beaulieu (1866-1929)

John Montagu was the son of the first Baron Montagu of Beaulieu and became the second Baron in 1905. He was educated at Eton and Oxford and, after leaving university where he was a keen rower, he became a practical engineer. He worked for the London and South-Western Railway and later put this railway talent to use, driving trains during the General Strike of 1926.

He served two terms as M.P. for the New Forest, being first elected in 1895. In the following election of 1900, he made great play of his use of a car for electioneering. He could attend several meetings in one day, a significant advantage over his rivals. He gave up his parliamentary seat in 1905 upon elevation to the House of Lords. He was an energetic and practical man and loved to supervise his magnificent estate at Beaulieu, christened 'A Little Kingdom in the Forest' by biographer, Paul Tritton[62], as if demands of life as an M.P., and later a publisher, were not enough.

A central early member of the Royal Automobile Club, John Montagu took part in the Thousand Mile Trial, raced in Europe with Rolls as early as 1899 and founded *Car Illustrated* (1902). Claude Johnson and Charlie Rolls were fortunate to be forming their new partnership when *Car Illustrated* was starting publication. Montagu wanted an upmarket, splendidly illustrated and photograph-packed

62 *'John Montagu of Beaulieu', Paul Tritton (Montagu Ventures Ltd., 1985).*

magazine and so it became. He knew that he could count on Rolls. J. T. C. Moore-Brabazon, the novelist, Mary Kennard, and others to contribute. The magazine contained descriptions of elegant houses, their owners and their cars, and this was just what Rolls, in his turn, needed to sell cars in general and later Rolls-Royce cars in particular. Montagu edited and owned *Car Illustrated* up until the Great War.

When Rolls and others began to make ballooning fashionable, the new sport became a source of glamorous additional material in *Car Illustrated*, as did powered flight when its time came. Glamour came in various shapes and sizes, the first issue of the magazine in 1902, included an article: 'The Car made its curtsey to the public' and Montagu achieved a coup by driving the new King round the Beaulieu estate with a picture of their drive together gracing the cover. On another occasion, however, Montagu and the monarch fell foul of a recalcitrant tollkeeper at Lymington. The tollkeeper, robbed of a toll early in the day, had shut the gate in protest. 'King, or no King', he declared to the duo, 'who was it who rushed my bridge?' Only after a few grumbles and payment of the fee, did he let the King pass…

Montagu married Lady Cecilia Kerr in 1889. She died in 1919 and bore him two children, Helen in 1890, who became an actress and was a disappointment to the couple, and another daughter, Elizabeth, in 1909.

Montagu was a visionary of motoring, he proposed motorways back in the 1920s, and he was the prime mover in the passage of the 1903 Motor Car Act. This increased the speed limit from 12mph to 20mph, not enough in most motorists' eyes but all that could be obtained in the face of a reactionary establishment. It also introduced car registration.

In 1915, commissioned to be an adviser on transport to the Indian government, he was en route to India when the ship he was travelling on, the *S.S. Persia*, was torpedoed off Crete. His long time personal assistant and mistress, Eleanor Thornton, was drowned in the sinking, and Montagu himself spent three days in an open boat before being rescued. He returned to London to read his own obituary in the papers. It is commonly believed that Eleanor was the model for the Charles Sykes creation, the Spirit of Ecstasy or Flying Lady, which became the mascot on Rolls-Royce cars.

In 1920, aged fifty-four, Montagu married his second wife, Pearl Barrington-Crake, who was thirty years his junior. They had three daughters, Anne, Caroline and Mary-Clare, but when he was sixty, his wife bore him a long-hoped-for son and heir, Edward, the third and current Lord Montagu. Edward's own longevity was more than matched by his mother, who remarried after John Montagu's death in 1929 and lived until 1996, when she died at the age of a hundred and one. Edward is responsible for the foundation of the National Motor Museum at Beaulieu and, as a consequence, the Montagu name is synonymous with the history of British motoring to this day.

J. T. C. Moore-Brabazon
later
Lord Brabazon of Tara, G.B.E., M.C., P.C. (1884-1964)

John Theodore Cuthbert Moore-Brabazon, happily for writers, was universally known as Brab. Born in London, he went to Harrow and Trinity College, Cambridge where he met Charles Rolls. Of Rolls he said: "While at Cambridge I had spent my days as a mechanic to Charles Rolls, who became my greatest friend, and his association with the great Royce carried their two names throughout the world as exemplifying all that was the best in automobile engineering.'

Moore-Brabazon once worked in the French Darracq factory learning about car tyres. In France, he was also found guilty of driving too fast and received a two-day prison sentence that he never served. He drove a car on the opening day of Brooklands and was leading the first race when his car caught fire, thus missing out on a major prize. He later won the last Belgian Circuit des Ardennes, driving a Minerva. He knew Rolls was mean with money, but said that he loved working for him and paid his own expenses down to the last farthing.

Brabazon took up ballooning in 1902 where he met his future wife, Hilda Krabbe, who was keen on both him and balloons. Together with Rolls, they bought an early spherical balloon, *Venus*, from Short Brothers enhancing the latter's reputation as the first, gifted, British balloon manufacturer.

Rolls and Brabazon began to make gliders of high efficiency. Rolls somehow obtained permission to use the Albert Hall as a test arena, and the duo went there frequently to launch gliders from the boxes and watch them glide slowly to the floor. Brabazon began his flying activities in Sheppey. He flew three miles in France and then won a major U.K. prize for making the first, circular mile flight in Britain in a Short biplane. Later he made the first transport flight, attaching a bucket to his plane in which was a rather nervous pig – thus establishing that pigs could fly. He was the first licensed U.K. pilot, Rolls being the second. Brab celebrated his achievement with a cherished number plate, FLY 1.

He did not fly at Bournemouth on the first day of the 1910 meeting. He was sickened by Rolls's death and decided there and then to give up flying, to the great relief of his expectant wife. He only resumed flying at the outbreak of the Great War in which he won a Military Cross for reconnaissance work.

In later life he served twenty-two years as an M.P., was Minister of Transport in 1940 then, briefly, Minister of Aircraft Production, a post that brought him back into contact with Rolls-Royce. He was ennobled in 1942 and was later a Privy Councillor and then Knight Grand Cross of the British Empire.

An excellent golfer, Brab was captain of the Royal and Ancient at St. Andrew's. In his later years he took up tobogganing and made his last descent of the St. Moritz Cresta Run when age seventy. He drove a 300SL Mercedes across Salisbury Plain at over 100mph shortly before his death in 1964.

Lord Northcliffe (Alfred Harmsworth) (1865-1922)

Alfred Charles William Harmsworth, (later first Baron Northcliffe), the son of a Dublin barrister, was one of fourteen children, Harmsworth's contribution to the motoring cause, and to Rolls-Royce in particular, was inestimable. Although at one stage he was offered the use of a Silver Ghost for free, he refused. He maintained his independence but could well claim to be, after Rolls, Royce and Johnson, the fourth man in the Rolls-Royce success story.

Harmsworth's *Daily Mail* became a smash hit despite being described by Lord Salisbury, Prime Minister at the time, as 'written by office boys for office boys'. The first issue exceeded four hundred thousand copies. After Harmsworth had acquired the *Daily Mirror*, *The Observer* and *The Times* and then *The Sunday Times*, Prime Ministers were more circumspect. His brother, Harold, later Lord Rothermere, left a secure Civil Service job to run the business side. They bought forests in Canada to secure future needs for newsprint. One of their few mistakes was to found a newspaper for gentlewomen, the *Daily Mirror*, which reflected the interest of the fair sex in manners and appearance. Having lost a fortune on the venture, it was quickly revamped and made money, as it does today, from a somewhat less genteel readership.

His sponsorship of the Thousand Mile Trial in which Rolls won the Gold Medal was crucial in sealing his relationship with Rolls, as was his close friendship with Claude Johnson. The wives of both Northcliffe and Johnson may have put up with quite a few infidelities. Northcliffe certainly had a mistress, his temporary secretary, Kathleen Wrohan. She probably knew Eleanor Thornton, Lord Montagu's secretary (and mistress) at *Car Illustrated*.

Harmsworth's motoring exploits were mixed and he was nearly killed in a car accident in 1899. In 1903 he lent his car to Mercedes to race in the Gordon Bennett race following a disastrous fire at their works, prior to the 1903 Gordon Bennett race in Ireland. His brother, Hildebrand, was involved in a cause célébre when his chauffeur killed a young child in a hit and run accident, creating a national furore against motorists. Alfred and Hildebrand got the chauffeur to own up and accept a prison sentence; another brother, St. John Harmsworth, was paralysed with a broken spine when his chauffeur-driven car overturned in fog.

Following the Race to Death – Paris/Madrid in 1903 – Harmsworth worked with Johnson to stress the safety of cars. The ill-fated Legal Limit was a knee-jerk reaction to this campaign. Looking back at the 1896 Red Flag Act, Northcliffe castigated the politicians. 'As one of the agitators for the abolition of the preposterous Red Flag, I have always felt that had the restrictions been removed, Britain would have gained almost a monopoly in the motor industry. We should not have been subject to the incursion of many millions of pounds worth of foreign cars, for our inventors, manufacturers and mechanics are as good as any in the world'.

Harmsworth/Northcliffe sponsored many aviation prizes. The race between Louis Paulhan and Claude Grahame-White in April 1910 attracted massive crowds along its route, much to the chagrin of Rolls, who was awaiting delivery of his own aeroplane. Paulhan won a prize of £10,000, almost £1 million today.

In later life Northcliffe's newspapers led to the change of government during the Great War in 1916 when Lloyd George became Prime Minister. Lloyd George offered him a place in the Cabinet, but Northcliffe preferred his independence. Such was the anti-German sentiment in his newspapers that prior to the Great War a rival newspaper stated: 'Next to the Kaiser, Lord Northcliffe has done more than any living man to bring about the war'. The Germans reciprocated by dispatching a warship to shell Northcliffe's home at Elmwood, near the Kent coast, in an attempt to assassinate him. The residence still bears a shell hole unrepaired out of respect for his gardener's wife, who was killed in the bombardment. In 1918, having finally persuaded the U.S.A. to enter the Great War, he was created Viscount Northcliffe.

Northcliffe founded a trophy for international motor boat racing. He became a huge enthusiast of the Rolls-Royce Silver Ghost and suggested that, as in American cars, the starting handle be dispensed with.

Northcliffe, in Western Australia, was named after him in a scheme that promised land to British settlers prepared to emigrate and develop the land around it. In later life after Alcock and Brown flew the Atlantic in 1919, to win the last great Daily Mail aviation award, in the Vickers Vimy biplane powered by two Rolls-Royce engines Northcliffe was adamant that Royce was the greatest engineer of the age and should receive far more public recognition. He asserted that the name Rolls-Royce was 'the finest piece of British propaganda that we have'. On Northcliffe's untimely death at fifty-seven, Rolls-Royce lost its most staunch and influential supporter.

No wonder Henry Royce a man of few words wrote 'I feel we shall miss our old friend Northcliffe'.

Such was Northcliffe's regard for his workforce he bequeathed each three month's pay – all six thousand of them.

Sir Frederick Henry Royce, First Baron of Seaton, O.B.E. (1863-1933)

When Charles Rolls died in a flying accident near Bournemouth in July 1910, Henry Royce was living at the Knowle (now Quarndon House) at Quarndon, north of Derby. The house was rented by Rolls-Royce Ltd. and Royce was building a house nearby on Burley Road. The Rolls-Royce factory was south of Derby. Royce was married to Minnie (née: Punt). They had no children, but a niece who lived with them. Violet was the daughter of Minnie's brother who lived in South Africa. Violet's brother, Errol, lived with the Claremont family, Claremont being Royce's partner, and Claremont's wife was Minnie's sister.

In 1911, Royce went on holiday to Overstrand, near Cromer, in Norfolk. While on holiday, he was taken ill and transferred to a hospital in Norwich. He returned to Overstrand to convalesce. This is where Nurse Ethel Aubin appears on the scene. He was looked after by Dr. Dent, who reported that Royce was suffering from a nervous breakdown and was nursed by Nurse Aubin. It is probable that Royce was suffering from both digestion problems and stress/depression due to over-work over many years.

When he had recovered, Royce and Nurse Aubin travelled to Tours by train, where they were collected by Claude Johnson, Managing Director of Rolls-Royce. Together the three of them travelled around France and Italy in a Silver Ghost, staying at the Villa Jaune in Le Canadel, Johnson's house. In December 1911, Royce and Nurse Aubin took a ship across the Mediterranean to Egypt, where they wintered. On returning to France in Spring 1912, he and Johnson returned to Le Canadel and Royce decided to construct a villa nearby where he would spend future winters.

Back in England, Royce returned to his wife, Minnie, and Violet in Crowborough (south-west of Tunbridge Wells). He brought Nurse Aubin with him but, as might be expected, this was an unhappy situation. According to Violet, Minnie had a horror of illness and saw little of Royce, and Nurse Aubin controlled Minnie's and Violet's access to him.

That October, Royce and Nurse Aubin returned to Le Canadel where Royce started designs for his 'Villa Mimosa'. R. W. Harvey-Bailey helped with the design and construction and, at the same time, designed a new four-speed gearbox for the Silver Ghost under close supervision from Royce. This followed problems in the 1912 Alpine Rally, when a Silver Ghost, with a three-speed gearbox, had been unable to climb a steep hill. Harvey-Bailey's four-speed gearbox with a lower first gear for the 1913 Alpine Rally was, however, a spectacular success.

Late in 1912, Royce was again taken ill and returned to London where he had a colostomy operation. In 1913, he returned to his wife at Crowborough, again with Nurse Aubin, but to prevent family disharmony, Johnson arranged for Royce and Nurse Aubin to move to St. Margaret's Bay, near Dover, where Johnson had a house. Minnie and Violet continued to live at Crowborough until 1921 when they moved to Bexhill-on-Sea where Minnie died in 1936.

Royce returned again to Le Canadel in Spring 1913. Villa Mimosa was under construction. One of Royce's engineers designed and built the electrical and water collection system. The electrical system consisted of an unreliable French petrol engine driving a Royce dynamo but, due to Royce's frugality, the unreliable engine and generator were still in use a decade later. He returned to England in July 1913 but was back at Le Canadel later in the year to winter in his new holiday home.

When World War I started in August 1914, production of the Silver Ghost virtually ceased. Almost all the cars produced during the war were armoured cars. There was also demand for Rolls-Royce to produce an aero engine. Royce was reluctant because of the death of Rolls but the company really had no choice since it would have been 'out of business' producing only a handful of Silver Ghost cars. Rolls-Royce started to design its first aero engine, the Eagle. There was pressure to produce a radial, air-cooled engine but Royce wanted to use the technology of the six-cylinder Silver Ghost engine to achieve a power of 200bhp. The Eagle, was a V12 (two six-cylinder engines in a V), with the same bore as the Silver Ghost, but with a longer stroke. It had overhead valves that were more efficient than the side-valves of the Silver Ghost. A six-cylinder version of the Eagle was used in airships. Most of the aero engines produced by Rolls-Royce, both during Royce's lifetime and through the World War II, were V12s of varying capacity.

After the war, Royce returned to producing cars and tended to neglect design and development of the aero engines. Most of the U.K. aircraft manufacturers had their own engine divisions, which they favoured over Rolls-Royce engines.

At this time, Rolls-Royce believed demand for the large Silver Ghost would diminish, so the company developed the smaller 20hp car. This had a 3.1 litre, six-cylinder engine with overhead valves as opposed to the Ghost's side valves. It produced about 60bhp, similar to the original Ghost engine – but at twice the power per litre. This engine was used in small Rolls-Royce cars, in increasing capacity and power, until 1959.

Like all pre-World War II car manufacturers, Rolls-Royce produced the engines and chassis; customers had a choice of body, using different coachbuilders with styles: saloon, limousine (chauffeur with a glass division between the driver and passengers) and convertible (called 'the Tourer'). The early 20hp had a three-speed gearbox and only rear wheel brakes (like the contemporary Silver Ghost), but in 1924 Rolls-Royce introduced four wheel brakes on the Silver Ghost, and, soon afterwards, these brakes were introduced on the 20hp in addition to a four-speed gearbox.

After the Great War, the Silver Ghost became increasingly old-fashioned, particularly the side-valve engine. In 1925, the New Phantom (subsequently called the Phantom I) was introduced with an overhead valve engine. And, in 1929, both the 20hp and Phantom I were replaced with the 20/25hp (a larger engine) and Phantom II (principally a new chassis).

About this time the company began to concentrate on aero engines once more, in particular the R engine, used in the Schneider Trophy races on a Supermarine S6, built near Southampton. The R engine was large and very advanced. It was a 37 litre V12, producing up to 2,800bhp. It won the Schneider Trophy against the Italians, achieving 328mph in 1929 and 379mph in 1931.

Towards the end of Royce's life, he became involved in the design of the V12 engine in the Phantom III (car) and in the Merlin aero engine, a slightly smaller R-type engine of 27 litres. The Phantom III engine was advanced but was not a success.

During the depressed early 1930s, customers moved to the smaller and less expensive 20hp/25hp. There were also problems with the carburation, the unreliable hydraulic tappets, and the aluminium construction. The Merlin aero engine, however, was an outstanding success. It was used in both fighter and bomber aircraft. From 1,000bhp at the start of World War II, its power doubled by the end of the war without any increase in the engine's capacity.

Royce had moved to St. Margaret's Bay in 1913, but in 1917 he and Nurse Aubin moved to Elmstead at West Wittering (south of Chichester) where he lived until his death in April 1933. His last visit to Le Canadel, pre-World War I, was in 1914. He returned in late 1919 and spent every winter there until 1931/1932.

Claude Johnson and most Rolls-Royce employees were pleased when Royce left Derby for the last time in 1911 – Royce returning just once (or possibly twice) before death, although he attended Board meetings in London. Royce was a perfectionist. If he disapproved of what an employee was doing, he would sack him – and the manager would have to reinstate the employee and calm the situation.

Once Royce was away from the Derby factory, he was free to concentrate on the design of the cars and aero engines. He employed a small team of engineers to produce drawings, which were then modified to suit his suggestions. The drawings would be sent back to Derby to produce even more detailed drawings, and then the parts were manufactured.

Many of the senior designers, who worked closely with Royce, lived in West Wittering. A smaller number moved to Le Canadel in the winter, usually, it appears, without their wives. The younger designers tended to be unmarried in any case. At Le Canadel, the Rolls-Royce villas are situated along the Avenue de la Corniche. Le Canadel is on the south coast of France between Toulon and St. Tropez, and they overlook the Mediterranean.

A hundred years after Royce first went there, Avenue de la Corniche is virtually unchanged and, beside the main road, is a garage where the cars were stored and serviced. Next to Royce's house was the drawing office. Close by are Villa Mimosa, Royce's villa, and Villa Jaune, owned by Claude Johnson. Even today, Le Canadel is quite remote, the nearest shops being about three miles away. For many of Royce's staff it was rather a lonely existence, and it needed a special person to survive. Royce was a taskmaster: 'Why do staff need time off when they are away from home'. They would work in the mornings without Royce and he would arrive in the afternoon to comment on their drawings. Work would often extend into the evenings and they would work on Saturdays and even Sundays.

Royce expected his chauffeur, Frank Dodd, to be available seven days a week. One day at Le Canadel, Dodd decided to take a Sunday afternoon off and to walk up the mountain. While he was away, Royce wanted to send a telegram to Derby and had to ask a passing car to take it. Dodd was in trouble, he was sent back to Derby three days later. Unusually, Royce relented and asked for his return. Dodd remained with Royce until his death and even attended Royce's funeral along with Nurse Aubin and Royce's solicitor – the only people to do so.

Rolls and Royce were together for just six years before Rolls died, Royce in Manchester and Derby, Rolls in London or travelling the world. And their period 'together' was really shorter than this because Rolls moved on to balloons and aviation.

Rolls was fifteen years younger than Royce when they met in 1904. Both were engineers, but Rolls was more academic and Royce was more practical. It is clear that they got on well from their first meeting. Subsequently Rolls described Royce as 'the greatest motor car designer in the world'. There is little documentation of their first meeting but Violet Punt describes Rolls visiting Royce at his home in Quarndon, Derby, for tea and Rolls requesting 'lots of thick bread and butter, Vi'. As a sign of their friendship, Rolls sent a silver Vesta case to Royce in 1909 to commemorate the fifth anniversary of their first meeting. Since both of them were 'careful with their money', this generous gift was a significant mark of appreciation.

(Kindly contributed by David Towers of the Rolls-Royce Enthusiasts' Club)

Sir David Salomons (Second Baronet) (1851-1925)

David Lionel Goldschmid-Stern-Salomons was a scientific author, wealthy barrister and one-time High Sheriff of Kent. He succeeded to the Baronetcy originally granted to his uncle, David Salomons, in 1873 when aged twenty-two.

His house, Broomhill, included large workshops where he investigated electromotive force and carried out countless other experiments, taking out patents for electric lamps and current meters amongst other things. It was said that his workshops contained sixty thousand tools and that, from them, he could manufacture anything from a watch to a steam engine. In February 1896 when Charles Rolls was just eighteen, he spent a week at Broomhill.

Rolls was fascinated. Some months before his visit, Sir David had acquired a Peugeot motor car, one of the earliest in Britain, and he had organised the first Exhibition of Motors (all four of them!) in Tunbridge Wells in 1895. Like Rolls, Salomons had installed his own electric light, an electric cooker and electric alarms.

Salomons was an early opponent of Harry Lawson of the Motor Car Club (he despised Lawson's commercial avarice) and founded the 'Self-Propelled Traffic Association' (S.P.T.A.) in 1896, in order to develop motoring theory. Following the establishment of the Automobile Club of Great Britain and Ireland, he agreed to the S.P.T.A. being absorbed a few years later, but it was to the S.P.T.A. that the young Rolls originally subscribed. Salomons was on the Judges panel for The Thousand Mile Trial.

In later life, Salomons amassed the largest private collection of watches by the greatest watchmaker of all time, the Frenchman, Breguet and, the year before his death, he donated one of his finest pieces to a museum in Paris. It was subsequently stolen and only recovered when the unwise thief took it to a renowned Paris watch-specialist for repair. After his death in 1925, his wife took what was left of his collection to Sothebys but was dismissed from the office on the grounds that no one could ever have acquired such an incredible collection.

Frederick Simms (1863-1944)

Frederick Simms was educated in Britain and abroad. He took an early interest in the internal combustion engine and met Gottlieb Daimler in 1888. Daimler entrusted him with the exploitation of its patents, and he founded the Daimler Motor Syndicate in 1893 and became its Chairman three years before the Emancipation Act. He coined the words 'motor car' and 'petrol' – other early names for motor car included: 'Petrocycle', 'Motor Fly', 'Olio-Locomotive', 'Volvite', 'Electro Bat', 'Non-Equine Automatic Car' and 'Autocar'.

When the Daimler Motor Company was formed in 1896 he became its first consulting engineer. He was a director of Daimler from 1897 to 1903, and was the first to suggest the concept of an automatic (float-feed) instead of surface carburettor.

Simms imported the first Panhard car, fitted with a Daimler engine, into Britain. He also drove with Evelyn Ellis in June 1895 on a fifty-six mile drive to Datchet, probably the longest journey made by any motor vehicle in Britain at that time. He recalled: 'Whole villages turned out to behold open-mouthed the new marvel of locomotion. The departure of coaches was delayed to enable their passengers to have a look at our horseless vehicle. Petrol works out at a little over one halfpenny per mile'.

He was responsible for the organisation of the Exhibition of Motor Vehicles at the Imperial Institute in 1896 where he explained the workings of cars to his Royal Highness, the then Prince of Wales. He founded the Motor Car Club in 1895 – which was largely hijacked by Harry Lawson – and took part in the Emancipation Run, which was a bit of a shambles, in November 1896.

As Lawson's Motor Car Club and Sir David Salomons Self-Propelled Traffic Association were at odds, Simms felt that another club was necessary so he, with Charles Harrington – Moore, started the A.C.G.B.I., predominantly funded from Simms's own resources. Charles Rolls was a founder member. Simms was largely responsible for the Richmond Exhibition in the summer of 1899, which lost some £1,500, although the finances were restored due to the generosity of Lord Northcliffe. At Richmond, Simms demonstrated a Maxim gun fitted to a motor quadricycle.

He designed and made the first single cylinder engine suitable for a motorcycle, and designed the first motor lawnmower, and formed the Society of Motor Manufacturers and Traders in 1903 and became its first president. Seven years later he formed the aero section of the same society, which held the first international aero exhibition in London and where Charles Rolls showed his aeroplane to the new King, Edward VII.

Simms patented the airplane joystick and invented and patented the first motor car bumper in 1906. He designed the first motor plough and tractor of caterpillar type in 1902 and built up the Simms Motor Units Company from 1913.

On the twenty-fifth anniversary of the formation of A.C.G.B.I., Frederick Simms was handed an illuminated address and a portrait by the Duke of Windsor at a dinner to celebrate his contribution to British motoring.

Charles Sykes (1875-1950)

Charles Robinson Sykes was an English sculptor, best known for designing the Spirit of Ecstasy mascot, which is used on Rolls-Royce cars. He was born in Brotton, a village in the ironstone, mining district between the Yorkshire Moors and Teeside.

His father and uncle were talented artists, and he received every encouragement to take up art as a career. His father, Samuel, was able to send him to Newcastle's Rutherford Art College, where he was supposed to supervise some of the decorating business staff, which he did not want to do, so he left in 1898 and won a scholarship to the Royal College of Art in South Kensington. He developed his drawing and painting abilities, studied sculpture and made experimental castings in gold, silver and bronze.

He became an artistic all-rounder, assured himself of a worthwhile career, acquired a taste for London life, and, due to the inability of Cummings Beaumont, publisher of a Northumbrian county magazine, to pay the bill for some sketches commissioned from Charles, as compensation Sykes was introduced to John Montagu, M.P. Montagu had just launched *Car Illustrated* and motor mania was at its height. Claude Johnson, who had been secretary of the A.C.G.B.I., had become a senior manager with Charles Rolls and took a close interest in Montagu's new magazine, realising its potential to promote Rolls-Royce Ltd. He also became aware of the talents of the gifted young artist from Tyneside. Sykes's Christmas illustration was so stylish that Johnson wanted to use Sykes's works to promote Rolls-Royce cars.

Johnson had previously seen the marble statue of Nike in the Louvre, and appreciated its stunning lines and style. Meanwhile, Sykes had produced a team trophy statue for John Montagu, to donate to the winning team in each year's Gordon Bennett road races. This was a female figure, cast in silver, holding a silver-winged bronzed motor car.

Rolls-Royce decided on a one car policy and decided to produce just the Silver Ghost, and Johnson used Sykes to produce promotional images. The Rolls-Royce 1910 catalogue contained six oil paintings of Rolls-Royce cars entitled 'Arrival at the Opera', 'Arrival at the Country House', 'Arrival at the Golf Links', 'Arrival at the

Meet', 'Arrival at the Covert Side' and 'Arrival at the Salmon Stream'. The rights to all six were assigned to Rolls-Royce Ltd. between June 1909 and April 1910.

The company acquired copyright to Sykes's several other works, and in 1911, when Johnson became concerned about inappropriate mascots placed on Rolls-Royce cars by Rolls-Royce owners, Sykes completed the most famous commission of his career, the Spirit of Ecstasy.

A special edition, known as The Whisperer, was produced for John Montagu. It indicated a figure intent on keeping a secret, almost certainly referring to the relationship between John Montagu and his private secretary, Eleanor Thornton, who is thought to be the model for the Spirit of Ecstasy. The more famous model, originally known as The Spirit of Speed but then known as The Spirit of Ecstasy, became standard issue on Rolls-Royces from that point onwards.

Sykes was married, but in the bohemian community in which he lived, may well have been close to Eleanor Thornton himself at some time, given her bohemian lifestyle and love of life.

The Wright Brothers
Wilbur Wright (1867-1912),
Orville Wright (1871-1948)

Wilbur and Orville Wright were two of seven children, although two of their siblings died in childbirth. Their father was a bishop of an American sect and their mother was of German/Swiss descent.

When aged eighteen, Wilbur was struck in the face by a hockey stick and badly hurt. He had intended to go to Yale but stayed at home, caring for his mother who died four years later of tuberculosis. Orville was then eighteen and Wilbur twenty-two. Although not at university, Wilbur read extensively and, meanwhile, Orville dropped out of high school and started a printing business (aged eighteen). They opened their bike shop in 1892.

They only flew together once, in May 1910, having, when their experimenting began, promised their father that they would never fly together. Much later when they took him up in a plane at the age of eighty-two, elderly Bishop Wright called to his son: 'Higher Orville, Higher'.

After they became famous, they became embroiled in law suits against Glenn Curtiss, who had won a Gordon Bennett race, and also Louis Paulhan, who had won the London/Manchester race. At one point during this nasty dispute, Curtiss's lawyer suggested that if someone jumped in the air and waved their arms, the Wrights would sue. The patent wrangles took their toll on Wilbur who died of typhoid, in 1912, worn out by legal issues and Orville and Katherine Wright always believed Curtiss was partly responsible for Wilbur's premature death. Bishop Wright said of Wilbur: 'A short life full of consequences and unfailing intellect, imperturbable temper, great self-reliance and great modesty'.

The patent war ended at last but side issues lingered on into the 1920s. Ironically, the Wright Aeronautical Corporation and the Curtiss Aeroplane Company merged in 1929. They were criticised by others apart from Curtiss for their protracted legal disputes, and their friendship with Chanute, an early mentor, who had visited Kitty Hawk, sadly ended as a result.

The brothers sold the patents to the Wright company in November 1909 for $100,000 and received one-third of the shares in a $1 million stock issue, and were also to receive a ten per cent royalty on every plane sold. Wilbur was President and Orville was Vice-President, and the company set up a factory in Dayton and a flying school and testing ground at Huffman Prairie.

There was a problem with the stability of the early planes. The brothers solved most, but not all of the problems. They hired a team of trained pilots, two of whom were killed at the end of 1910 and four more died in crashes afterwards. The death toll reached eleven by 1913. Eventually the U.S. Army called into question the safety of the Wright aircraft.

Orville made his last flight in 1918 as a pilot.

He also retired from business and eventually became the elder statesman of American aviation.

The brothers' relationship with their sister, Katherine, was unusual. Following the early death of their mother she effectively took her place. She had always looked after their home life, and Orville after the death of Wilbur in particular, neglecting her own personal happiness. She finally married in 1926 and left Dayton to live in Kansas City. Orville refused to have anything to do with her thereafter. He did not attend the wedding. There had, at some stage, been a pact between the brothers and Katherine that none of them could marry without the agreement of the others and she had broken her promise. He at last saw her, at the behest of his older brother, Lorin, just before she died in 1929. Orville's last flight was in 1944 with Howard Hughes, the reclusive business magnate and aviator.

Orville died in 1948 following a heart attack[63], and is buried with Wilbur and Katherine in Dayton cemetery.

Ohio and North Carolina both take credit for the Wright brothers, Ohio because the brothers built and developed their planes in Dayton, and North Carolina because Kitty Hawk was the site of the first flights. Ohio carries the legend, 'The Birthplace of Aviation Pioneers', on its license plates, referring to the Wrights and also to Neil Armstrong and John Glenn, both born in the state. Neil Armstrong was the first man to walk on the moon, and John Glenn the first American to orbit the Earth and later also the oldest astronaut when aged seventy-seven. The state of North Carolina uses the slogan 'First in Flight' on its license plates.

Sadly, the Wright home in Dayton was badly damaged in the Great Dayton Flood of 1913, and many photographs of the brothers' progress towards powered flight were destroyed.

63 *Coincidentally, John Downey of the Coast Guards at Kitty Hawk, who took the picture of their first flight back in 1903, died the day after Orville.*

Selwyn Francis Edge.

Ernest Claremont.

Henry Edmunds.

Harry Ferguson.

Frank Hedges Butler.

Charles Jarrott.

Claude Goodman Johnson.

John Douglas-Scott-Montagu M.P. (Second Baron Montagu)

J.T.C. Moore-Brabazon (Lord Brabazon of Tara).

J.T.C. Moore-Brabazon (left) with C.S. Rolls (in fancy dress).

Lord Northcliffe (Alfred Harmsworth).

Sir Frederick Henry Royce.

Wilbur Wright

Orville Wright

Wilbur and Orville Wright.

Appendix 1

Speech by C. S. Rolls at a dinner at the Trocadero in London, 3rd November, 1905 to celebrate the performance by Rolls-Royce and Percy Northey in the TT race of September 1905:

'I would like to say a few words of introduction, as it were, to Mr. Royce – I say introduction for although you have frequently heard his name in connection with the excellent motor car manufactured by him and with which I have the honour to be associated, yet the greater part of those present in this room have never before had the opportunity of making his actual acquaintance; indeed there are but few who know him for Mr. Royce is of a very retiring disposition. He is one of those unassuming, hardworking men, who devote their lives to the study and solution of difficult and mechanical problems and to whom directly are due the general advancement of civilisation and the high position which Great Britain holds at present in the engineering world.

You may ask yourself how it was that I became to be associated with Mr. Royce and Mr. Royce with me. Well, for a considerable number of years I have been actively engaged in the sale of foreign cars, and the reason for this, was I wanted to be able to recommend and sell the best cars in the world, irrespective of origin, and the cars I sold were, I believe, the best that could be got at that time, but somehow I always had a sort of feeling that I should prefer to be selling English, instead of foreign goods.

In addition, I could distinctly notice a growing desire on the part of my clients to purchase English-made cars; yet I was disinclined to embark on a factory and manufacture myself, firstly on account of my own incompetence and inexperience in such matters and secondly on account of the enormous risks involved, and at the same time I could not come across any English-made cars I really liked.

Although I had numerous offers of sole concessions and sole agencies and so forth, on terms which represented a far higher rate of profit than I was working for with my foreign cars, yet the majority of British manufacturers at that time all seemed to suffer from the same thing, what I might call their sheer pigheadedness, that is to say they had a deep-rooted objection to copying the foreigner, who had many years more experience.

Being intimately acquainted with best foreign practice, and having followed pretty closely the gradual evolution of the motor car and the improvement and perfection of every detail by the French specialists whose names are household words, it used to annoy me considerably to see the average English motor car builder bringing out, for example, as a wonderful new improvement, a device which anyone who had followed the movement closely enough knew had been tried and discarded in France perhaps five years previously. Many manufacturers went over ground, which they could have saved had they chosen to take advantage of the foreigner's experience; and this together with bad finance has undoubtedly been the chief causes of the backwardness of British automobile manufacturers during the early years of the movement.

Eventually I was fortunate enough to make the acquaintance of Mr. Royce and in him I found the man I had been looking for for years.

Mr. Royce, whose firm – a firm of longstanding, much respected and of the highest repute in the motoring world – have been renowned for their electrical cranes, dynamos, electro motors and various kinds of mechanical work, down to scientific instruments requiring the utmost precision and the very highest quality of workmanship.

Well, Mr. Royce, like myself, always had a hankering after the designing and making of mechanical carriages, and not long after we met each other, arrangements were made whereby he commenced the manufacture of various types to suit my special requirements, and I won't say he has suited me in quantity, for we could have sold double and treble the number. I see no chance of getting satisfaction in this respect for a considerable time to come, but in quality and other respects he has more than fulfilled my requirements. In addition to carrying out the general ideas and designs that have come from my side – that is from my able colleague, Mr. Claude Johnson, and myself – his extraordinary genius – for Mr. Royce is no ordinary man, but a man of exceptional ingenuity and power of overcoming difficulties – his extraordinary genius has enabled him to effect clever improvements in general and in detail, which had been possessed in no other make of car.

The result is the vehicle, which you now know under the joint name of Mr. Royce and myself, and which I think I may go as far as to say is now to be reckoned amongst the first rank of automobile manufacturers in the world, having established for itself, in a very brief period, honest reputation for silence, simplicity and high quality. This success has been due, in no small measure, to the fact that Mr. Royce is an unprejudiced man, and in possessing originality to the very highest degree, is not too proud to acknowledge the valuable work and experience of our friends across the Channel and to benefit thereby.

This, I think you will agree, is a very unusual thing to find in a British engineer, and it has enabled us to start on even grounds with the foreigner and level with him, for I venture to say that no engineer, however able he may be, could possibly set to work and design a motor car with anything but failure awaiting him, unless he is thoroughly well-acquainted with, and is prepared to benefit by, the corresponding work that has been done by his Continental rivals, for otherwise he must waste years covering old and useless ground, which has been traversed and abandoned by others. He will thus be following along always two or three years behind them – if you understand what I mean – instead of being on a level with them.

You will thus understand the reason why we have always been anxious to make it clear that although it is a new car, the Rolls-Royce is not an experiment, for we have not started off by thinking we knew more about it than anyone else, but we started out with the full knowledge of what we were doing and what is even more important, what other people were doing and had done. The car has thus embodied all such modern improvements as we know had been proved to be right, and the only real improvement we wished at first to devote our attention to, were in the direction of simplifying and standardising the number of working parts and silencing and balancing the engine. In regard to the extraordinary silence of the Rolls-Royce, many of our rivals content themselves by telling people we do this by shutting up the exhaust at the expense of power.

Well, it would take too long to explain to you how it is done, but I can only assure you that this is not the case; if it were, we should never be able to get the hill climbing power we do out of the Rolls-Royce; we should never be able to climb such hills as Hind Head, Guildford High Street, Hogs Back and Richmond Park test hill of 1:7.8 on a top speed, with a standard gear, of 33mph.

With regard to the notable absence of vibration on our cars, well, I suppose there is no one who has devoted closer or more careful study to the important questions of balancing than Mr. Royce. This is what accounts for it. Indeed, it seems to me no one actually in the automobile business has really attacked and gone properly into this matter from a theoretical point of view, for correct balancing of internal combustion engines is one of those things that cannot be attained properly by practise without the use of theory.

It's hardly incumbent on me to say more about the merits or otherwise of the Rolls-Royce, if indeed as much as I have already said; suffice it to say that in consequence of the utter impossibility of coping with the demand, there has been, for the cars this year, and the fact that in some types we are already quoting September 1906 (it is now November 1905) as the earliest date we can possibly deliver. Arrangements are rapidly being made to extend and also to still further equip our present works with more of the latest automatic machinery. I might maintain, however, that the present works already possess some of the most perfect gear cutting machinery in the world, and to this fact, together with the system of supervision in general organisation of the works, are due, in a great measure, the silence and sweet running of the gearing and general mechanism of the Rolls-Royce car'.

Appendix 2

This describes the flights made by Griffith Brewer, C. S. Rolls and Frank Hedges Butler with Wilbur Wright on 8th October, 1908.

Four Englishmen in a Plane

In October 1908 *Automotor* carried the following article:

An incident of extraordinary interest and historic importance took place at Auvours on Thursday, 8th October when Mr. Wilbur Wright took as passengers on his aeroplane four Englishmen in succession. They are the first residents of the United Kingdom who can claim to have flown and returned to the same starting point, and its only appropriate that the veteran aeronaut, Mr. Frank Hedges Butler, had the record duration with a flight of four minutes thirty-one seconds.

The Honourable C. S. Rolls... made a flight lasting four minutes twenty-seven seconds while Major Baden-Powell and Mr. Griffith Brewer were aloft for four minutes twenty-five and four minutes twenty-two seconds respectively.

Subsequently Mr. Griffith Brewer entertained Mr. Wright and his compatriots at luncheon, when the famous aviator related some of the more interesting experiences of the days when he was learning the art of flight at Dayton and Kitty Hawk.

Wilbur Wright had taken various passengers up from mid-September, the first being the English-born *New York Times* correspondent, Mr. Dickin.

The day before the Englishmen flew, he took up first Mr. Hart O. Berg, an American associate and then Mrs. Edith Berg (who thus became the first woman in the world to be flown) followed by three others.

Wilbur Wright took the English quartet, one at a time.

Griffith Brewer described his flight: 'I then enjoyed the greatest thrill that had ever been my lot to experience. The weight was hoisted up on the pylon, the propellers were started, being driven from the engine by the chains and then the machine was released and we were catapulted along the rail. The machine became airborne and we raced down the field, level with the treetops. We turned on a purpose bank and came back down the field and finally landed near the spot from which we had started. I had no thought of danger. I had a feeling of perfect confidence and admiration for the skill of the birdman. During that first flight I remember wondering whether we would really rise from the rail and then a feeling of elation when the grass slipped away backwards and downwards, and the machine seemed to be sitting on nothing. There was no sense of travelling except for the appearance of the earth moving backwards. On looking upwards, without the sense of movement, inherent in all other vehicles, which are supported below on wheels or on water.

In spite of knowing the theory of banking on a turn, I remember marvelling at the machine not slipping inwards when inclined to such a steep angle.

I'm afraid, however, that my keenness of observation of the flight's sensation was stifled by my greater interest in the man, and the predominant sense was one of wonder that the same man could calmly invent such a mechanism and yet fly it with such consummate skill'.

Rolls made his first flight immediately afterwards, then Butler and, later in the day, Major Baden-Powell .

One of the earlier passengers, the day before Rolls, was a Mr. Katznatoff, Chamberlain to the Tsar of all the Russias. Clearly the implications of the Wrights' achievements were appreciated across several continents.

C. S. Rolls himself wrote in *The Times*: 'Once clear of the ground, the feeling of security was perfect and I was able to watch with great interest the movement of the operating levers. We tore along at a speed of 40mph and soon came to the first corner. Here, a point of interest to motorists, was demonstrated, namely, that no matter what speed a curve is taken, the machine 'adjusts its own banking', so to speak. At the will of the operator, it tilted up gracefully when taking a turn, demonstrating that taking a curve on a flying machine will, instead of being more dangerous, be actually safer than on an automobile.

On this occasion, our flight was more than usually interesting by reason of some strong side gusts that attacked the flyer on certain parts of the course. The relevance of these and other undulations of the atmosphere rendered very close attention necessary to the two levers controlling the equilibrium and altitude; I noticed that both these were kept constantly on the 'joggle' with slight movement.

One has been accustomed to consider the atmosphere as a mass of air, increasing in density with its altitude, but otherwise uniform. Experience on a power-driven flyer, however, shows that, far from being the case, the atmosphere near the earth's surface – even in what we call calm weather – is made up of spiral movements of varying diameter, sometimes vertical and sometimes horizontal, undulations of all sorts, little hills and valleys, and 'streams' of air; in fact one might call it a new world conquered by man – a world with scenery of great variation, which, though invisible to the eye, is nonetheless felt by the operator of a flying machine.

To maintain equilibrium and steering control, while battling with these complex movements of the air, has been the great problem, which for centuries has baffled human ingenuity and which is now solved by the Wright brothers after years of systematic study and experiment'.

In *The Sportsman* of 13th October, Frank Hedges Butler let his imagination soar, following his turn at Auvours. He wrote: 'Like a bird in a cage, yes! I have flown! To look back seems like a dream, but I have seen Mr. Wilbur Wright fly for over an hour, by day and by night. I have also seen sixteen passengers, including two ladies, make a flight with him. One asks what it feels like to fly; the answer is, there is no sensation whatsoever: it is as if man has always flown. To give an idea, it's like gliding over sparkling water where you can see the bottom.

A perfect feeling of security and stability; turning the corners and tipping the wings is like skating on the outside edge. Wright feels his levers and looks at his planes as a skipper looks at his sails to see if they are full.

The great problem of the navigation of the air, which is now solved, must proceed. Future battles will be fought in the air, and a new aerial force, different from the army and navy, will be formed. Lighthouses on land will be erected by the Trinity Board to mark the way at night. Lamps on aeroplanes or flyers will be used; with smaller planes, speed will be terrific – 200mph. Twenty-one miles across the Channel means very few minutes; the winds at sea blow steadier than on land. Aeroplanes can be made to float on the water and raise themselves. No reason, if now they can carry equal to three passengers, an aeroplane should not carry more with larger planes and engines. The North Pole, tropical forests of

Central Africa, Australia and the Sahara Desert will be new fields for the explorer to glide over.

May the brothers, Orville and Wilbur Wright, live for many years to continue and improve their great invention of the age, the heavier-than-air flying machine'.

Major Baden-Powell, brother of the founder of the Scout movement, was last and it would have been a most interesting dinner party that evening as the four of them jointly relived their experiences of the day with one of the extraordinary brothers, Wilbur Wright.

Bibliography

Anon. Etiquette for a Chauffeur. *Copperbeach Publishing Ltd: 1997*

Bastow, D. Henry Royce – Mechanic. *Rolls-Royce Heritage Trust: 1989*

Bennett, E. The Thousand Mile Trial. *Elizabeth Bennett: 2000*

Berget, A. The Conquest of the Air. *William Heinemann: 1909*

Bird, A & Ian Hallows. The Rolls-Royce Motor Car. *B. T. Batsford Ltd: 1964*

Bird, R. The Birth of Brooklands. *Self-Published: 2007*

Bouzanquet, J. F. Fast Ladies – Female Racing Drivers. *Veloce Publishing*

Lord Brabazon of Tara. The Brabazon Story. *William Heinemann Ltd: 1956*

Melbourne Brindle, Artist. Twenty Silver Ghosts The Incomparable Pre-War I Rolls-Royce *(Text by Phil May)*

Brendon, P. The Motoring Century. The Story of the Royal Automobile Club. *Bloomsbury: 1997*

Brewer, G. Fifty Years of Flying. *Air League of the British Empire: 1946*

Bruce, G. Charlie Rolls – Pioneer Aviator. *Rolls-Royce Heritage Trust: 1990*

Bullock, J. Fast Women The Drivers who changed the face of motor racing. *Robson Books: 2002*

Buist, H. M. Rolls-Royce Memories. Cambridge University Press *and reprinted by the Rolls-Royce Enthusiasts' Club*: 1980

Butler, F. H. Fifty Years of Travel by Land, Water and Air. *T. Fisher Unwin Ltd: 1920*

Clarke, T. C. A Manchester Life with Rolls-Royce and W. T. Glover & Co. *The Hulme Press: 1995*

Cooper, R. Images of Shelsley 90 Years of Britain's Oldest Motoring Event. *The Midland Automobile Club*

Davies, S. C. H. Atalanta: 1960

Driver, H. Lord Northcliffe and the Early Years of Rolls-Royce. *The Rolls-Royce Enthusiasts' Club: 1998*

Edge, S. F. My Motoring Reminiscences. *G. T. Foulis*

Evans, M. In the Beginning The Manchester origins of Rolls-Royce. *The Rolls-Royce Heritage Trust: 1984. Second Ed: 2004*

Fasal, J.M. The Rolls-Royce Twenty. *John Fasal: 1979*

Fasal, J.M & Goodman, B. The Edwardian Rolls-Royce – Volumes I and II. *John Fasal: 1994*

Ferdinand & Kasmann. 100 Years of the Land Speed Record 1898-1998. *Auto Review*

Fraser, C. Tractor Pioneer – The Life of Harry Ferguson. *Ohio University Press: 1973*

Funnell, B. The Team Panhard The Story of C. S. Rolls 8hp 1899 Panhard et Levassor

Garnier, P. & Allport, W. Rolls-Royce The Story of the Best Car in the World. *Temple Press: 1978*

Grahame-White, M. At the Wheel, Ashore and Afloat. *G. T. Foulis & Co. Ltd.*

Harvey-Bailey, A. Rolls-Royce – The Formative Years 1906-1939. *Rolls-Royce Heritage Trust: 1982*

Harvey-Bailey, A. & Evans, M. Rolls-Royce-The Pursuit of Excellence. *Sir Henry Royce Memorial Foundation: 1984*

Holliday R.R. Racing Round The Island *(David and Charles 1976)*

Holmes, R. Falling Upwards – How We Take To The Air. *W. Harper Collins: 2013*

Jarrott, C. Ten Years of Motors and Motor Racing. *G. T. Foulis & Co. Ltd: 1906*

Jackson, D. D. The Aeronauts. *Time Life Books Ltd.*

Johnson, C. The Early History of Motoring. *Ed. J. Barrow & Co. Ltd: 1927*

Kelly, F.C. The Wright Brothers. *Dover Publications Inc: 1943*

Levitt, D. The Woman & The Car. *Bodley Head: 1909*

Marr, A. The Making of Modern Britain. *Macmillan: 2009*

Meynell, L. Rolls-Man of Speed. *J. B. Rol*

Meynell, L. First Men to Fly – The Wright Brothers. *Werner Lauri: 1955*

Miller, F. P. Dorothy Levitt. *Aphascript Publishing: 2010*

Minchin, G. R. N. (M.A.) Under my Bonnet. *G. T. Foulis & Co. Ltd: 1967*

Minchin, G. R. N. (M.A.) The Silver Lady. *G. T. Foulis & Co. Ltd: 1961*

Montgomery, B. The Irish Gordon Bennett Race 1903. *Dreolin Specialist Publications Ltd.: 1999*

Morriss, H. F. Two Brave Brothers. *H. F. Morriss*

Morriss, H. F. Minister, Mayor and Merchant. *H. F. Morriss*

Morton, C. W. The History of Rolls-Royce Motor Cars.Volume 1 1903-1907. *G. T. Foulis & Co. Ltd: 1964*

Lord Montagu of Beaulieu. The Early Days of Rolls-Royce and the Montagu Family. *Rolls-Royce Heritage Trust: 1986*

Lord Montagu of Beaulieu. *(Researched by Michael Sedgwick)* Rolls of Rolls-Royce. *Cassell: 1966*

Nixon, St. John. Romance Amongst Cars (R.A.C.). *G. T. Foulis & Co. Ltd: 1937*

Nockolds, H. The Magic of a Name. *G. T. Foulis & Co. Ltd.*

Oldham, W. J. The Hyphen in Rolls-Royce. *G. T. Foulis & Co. Ltd: 1967*

Sir Max Pemberton. The Life of Sir Henry Royce. *Hutchinson & Co.*

Sir Max Pemberton. Lord Northcliffe – A Memoir. *Hodder and Stoughton*

Pugh, P. The Magic of a Name – The Rolls-Royce Story. *Icon Books U.K: 2000*

Rolls-Royce Catalogue 1910/1911. *E. P. Publishing Ltd: Reprint 1973*

The Society of Motor and Manufacturers Traders Catalogue – Olympia Exhibition 1905

Tritton, P. The Godfather of Rolls-Royce The Life and Times of Henry Edmunds. *Academy Books: 1993*

Tritton, P. The Life and Times of Henry Edmunds (an updated version of the 1993 book). *Rolls-Royce Heritage Trust: 2006*

Tritton, P. John Montagu of Beaulieu. *Montagu Ventures Ltd: 1985*

Lady Troubridge & Marshall, A. John Montagu of Beaulieu – A Memoir. *Macmillan & Co. Ltd: 1930*

Ullyett, K. The Book of the Silver Ghost. *Kenneth Ullyett & Craft Publications Trust Ltd: 1963*

Venables, D. Brooklands – The Official Centenary History. *Haynes Publishing: 2007*

Williamson, C. N. & A. M. The Lightning Conductor. *Methuen: 1902*

Index